THE ENGLISH

The countryside and its people

MICHAEL WATKINS

PHOTOGRAPHS BY PETER PUGH-COOK

ELM TREE BOOKS
London

First published in Great Britain 1981
by Elm Tree Books/Hamish Hamilton Ltd
Garden House 57-59 Long Acre London WC2E 9JZ
in association with Arrow Books Ltd

British Library Cataloguing in Publication Data

Watkins, Michael
   The English.
   1. Villages – England
   2. England – Social life and customs
   I. Title
   942′.00973′4   DA588

   ISBN 0-241-10547-1

Set in Linoterm Times by Book Economy Services, Cuckfield, Sussex
Colour separations by Dot Gradations Ltd, Chelmsford, Essex
Monochrome origination by Culver Graphics Litho Ltd, Lane End, Bucks
Printed in Great Britain by Hazell, Watson & Viney Ltd, Aylesbury, Bucks
Bound by William Brendon & Son Ltd, Tiptree, Essex.

CONTENTS

Introduction

I The Yeoman   12

II The Shepherdess   24

III The Lifeboat Coxswain   36

IV The Builder   48

V The Gamekeeper   60

VI The Nature Warden   74

VII The Lock-keeper   86

VIII The Lobster Fisherman   100

IX The Landowner   114

X The Meals on Wheels Helper   128

XI The Village Schoolteacher   144

XII The Thatcher   158

XIII The Publican   174

XIV The Coal Miner   188

XV The Shopkeeper   202

XVI The Country Journalist   218

XVII The Gardener   232

XVIII The Parson   244

For Cuckoo Bradley-Williams,
an English girl

INTRODUCTION

The question is: Who are we?

Once we knew; now we are less sure. Our corporate or individual sense of identity has become blurred. Of course, there were always joint perspectives: one for townsmen, another for countrymen, with scant tolerance or charity between them. But within the rigid overall framework, one's place in society was largely ordained – a state which obtained from earliest days until the 'old queen' died.

Rich or poor, high or lowly, man has exercised freedom of choice since his release from feudal villeinage; but circumstance and duty more often than not manacled him to his birthright. The Englishman knew his place and infrequently strayed from the security, the protectiveness it offered. Exceptions were the rarity, but exceptions there were since the Peasants' Revolt. Think of Peterloo, the Reform Riots, the Chartists.

As the Victorian era ended – perhaps a little earlier, perhaps a few years later – the issue of society was confused by the appearance of a new strain. A mutation came into existence – the *sub*-urban man, searching for the best of both worlds, often settling for the worst of each. Yet he survived, creating a whole sub-species to disturb the social balance more dramatically than the two world wars which shoulder so much of the blame.

It was unusual for the suburbanite to put down roots in the way of village England; he became semi-nomadic, moving with the fluctuations of his fortune, 'bettering' himself when times were good, contracting when they were not. Nevertheless, he was an original – with invincibly unoriginal ideas, borrowing impartially from both his peers and inferiors. His architecture could be florid; then again it could be quasi-Tudor, cottage style. His inspiration was drawn from the Establishment; his muse convention.

He was feeling his way cautiously. He was not a revolutionary, his last wish was to cause offence. What he wanted more than anything was to be unremarkable; his idealism lay in respectability . . . the noblest of all virtues.

At this stage of evolution he was docile, timid, not particularly vocal, merging into his habitat. Above all, he was vulnerable; and it was this rather endearing quality which drew attention from the predators swooping in from their commercial eyries.

The rich knew what they wanted and could afford it; the poor were conditioned to be content with what they had. The suburbanite, on the other hand, was not precisely sure what he wanted but could be persuaded, marginally at any rate, that he could afford some of it. Some of what? It was here that advertising, the new smokeless industry, came into its own.

It was advertising, in substance, which made the suburban man what he is. It made him sartorially aware, steered him towards the car he drove, the sherry he drank, the golf club he joined; it even influenced his choice of vote. Consumer capitalism may have been founded on the existence of a working-class market, but it was for the suburban middle class that a multiplicity of choice – 'brand image' - was popularized.

By the 1950s the prototype sub-urban man had reached such a point of sophistication that he was ready to colonize new territory; in such manner did the suburbanite graduate as the commuter.

Village England, unchanged for centuries, was not only threatened – if that is not too strong a word – by the commuter; the weekender was staking his claim, retireds needed space. They constitute the 'overners', 'interlopers', 'incomers', so called by those born and bred along the way of this journey into England. They are not ecstatically welcome and they are not vociferously unwelcome; mostly they are tolerated as objects of mild curiosity, sometimes scorn, sometimes envy. Occasionally they are resented, especially weekenders, two-home itinerants whose affluence forces up property values, depriving young villagers of their heritage. Often they contribute nothing to the place of their adoption, translating their own ways rather than experimenting with the customs of their hosts.

In this book the country journalist tells a story of an old fellow being interviewed as the village ancient. 'You must have seen a lot of changes in ninety-six years?' he was asked. 'Aye,' the sage replied, 'and I've opposed every one.' The journalist acknowledges the perennial trap of all old men, yet his own personal statement remains: 'In my young days we believed in Beecham's Powder and instinct.'

In plainer words . . . the good old days. But the good old days were very often putrid; and not always as innocent and God-fearing as the myth perpetuates. Laurie Lee reminds us that where communications were bad, incest flourished. There is nothing new about permissiveness, only in the disproportionate amount of publicity it receives. There were always those beyond temptation; Daft Willie was one: 'He has not done a great deal with his life. And now he is old, no one wants him; possibly he was never very desirable, being simple. He never walked a girl after church or held hands at summer fairs, watching Punch and Judy on the sands. No girl ever traced the lines of his face with willing, eager fingers or wished him in her bed. They would have called him Daft Willie, giggling behind his back, and spread their thighs for handsome boys who knew a thing or two. Willie missed all this and so his loins remained inert. Those pert and predatory girls of long ago who could have made of him a man, left him instead a eunuch; so he turned in on himself, to his own language hard to follow, and to silence.'

Mrs Bray, who moved into the big house when she married seventy years ago, exclaims, with all the hauteur of Lady Bracknell, 'Would I *move*! It's a very suburban habit all this moving . . . quite deadly.'

'It's important to restore lovely things,' says Frank Axe, the builder. ' . . . It may all come back . . . I can't believe that mass-production is the final answer . . . we've got to care more.'

'I don't miss the flowers and sky so much,' says blind Maud. 'I remember all that, it doesn't alter. What I miss is growing old with my husband. I remember him as he was thirty-seven years ago. He can see my wrinkles and knows I'm old – but he's still young to me, he hasn't changed.'

Reg Honeybun, publican: 'Those people in the town worry. They sit up looking at each other, then one says what's the time? And they look at the clock and say is that all, we can't go to bed yet then. I've never known about time . . .'

Wilf Simcock, coal-miner: 'We knew real poverty, but we were still taught manners . . . there aren't many Tolpuddle Martyrs left.'

Oliver John Morris, gardener: 'I'm a stranger in my own village . . . in my time the place was alive, you heard the sound of children playing on the green, laughing. There's no kids today, not on the green – they're untidy in a beauty spot, so they're hidden away on council estates.'

Times have changed, that is what they are telling us; as if we didn't know. So they cling to the past, reassured by the world they once inhabited, remembering sixty years ago more clearly than last week. It was their own special world, the world of the village; you were born to it or you were an intruder. There was no other way.

Who are we? That was the question. And really we don't know, for we are fast becoming a tribe of separate isolated selves. In all the ages of man – Stone Age, Age of Reason, Age of Enlightenment – this must surely be the Age of Self. The class system, for better or worse, is undermined; the family structure, scarcely for better, is disintegrating. We are becoming units of one, self-orientated, self-absorbed. There is a tendency to fake interest in the environment, the Third World, abortion; we scale butter mountains, declare farcical cod wars, invest green pounds; populations die of malnutrition, while, in its wisdom, the *Guinness Book of Records* relates that Bobby Acland of the Black Raven in Bishopsgate, City of London, consumes 1,000 bottles of champagne per annum.

Aunt Emma, she say: 'We're all sent here to help others.' Grandad, he say: 'Well, what are the *others* sent for?'

This is the basic comment on who we are: givers or takers – as has always been

9

the case; it is merely that the takers are gaining ground. The epidemic of more, of wanting more, of claiming more as right rather than merit, is spreading. There are pockets of resistance and these occur in the country, in the village, with greater stamina than in the city.

Children of a future age may satisfy their need for acquisition in cities, but it is unlikely, at the final count, that they will find peace there.

Towards the end of *Candide*, Voltaire summarizes a parallel dilemma:

Pangloss takes every opportunity of reminding his friend Candide of his success in life – '*All the events in this best of possible worlds are connected. If a single link in the chain were omitted, the harmony of the entire universe would be destroyed. If you had not been expelled from the castle, with those cruel blows, for your love of Cunegonde; if you had not been imprisoned by the Inquisition; if you had not travelled over America on foot; if you had not plunged your sword into the Baron; if you had not lost all the sheep you brought from Eldorado, together with the riches with which you were laden, you would not be here today, eating preserved citrons and pistachio nuts.*'

'*That is very well said, and may all be true,*' replies Candide, '*but let's cultivate our garden.*'

MICHAEL WATKINS
TARSTON HALL
NEEDHAM MARKET
SUFFOLK
SEPTEMBER 1980

The Yeoman

CHAPTER 1
THE YEOMAN

Leslie Lewis

New Year's Day was greeted with restrained enthusiasm in the Herefordshire village of Dilwyn. There were even those who would have preferred to cancel the whole business, to remain stoically with the old model, disdaining January 1st. The devil you know . . .

Because the past year had not been an unqualified success: the Phantom Fire-Raiser had struck again, a couple of barns in his tally, two or three hayricks, escaping undetected as was his elusive custom; the poachers had a bonanza too, not the local poacher who enjoys an esteemed place in folklore, but townsmen with high-powered getaway cars and high-velocity rifles – they even winged a keeper one black night. To say nothing of the ramblers who left gates open so that cattle strayed from here to Leominster.

But this first day of January, now here was something else. Fourteen degrees of frost were recorded in places. This frost, appearing as an exquisite decoration, could be cruel. Snow came next, all in the same twenty-four hours, driven by a north wind into drifts deep enough to swallow a platoon of marines. Icicles hung from gutters like stilettos and somewhere an old lady, living alone, was stabbed by winter's ferocity. They called it hypothermia – which meant she froze to death.

There was no let-up for days. A metallic sky was welded on to a starched, unyielding landscape. When the wind dropped, the only sound was of silence. No birds sang; it was too cold for such frippery. Yet up at the big house on the hill Mrs Bray was in full song, as cheerful as when her rhododendrons are in bloom. She was not singing to keep up her spirits, for her spirits have no need of elevation – they are always up, there being no other place for them. The pipes had frozen, a burst was imminent, and Mrs Bray was dressed in much the same way as she is for glorious June or February fill-dyke. She is not a person given to making concessions.

The heating at Henwood, the Georgian house on the hill, was not turned up, for the good reason that there is no heating. Kitchen flags were dungeon chill, and in the dining room, beneath portraits of long-dead Brays, stern of countenance, Oxford coarse-cut marmalade congealed into frozen stickiness in the jar. In the drawing room a coal fire glowed wanly; about a hundred yards away, at the other end of the room, an ancient single-element convector heater chattered away, its weak breath coaxing the threaded Christmas cards into a tremble.

From a sofa, humped and rumpled as an old elephant, Mrs Bray pours afternoon tea from a silver pot, passes Messrs Peek Freans Family Assorted biscuits which shed sugary crumbs over the carpet: 'Cold? *Is* it cold?' She considers the proposition briefly but none too seriously, as if it seems to her as unlikely as a Whig revival. 'I hadn't really noticed. There's not much time for these things . . . it's a very modern practice to worry about the weather. It's all to do with changing attitudes. There's no love of work these days – or pride. When I came to this house seventy years ago with my husband, we had a wagoner, Hayson was his name, he used to wear a smock and his wages were twelve shillings a week. They had seven children and Mrs Hayson sent those children to school in freshly laundered pinafores each day. On Monday they took a penny to hand to the schoolmaster for a week's learning. They left school at twelve, and my word they'd learned something – they could write beautifully too. Cottagers didn't grow flowers then, that would take up valuable vegetable space. Everyone kept a pig in the backyard. Everyone brewed beer as well – one of the men, Montague, made it out the back here . . . Montague's Sunlight, they called it.

'No motor cars, of course. We had dog-carts and we'd walk to church through the trees, it was like the Black Forest – all felled now. Three living-in maids in the house . . . now there's just me. Well, there must be change . . . we stopped using the oast houses in 1932, I think it was. And everyone lives so well now, new curtains every year in the cottages – their sitting rooms are far grander than mine.'

Mrs Bray sips her tea, snorting merrily at the topsy-turvy world about her. Her back is straight, ramrod straight as old Queen Mary's, her eyes bright as a jackdaw's. No, a few snowflakes would be unlikely to spoil Mrs Bray's week.

'Would I *move*!' She makes the word sound a profanity. 'What would I do with my bits and pieces . . . country people like continuity. It's a very suburban habit all this moving . . . quite deadly.'

Bray, Lewis, Moore, Bevan, Lane, Griffith, Bradstock: these are the names hereabouts, strong yeoman names whose sons and daughters grew up together, married and intermarried, binding land and fortune together in dynastic knots. Unravel them at your peril. They are a tough breed, these yeomen, wary of strangers and of frills, clannish; with more victories to their credit than defeats.

Neither are they newcomers to the land; it has all taken time. A lot of time, sweat and muscle have fertilized their soil. Open the 1851 volume of *History, Topography and Directory of Herefordshire*: there, under the entry for Dilwyn '12 miles north-west from Hereford, and 16 north-east from May, in the Hundreds of Wolphy and Stretford, Weobly Union, Weston deanery, Hereford archdeaconry and bishopric . . .', are listed farmers – George Bray, Henry Moore; and there, under 'Miscellaneous', is William Lewis, blacksmith. The population was 1,112 then and the parish covered 5,973 acres. The soil, we read, is clayey and loamy, and Captain Daniel Peploe Peploe was Lord of the Manor; and Mr John Deane, postmaster, accepted letters from Leominster at a quarter to 12 am, despatching them at a '¼ past 3'.

It reads like an idyll: on Sunday the vicar, the Reverend Henry Charles Morgen, MA, whose stipend was £400 annually, conducted his services, assisted by curate James Powell; on Monday the youngest members of their congregation, pinafores spotless no doubt, attended the Dilwyn National School for Boys and Girls. God was in his heaven, the Queen upon her throne, and all was right with the world. There was croquet on Capt. Peploe Peploe's lawn, and bondage in his fields. A breed of cattle known as Herefords was coming into fashion.

Earliest records of Hereford breeding can be traced as far back as Richard Tomkins, who died in 1723, bequeathing his cow Silver to his son Benjamin; although it was some while still until the formation of any sizeable herd. One such was the Haven Herd, founded by Thomas Lewis in 1822. In addition to perfecting a strain of beef cattle, doing his best to propagate his own species of Lewis, Thomas also raised his dead brother's children. There came a time, however, when Thomas held a Dispersal Sale of his herd; in 1888 it was, sixty-six years after he went into business. It was one of his nephews, James Lewis, married as chance would have it to Margaret Bray, who purchased certain reliable stock at the Sale, among which was lot 9, Teresa 2nd, a cow born in 1882. Teresa was destined to become ancestor of both the Tiny and Thrush families so prominent in the Haven Herd today.

All very neat and orderly, one might think: the dynasty gathering strength. Yet had it not been for the meticulous intervention of an outsider from Shropshire, the Haven Herd, and others too, might have remained in an awful muddle. T. C. Eyton, Esq., Gent., of Donnerville, near Wellington, wished to establish a herd of his own. Let him tell his own story: 'Having always been an admirer of Hereford cattle, and anxious to possess a herd of them, I proceeded into Herefordshire with a view to purchasing some, but found so much confusion among pedigrees, that I at once determined to compile a Herd Book . . .'.

Published in July 1846, *The Herd Book of Hereford Cattle* provides comprehensive records of breeding progress, esoteric but to the point: 'Young Victory, MF, calved 1837, bred by Mr J. Rickets, by Victory, dam, Dainty, bred by Mr Rickets, by Radical, g.dam, Mottle, bred by Mr Rickets, by a bull of his own.' Ah, but what's this, the very next entry: 'Victory, calved – bred by Capt. Peploe Peploe.' So even the squire, Capt. Peploe Peploe, had been clever in climbing on to the bandwagon.

The authorities have been kind to Dilwyn, allowing the brave new road to by-pass the village, so that noise and fumes are at arm's length. Dilwyn remains unchanged, unviolated, manacled to the past which welcomed Thomas of Colchester as priest in 1275. The cottages are of lath and plaster, timber framed, painted black and white as in the style made famous by Weobley, a couple of miles across the fields and looking rather like the Hollywood version of Village England. Weobley is a place not to be underrated: any village which, with a population of 5,000, returned two Members of Parliament until the Reform Bill, must have a bit of pull somewhere – which is why perhaps Weobley seems to lord it over Dilwyn to this day. The world comes to Weobley, leaving Dilwyn slumberous.

A way out of Dilwyn is Bill Jones' pride and joy; for Bill Jones, churchwarden and gravedigger, became Jones the Builder too, erecting a fine redbrick house in 1961. Called Little Haven, this is where Edward Lewis has lived since moving from the old house – the house in which the family settled 300 years ago – to make room for his son Leslie. Such is the way of the yeoman. So Leslie shares the Haven with his three children and with his sister, Sybil; and one day, God willing, he will stand aside for his elder son, Edward.

In 1914 Edward senior went off to the Kaiser's war, a private in the Ninth Devonshire and Shropshire Light Infantry: 'I don't remember all that much . . . only thing I seem to remember is burying the poor devils. I've read that in one battle there were more killed than in the whole of the Second War and I'd believe it too. I remember the wet and the trenches, the mud and the hunger . . . we were more hungry than frightened, we shared a loaf of bread among fourteen men, that's all there'd be some days. But I wasn't really there, I was still on the farm in my mind – I never really left Dilwyn. But all the men left the farm for the front, so I went too. It was mother I missed most – she'd send me a loaf of homemade bread every week and when it came down the line we'd share it out. I'd change my baccy for food, I didn't smoke, but they'd pass a fag around, one pull and on to the next . . . a man would give his life for a fag.'

Then one day an officer told them the war was over and they could go home; so they packed up and made for Blighty. Edward Lewis took a train to Leominster, then walked the rest of the way, kitbag over his shoulder. King and Country gave him a couple of campaign medals, Dilwyn gave him a cigarette case, and he was unmaimed; so he had done well enough and settled down to breed Herefords, more to his liking than killing Germans.

Ten years later Edward took over the Haven Herd from his father. From then on he used a succession of stock bulls, including Westhide Forecast, bought in 1938, a grandson of Eyton Taurus whose sire Lion became Royal Champion at eight years of age and happened to be bred by Edward's uncle, George Bray. In 1949 Edward was joined in partnership by his son Leslie, and Favourite was the first bull they purchased, bred by Edward's cousin, Harry Moore . . .

15

Today Edward sits back, comfortable beneath a picture of his hero, Sir Winston Churchill. Edward's hair has turned white; it is his vanity, and a comb, pink as a heifer's tongue, sticks out of his breast pocket, ready to keep the profusion in place. Leslie has virtually taken over, yet the bond is between father and son, insoluble; it is in every word, every gesture and look.

Leslie was born in 1931 and went to the village school, from where he attended Worcester Cathedral School until he was sixteen. 'I was going on to agricultural college then, until father asked old Charley Coxon over Pembridge way for his advice. "If you want to spoil the boy," old Charley told dad, "you send him to Cirencester – that's gin farming." So I came home to work 160 acres of my own, looking after the horses, shires we had. One of them, Duke we called him, kicked me one day in the orchard – that woke me up. I worked with Wilfred Herbert, he was champion ploughman, still with us after forty-eight years, and Jack too – he's been here forty-three years.'

It was a short apprenticeship. At eighteen, the year he went into partnership with his father, Leslie suffered the first of two blows: 'It was that hot summer of 1949 and we had 300 hop-pickers down from South Wales – I often wondered if there was a carrier among them. A Monday afternoon it was and I didn't feel too good. One of the men said I looked poorly. "Take a Beecham's Powder, lad," he told me. But I just seized up, couldn't move . . .'

Leslie Lewis had polio and spent nine months in hospital. The six other cases with him all died. For years Leslie's legs were in calipers, then he graduated to crutches. Now he moves slowly with stick and elbow crutches. 'It gave me time to think; I knew I'd have to become another kind of farmer. I couldn't tackle hedging and ditching, so I took to administrative farming. Father was the practical one, with mother as Chancellor of the Exchequer. I studied the stock . . . we've about 750 acres here, with 500 head of cattle – 200 breeding cows and followers. I know every animal by name, its dam, its sire, going back three generations of pedigree. Some of the men can do it too. Take the Irishman, Eric – he's only got to look at a heifer once and he'll recognize it life-long. And he can spot illness a mile off . . . if one of his cows is calving, Eric will sleep in her manger.'

The Haven is a rambling place, mellow; clean as clean can be, well loved by Leslie and sister Sybil who keeps house for him. There are massive championship trophies, rows of leather-bound herd books, framed pictures of breeding bulls.

16

Leslie has chosen an armchair, his favourite, which places him in a corner, in shadow, on the defensive. There is an anonymity about him; his withdrawal palpable; his laughter mirthless and full of pain. But there is still a will to talk, to communicate; he gives the impression of a man who needs to reach out, but who has lost the knack.

'The scientists have taken over,' he informs. 'It's all politics and permits – we export fewer cattle than we did twenty years ago. There's a twelve months' quarantine to export to Australia because Blue-tongue disease could wipe out every herd of cattle in the sub-continent . . . but we don't have Blue-tongue here . . . it's in America. It's hard to sell to Africa because we seem to object to what's going on there . . .

'Horse breeding is easier, all a horse must be is fast. With cattle there's change all the time. Doctors say fat is bad for us, so we breed lean animals, they've got to put lean meat on. Thirty years ago the Ministry of Food were paying for heavy cattle, so we bred big hefty animals. In the fifties and sixties we bred smaller, early maturing cattle for the South American market – today we're back to taller, leaner animals for Europe. Ultimately we breed for the housewife – who is influenced by what she reads in magazines.

17

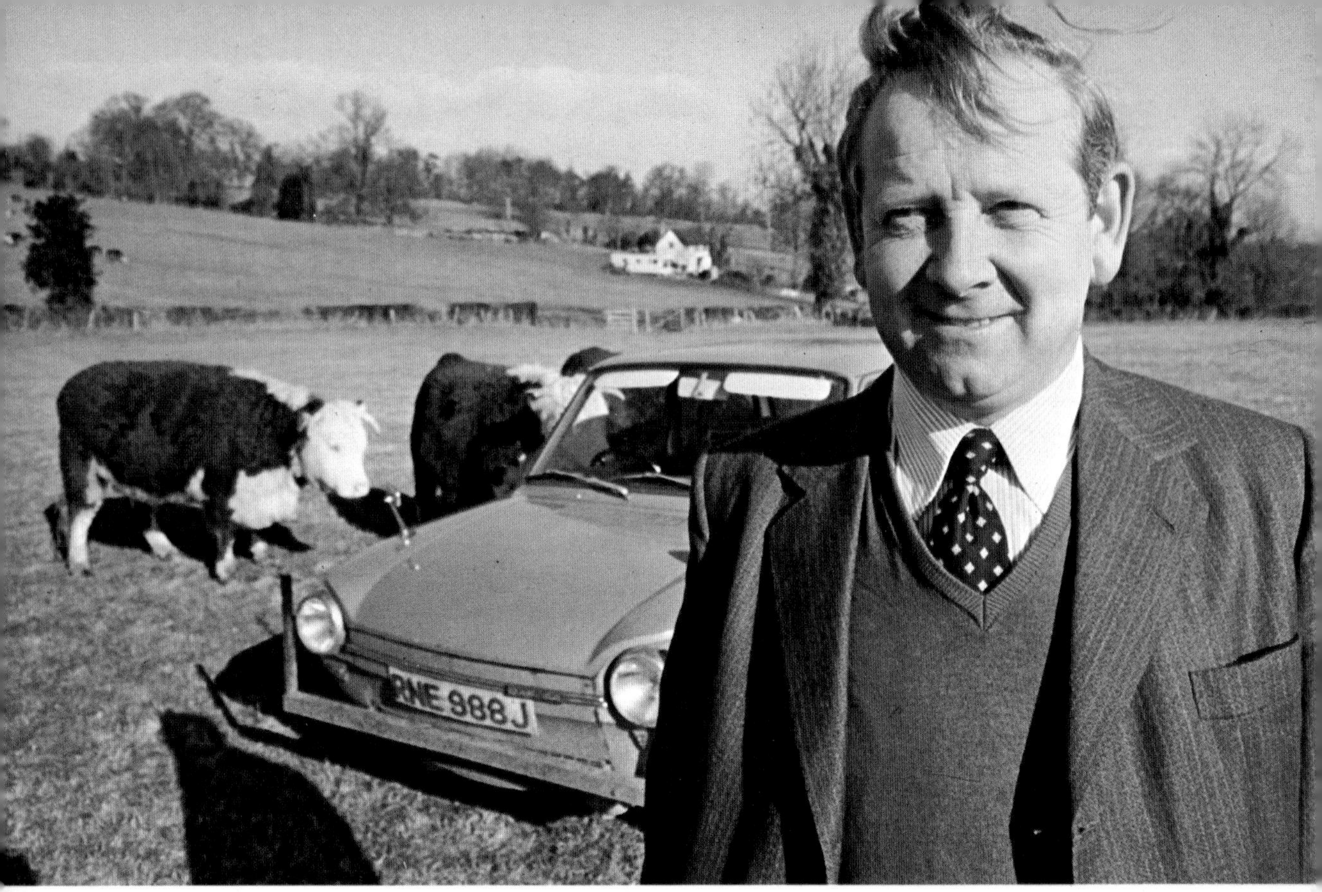

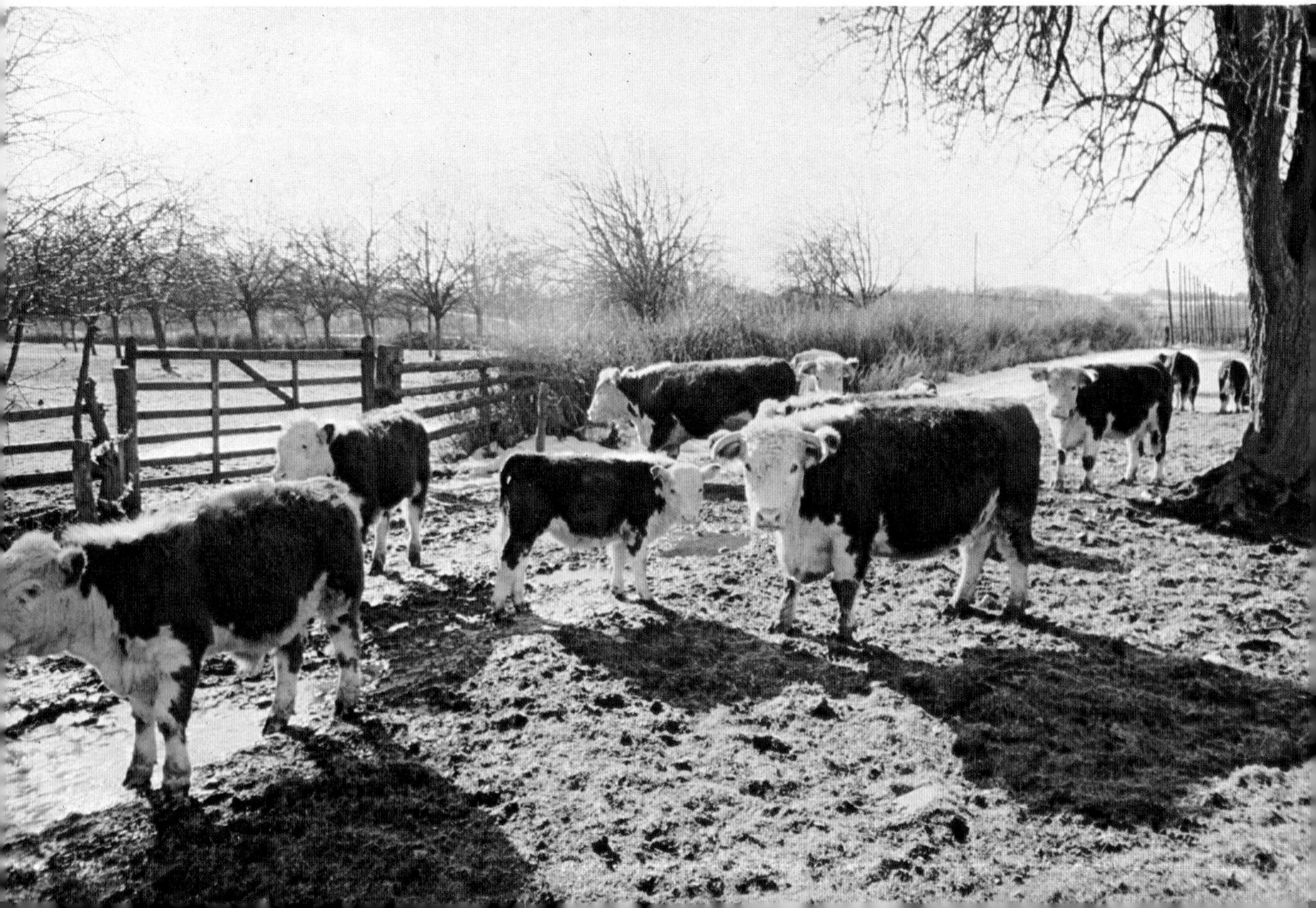

'Herefords are a lovely breed, they live anywhere, in heat and cold, a docile breed, they'd do anything for you – convert roughage into beef . . . you realize what an animal means to you when it reaches the end of its usefulness. We used to bury them on the farm – well, you can't do that any more. Nowadays the knacker comes over, shoots the beast and takes it away for sausages. I always make sure I'm off the farm that day.

'Foot and mouth is what we fear most. If it's detected you must slaughter the entire herd. The government pays full value, but you've lost a proud strain, a life's work. It's not just financial ruin, it's emotional ruin – a true stockman would cry. Me? My heart would break, that's all. We're not as hard as you may think – and father was never a hard man . . . he'd rather hurt himself than someone else. It's never been for money alone – money to me is just worry.'

Outside, the snow is returning, settling in fluffy, moist, Walt Disney flakes over hedgerows. Hedges grow tall here, a rare legacy of husbandry in times when every foot of land is at a premium. Cattle stand unperturbed, chewing rhythmically, soppy ruminants with nothing better to do. They have china eyes, mistily, softly vacant.

Leslie Lewis leans on his stick, each movement an effort, fearful to watch: 'There's so much talk about inflation, but there's no inflation in this business. Our herd record was in 1978, 12,000 guineas – yes, we still use guineas – for a bull,

Haven Lumberman. In 1946 the record at Hereford market was 12,500 guineas paid for Weston Masterpiece . . . no one's really making money from beef today.

'I remember when we drove cattle freely through the village – all the cottages were fenced to keep animals out. Today gardens are open-plan – an American idea,' he says darkly. 'We always drove cattle by road – you'd set off to Pembridge at 6 am leading a bull by the nose. In the other hand you carried a lantern so's when the bull tossed you over the hedge, you could light your way back. They say my aunt was the first woman to lead a bull to market, that was in 1917.'

He is still for a moment, staring ahead, his boots blancoed in snow: 'You may have wondered . . .' he begins. 'Perhaps you heard – my wife left me seven years ago. Went off with my best friend, we were at school together. It's very complicated because he farms the land adjoining ours – so it's difficult to get out and about in case we run into each other.' He laughs, a bitter sound. 'Sybil runs the house for me, but when the children go back to school, it's like a morgue.

'Marry again? Well, you don't know who to trust, do you? It knocked the confidence out of me – if I feel I'm getting close to someone, I retreat. I often wonder what went wrong, it's tempting to think "Why me?" Anyway, if I re-married, it'd probably be a failure. So it's the herd and sleep – and living through the children. All three are breeding from their own heifers, building up a herd. I have no views on my ex-wife . . . I don't think about her.' It sounds a lie, and probably is, self-deception treating the patient.

Loneliness is usually an urban affliction. In places where there are bingo halls and pubs, lamp-posts and people, you expect love; and when there is none, it is a shock. But there are no problems in the country, no expectations; it is just there to take, to take without guilt. There is God's earth to mess around with, growing vegetables or just sitting. There should be no such thing as trespass, or suffering; yet Leslie has found both on the land his family has farmed for 300 years.

'Pretty, isn't it?' he says, surveying his white dominion. 'But cattle don't get fat on snowballs.'

The Shepherden

CHAPTER II

THE SHEPHERDESS

Freda Iveson

Malcolm Stonestreet, Vicar of Askrigg, likes to tell a story about one of his predecessors, Uctred the Priest who, shortly after his arrival from France in 1175, went calling on the Earl of Richmond. Uctred, nimble of tongue, begged a parcel of land in Upper Wensleydale running into the Pennines; and here he built a house and a chapel. Here too he planted seeds of corn and vegetables, and attempted to breed sheep and cattle; he said his prayers and taught the faith. For eleven years he struggled, but he was not a hill-farmer – so he failed.

There is a calloused touch to these North Yorkshire Dales; nature has the last word here, not man . . . and the word is without charity. The long, silent hills are desolate, austere; their message is of warning more than welcome. For the soil is shallow, three to six inches at most, insufficient to support crops other than grass. Men have tried and, like Uctred, have been broken. Sheep may safely graze, cattle too – and there's an end to it.

'But it's no good thinking', insists the Vicar, 'that we're a dying village – or even a surviving one. We're a *fighting* village. Let anyone hear you call Askrigg dying, they'll stone you. They would too. As a community they're bloody-minded, cussed, difficult. They don't want leadership and they don't want to know what's going on in Leeds, let alone London. They're fiercely independent, but they're threatened all the same . . . threatened by the Big is Beautiful philosophy that wants to devour everything.

'Trouble is they don't know they're threatened . . . I know, but they don't. Their essential quality is that they belong to each other, they're from the same mould, shaped by the moors, the valley, wind and rain. By God, they're not a Yes Man people – they're sturdy, tough, weatherbeaten. It's a long winter, brief spring and autumn, the sun never really warms the land. Outsiders tend to think in terms of "Dark Satanic Mills" hereabouts, of deprivation. But the villagers define a deprived person as someone who doesn't live in Askrigg . . . they're fighters all right and I want to stay until the fighting is over – perhaps it never will be.'

A battle lost, a battle won – the difference is small at the final count. But such consideration devalues the cause not at all. On 23 January 1535 Lord Conyers and Sir James Metkalf summoned the men of Askrigg to attend Musters on Middleham Moor. Among the Archers stood Gawden Thirnbek with horse, Ninian Metkalf with horse, Olyn Fawcett with horse and harness; the Pikes included Jamys Wedderhelde with horse; while among the Bills, Richard Wedderhelde with horse and steilcapp, and William Wright with horse and salett (helmet) were willingly called to arms, as were their descendants in two wars of this century, shedding their youth and blood in foreign fields. No doubt they swore as they went down, disbelieving at the last gasp that anyone could better a dalesman.

In these parts the land and the people are one; confiscate his land and a man is nothing, he is emasculated. It is both his privilege and his right to take nourishment from common-land and moor; if he wishes to hew sandstone from the gill to build a cottage, or grave peat to warm his hearth, he is free so to do. Ownership of property in Askrigg is the only permit required. But his allotment, that which is his own by deed, is guarded jealously. Cross a dalesman's path if you dare. He is hemmed in by these hills, knowing little of the world beyond his sparse acres; his justice is rough justice, as his fealty is beyond question. He is his own man, and likely to remain so.

Askrigg has reared few sons to fame and fortune, power and glory. The muses of poetry and literature have found an unresponsive climate here; the academies of philosophy, politics, medicine and music have included few Askrigg pupils. Few, indeed! Why, none at all, if one cares for truth. Scholarship is not to the palate of this village; the chief concern is for survival, despite the Vicar's denials.

The scars of Ellerkin rise above Askrigg in Wensleydale; in the distance Baugh Fell, Whernside, Penyghent . . . closer are gentler hills: Lovely Seat, Dodd Fell, Nab End. Dry-stone walls cross the land, and cross it again and again, containing minute rock-strewn meadows, a thousand miles of wall marking a man's property, staking his claim since time was young.

At the centre of Askrigg is the church, drawing the village to the sanctity of her episcopal skirts. 'It is a majestic, usable, 600-year-old focal point in the market place,' says Malcolm Stonestreet. 'Unfortunately, it is a sanctuary and a place of comfort only. It does not provide the dynamic; it is a house of prayer – but is this enough?'

The Vicar is tall, evangelical by persuasion, a person generous with himself; he is a leg-puller, a teaser, gregarious and caring. If his ministry is one of suffering, it has not marked his face; he has the looks of a matinée idol. Preferring well-cut tweeds to clerical grey, he disdains dog-collar for jersey, wearing a crucifix around his neck. Out walking, he carries a shepherd's crook, using it in the way of a squire striding his broad acres; indeed there is something of the flamboyant eighteenth-century squire-parson about him. He comes from Kew in the deep, effete South; but for twelve years has made the dales his own. It bothers him that the dales may not yet have made him their own: 'I'm in transit, but it's become home. I'm "our Malcolm", accepted but not one of them.'

He is known as a bit of a character, a live-wire always raising money for this and that; holding concerts, plays and the like in church. 'Stunts', volunteers someone from Hawes, along the valley, 'he'll have a cocktail bar in church next.' But the Vicar seems unaverse to his image, nurturing it; he is self-aware, no plaster saint . . . and apparently well loved by Askrigg.

Up The Street and round the corner, Maggie-Joe Chapman – Joe was the name of her husband – remembers the day 'our Malcolm' introduced himself: 'He came bouncing up to me in church and said, "Well, then, I'm your new Vicar," and I said, "Now steady up young man, you heed my advice and take no notice of any of us." Very bouncy he was, for an incomer.'

Not much enamoured of 'incomers', is Maggie-Joe – although she is on pretty shaky ground, born as she was at Muker, a hamlet two or three miles up dale. But, as an octogenarian, she is entitled to a little licence. She hugs the fire in her stone cottage, her feet in woolly slippers that go flip-flop as she crosses the room to adjust the controls of her colour telly: *Blue Peter* is reduced to an incandescent pinpoint of light. 'No, I wasn't really watching – it's habit more than anything.

'Incomers,' she draws her breath in sharply, 'there's this couple who walk their dog up and down . . . do you know what it did? Its business on my front step – number two's on my clean doorstep. Well, when they'd gone I wrapped it up in a newspaper and took it back to their doorstep. The idea! I'd like to see them pushing a pram instead of pulling a dog – children are breeding well today,

28

beautiful children. Incomers . . . they're just like writers who come along picking your brains because they're so brainless themselves. We can chatter our heads off and all they do is put it in some book.'

She is gleefully vituperative, bowling down her foes like ninepins, hugely enjoying it all. She wears her age like a cloak; it makes her invulnerable. 'That woman at the shop – gone long ago. Always had her finger on the scales, just popped it down when she was weighing up your groceries – they're still up to their tricks very likely. Oh, I could tell you a thing or two . . . I'm very fond of the Vicar. Reminds me of our Billy – I caught him saying his prayers once and I said, "What are you praying for then, Billy?" and he said, "I'm praying for a bellyache so's not to go to school." '

She comes to the door, casts a sergeant-major look at the step, glowering at the ice-packed snow, an old lady with a vendetta against change. She has made her statement, contributing as much as any; three strapping sons she bore in three years, then a couple of daughters for good measure, looking after them all, making Joe a good wife to come home to. They are gone today, gone their way; and Joe is dead. So there is telly now, Wednesday visits from a kid sister of seventy-seven, and an occasional commando raid against new neighbours.

Four hundred and fifty people live in Askrigg, with another thousand around it; yet the village feels deserted, locked up for the winter. By Easter the tourists are returning, hikers, ornithologists, photographers; a mixed blessing. Good for trade, of course – the Askrigg Foundation Shop, another of our Malcolm's schemes for raising funds, does a roaring business in souvenirs. There is local pottery for sale, leatherware and paintings, crochet and tatting work, marmalade, biscuits, knitted goods and rather horrid looking creatures in clay. The coffee shop prospers, so too the King's Arms, and the picture postcard industry booms. Jennison Stocks, Warden of Low Mill, is happy because his Youth Centre will be sleeping twenty-seven boys and girls who will go canoeing, pot-holing, pony-trekking . . . but how the tourists clutter up the place, gawking at squat grey cottages, asking how you get to Gayle.

Anyone can find his way to Hawes, Bainbridge or Aysgarth, they're marked on the map, signposted even. But Gayle, at the foot of Sleddale and Burtersett below Wether Fell End, takes knowledge, perseverance. Mr Bartholomew has not placed it on his road map; Reader's Digest has been equally cavalier . . . for which omissions Gayle should be eternally grateful.

Look over your shoulder when leaving Askrigg, focus on the church and see what tricks light and distance play in these half-forgotten dales. Describing the scene in 1799 in a letter to Coleridge, Wordsworth wrote: 'The steeple of Askrigg was not quarter of a mile distant, but oh, how far we were from it.' It is much the same with Gayle, so near, so unapproachable; especially in snow. The snow is nothing along the A684 because this is the Milk Run, kept open at any cost; so ploughs gobble the stuff up, spitting it out into drifts heaped against walls – and lorries hurtle through to the Milk Marketing Board before the cream curdles.

Things are not the same at Gayle, which has not quite caught up with snow ploughs yet, so the lane scaling the dale is closed, there is a notice at the foot of the hill saying so. Men of Gayle look at Askrigg as if it were New York City, what with its coffee bar and Temperance Hall, Mobile Library and pub. Not that there are many men in Gayle, it being so isolated; but the souls who do live here belong as they would nowhere else. They are not cut out to be in another place.

One such man is Jim Iveson who, with Freda his wife, lives at East Shaw Farm, a stern-looking house put up in 1879, with few refinements for added comfort since. Ask how they met and when, their answer is vague: 'We met locally, didn't we? We've always known each other since the choir, since Sunday School . . . in 1957 we just got married. There's Alice too, our daughter, she's twenty-one, works at the Creamery in Hawes. She's done a lot of things, worked in a bank . . . she's been to Tenerife.'

There is a pencil sketch of Alice, done by a Tenerife pavement-artist; it shows a girl with strong profile, lean and determined. 'She's determined all right,' says Freda, 'can't stand the thought that we'd ever have to sell the land – but who would run it when we're gone? She had a boyfriend who was interested in farming, but it didn't work out. She's right, it goes against the grain to sell land, it's owning a little part of England that's yours to walk over – the tycoons can't take it from you. We don't really think about getting old – we'll go on until we're physically unable.'

This land, this precious plot, has made them what they are; as one day it will kill them, because they will never give up. It was hard come by: while Freda's father was earning a penny a hole mending dry-stone walls, Jim's father worked the gravel pits; but what he wanted was land, his own. Eventually he bought a field, and then another – which, as is proper, Jim took over when time was ripe. He married Freda, who was by then teaching Sunday School, settling to make a living from cattle and sheep. Jim looks after eight milking cows, Freda is shepherdess, guarding a flock of 170 black-faced Swaledale sheep. Together they make a living, enough to get by on; they would get by better if they sold out, drawing on the interest. It is a proposition they have never considered.

The snow makes it difficult to reach their house; it is an uphill trudge, leaning into the wind, cowering under a fusillade of hail-pellets. Drifts are five and six feet deep, so that it is good to come into the Ivesons' living room, to watch your boots steaming by the Aga. It is a sparse room with a sofa and a couple of upright chairs, no pictures or ornaments, just a clock to tell when it is time for tea. Freda wipes her hands, slices off a piece of fruit cake and a slab of Wensleydale cheese in equal portions, eating them together as is the way.

'These dales-bred sheep are tough,' she says. 'They clip a coarse wool, four to five pounds each, used to make Swaledale cloth and for stuffing mattresses. They can stand a lot of cold – we bring them down here to the lower slopes with the first snow, but sometimes we're taken by surprise when they're high on the moor, and every now and then they'll get buried in drifts. One was missing sixteen days a while ago – the dog sniffed her out of four feet of snow, quite bright she was. You could hardly cut the snow with a shovel, but I fed her vet medicine and milk . . . she'd probably been chewing her own wool. She wouldn't be driven, so I led her from a string through the horns, carried her over walls all the way down . . . I was that jiggered.

'There was one sheep, in 1947 it was, lasted seven weeks buried . . . they're sensitive animals, intelligent, they know what's what. I've always liked sheep, they rely on you 100 per cent – that's why April's my favourite time, when they're

31

lambing. It's eighteen hours a day then, I deliver them myself but they're good mothers. They clear up their own mess. No, they don't have names, but I know them all and they know me, they recognize my voice . . . they wouldn't come for anyone else. We just know each other – they've more sense than humans. Take the strikers in factories . . . they're to be pitied, they don't know where they're going – but my flock does. Strikers wouldn't and couldn't do what we do, I'd like to see them try. There's no downing tools in this job if you want to keep fed. We work as hard as our parents . . . we could make more money, but we eat well enough.'

Cattle and sheep are no respecters of clothes, so the Ivesons are virtually in rags, Jim's trousers held up by cord. Their complexions are burnished, scoured raw by wire-wool elements. In Knightsbridge they might catch a glance, but it is unlikely that they would expose themselves to London after their one experience: 'We went on the Underground, but didn't think much of that. People were like flies, heads down, they didn't seem to notice each other or anything else – like part of them was dead. There's a cinema at Richmond here, only thirty miles away – we go every year or so; and Alice went to a dance at Bishop Auckland, that's sixty miles. We think people in the south are a bit soft, pampered – they probably think we're heathens.'

Saturday is frantic because Freda and Jim will not work on the Sabbath, never have done, nor their parents before them. Anyway, there are two Sunday services

for Freda, who still sings in the choir and says a prayer for the sick – 'and them who think they're sick'. There is a contour-quaking Saturday breakfast of bacon and eggs, porridge, hot weak tea; outside, the farmyard muck has blended with frost into a tawny, crunchy-surfaced toffee mallow. Jim's cowshed is warm, stickily scented with milky magic.

On steep, snowy slopes Freda is humping bales of hay upon her shoulders: one bale to twenty sheep, that's eight-and-a-half bales up a slippery hill, the black-faces watching her every step, crowding about, shoving and pushing, housewives at a Debenham's sale. Three Border Collies, Jill, Ben and Bess, are watchfully at heel, haunches down, quivering, crawling in sudden lunges, longing for action. Across the valley, doom-laden clouds are scudding in from the west, obscuring peaks, a blizzard winging in from the Irish Sea. East Shaw Farm may be cut off by nightfall. Freda grimaces: enough is enough. The whole of Wensleydale has had a surfeit of winter.

Yet it is not summer Freda longs for. In the wicked month of August strange faces appear along the lanes; strange faces and strange number plates on cars from foreign places. Queues form in the shops of Hawes; Freda has even seen black people in the supermarket. Not that Freda has anything against blacks, it's just that she might not have them to tea; any more than she would folk from Northallerton, thirty-five miles away . . . she and Jim know their place, as others should know theirs.

It is spring that Freda loves, when lambing is over, with her charges safe and sound; when curlews are nesting in the meadows, when peregrine, kestrel and sparrow-hawk wheel and swoop after prey. Sometimes it is a buttercup spring, often pignut predominates; and there is thyme, cinquefoil, lousewort, yellow rattle and wood-geranium. This is Freda's time of year, her joyous time.

Jim and Freda own their land; yet one could say that it is the other way round – that the land owns them. They are in servitude to their possession; they would have it no other way. And when they die, the strength of the grass, the stone walls, the moors and the community will not have been lessened by their touch.

The Lifeboat
Coxswain

CHAPTER III

THE LIFEBOAT COXSWAIN

David Kennett

Alas, poor Yarmouth! Shy, demure Yarmouth, Isle of Wight; not that forward hussy of Norfolk's east coast, with her 'Kiss Me Quick' paper hats, furtive fumbling in the tunnel-of-love, her shamelessness and heart of gold. Oh dear, no; Yarmouth, IoW is a lady born and bred, as anyone can see.

Yet there was a time, for 162 years to be precise, when she would have been hard-pressed to qualify this breeding, to prove her pedigree. Historically speaking, she became a Displaced Person, undocumented, bereft of background. It was as though Yarmouth suffered collective amnesia: one day a heritage, a sense of the past, the next day none.

It all happened in a thoroughly reprehensible way one chill night in October 1784 when a certain Naval officer – a high sense of corporate rectitude having erased his name from church records – was dined by the Mayor and Corporation at the annual Court Leet Dinner. (It was custom for the Mayor to summon twelve local residents to form common jury for the Court Leet, for which duty they were rewarded by dining at the town's expense.) The Naval guest, with perverse gratitude, made off with the town chest, believing it to contain remaining stocks of wine with which he had been liberally entertained. Discovering, aboard ship, that the chest contained the dullest of registers and documents, the villain heaped the lot into the Solent.

So there you have it, a borough with no past, a town without history; until 1946, that is, when a slim volume, *Yarmouth – Some Records of an Ancient Town*, appeared, written by a retired Master Mariner, Captain A. G. Cole, who, after a life at sea, returned to the house, Landguard, in which he was born seventy-five years earlier. After travelling the world: 'It was to Yarmouth I returned when I "swallowed the anchor", and from Yarmouth I expect to take my departure on my last voyage.' Before setting out, however, on this final one-way Odyssey, he painstakingly reconstructed the life and times of his home-town, in so doing restoring the vulgarly appropriated birthright.

His researches were so diligent, his appetite for retribution so sharp, that he even exposed the Naval culprit by name: Lieutenant Charles Cunningham Crooke, of HMS *Expedition*, who in due course was sued by the Corporation for the return of the chest and contents or, alternatively, £10,000. On 19 July 1787 the case was tried at Winchester before the Sheriff and a 'respectable jury', who awarded £500, which was duly paid to the Corporation. Crime and punishment; but Yarmouth's recorded history remained at the bottom of the sea.

Or did it? The gallant Captain's investigations revealed papers found in the estate of a solicitor, Richard Clarke, which shed new light on the matter . . .

In these notes Mr Clarke remarks that in June 1785 he met Crooke in Newport, learning from him the loss of the Yarmouth papers, including the original Charter granted by James 1. Crooke denied taking the chest aboard ship, but said that it served the Corporation right because without the Charter he did not believe they could return Members of Parliament. At a later meeting, the rendezvous being the Newport Coffee Room, Crooke confessed to knowing where the chest was in the previous December when he was having the contents examined in London, but that the porter carrying them had been robbed . . .

Captain Cole concludes with restraint that 'Crooke does not seem to have been a man of high character', and that whether the treasure is in Davy Jones' locker or in a London safe, it is Yarmouth's loss. Who knows, it might turn up yet.

Which seems of only peripheral importance on a February day, with gale force north-easterlies raking spume off Solent rollers. The Lymington ferry is still running, slewing drunkenly into Yarmouth harbour, yawning its jaws to regurgitate an undigested stream of motor vehicles. Elemental alchemy turns slanting rain into sleet,pock-marking the quayside; mist closes, blotting out the mainland. At sea, sirens of unseen ships make low abdominal sounds, eerie, melancholy notes of a marine fugue. Yarmouth – made by the sea, living on the sea – battens down hatches.

High Street, The Square, Bridge Street are deserted; bar parlours of the George, the Bugle, derelict; Harwood's Yacht Chandlers have not sold a ha'porth of tar all morning. In his surgery Dr Gerald Hurley, stethoscope about his neck, draws on his umpteenth after-breakfast cigarette, cogitating gloomily that, 'The entire island's ill. You name it, they've got it – 'flu, back-ache, colds. It's the devil, this winter . . . I've not been so cold since the lifeboat took me out on exercise, with a helicopter flailing overhead like a damn sycamore pod. They winched me up in the cradle: "Let's see if the doctor can walk on water," yelled the coxswain – and I was lowered to the surface. Only they got it wrong and I got a ducking. He's a scoundrel, that coxswain . . . which pub did he take you to? None? Don't give me that . . . a scoundrel. Of the nicest sort, you'll understand.'

Somewhere in this house called Landguard, the dwelling Dr Hurley bought from that same retired Master Mariner, a woman is singing, accompanied on a piano. 'My wife's warbling again . . . it's something she does quite often,' the doctor explains loyally, somehow implying a condition from which Elizabeth Schwartzkopf is immune. 'We came from County Limerick twenty-five years ago, so we're still "overners", that's what they call strangers . . . "overners" and "yachties", they're the weekend sailors. We Irish are everywhere, like tics in America; but we're accepted here – they like you if you like them. Everything revolves around the sea, the sea and the lifeboat.' Gerald Hurley is honorary doctor of the lifeboat; he lets the fact slip out, an inconsequential aside, yet one he returns to not infrequently.

The gale is in full voice too, howling, moaning in Wagnerian fury; it buffets Town Hall, crashing against parish church, making no distinction between buildings sacred or secular. Not long ago the sea invaded Yarmouth, so that dinghies paddled along Quay Steet, leaving half-drowned Hillmans and Austins gasping for artificial respiration. Then the new breakwater was built and Yarmouth kept its cellars dry; but you can never tell what mischief spring tides bring. You can never take the sea for granted – which is why Charlie Attrill, Harbour Master, is out in his launch, checking moorings, seeing that ropes are not chafing. Standing with his back to the tiller, he strains against the wind, yellow oilskins branding him a maniac to be afloat in such weather. But there is no one else to do it: too bad if *Tamarisk* takes on water, if *Seaspray* slips her mooring, with no one to make safe. The 'yachties' are miles away, in gilded Throgmorton Street, patrician Pall Mall, well beyond earshot of halliards flapping against masts.

Yarmouth is compact, a borough in miniature, toy-town without much to worry about when the sea is docile. The Town Hall, rebuilt by Lord Holmes, Governor of the Isle of Wight, in the third year of George III's reign, seems a doll's-house before which it would be unsurprising to hear Larry-the-Lamb bleating at Mr Mayor. The Methodist Church, next door to Dr Hurley's conservatoire-surgery, is as fanciful as Hansel and Gretel's cottage; the Primary School has gingerbread tiles – and palm trees, with the look of dessicated shaving brushes, give the playground a tropical touch. As for the Ladies Lavatory, conveniently at the pier entrance – well, one can only stare in awe at such rococo for such simple needs . . . would it be impious to pray that Yarmouth's good ladies appreciate the care, the depth of ingenuity that went into the construction of such a loo?

To north and west waves lap and slurp at the town's foundations. From castle ramparts a stubby cannon points rudely across the Solent, primed to blast Sealink from the water at the touch of a fuse. Through streets and alleys, narrow as a puritan's smile, and there, in no time at all, is greenery, slopes no higher than hills in a child's pop-up picture book.

Along the coast, minutes by car, lies Freshwater Bay, cowering beneath the

gale's onslaught, not a soul at large. The Albion Hotel is boarded and shuttered, with the abandoned look of a haunted ballroom. The last waltz over, dancers steal away as the orchestra rest violins, Italian waiters pack their bags, taking their dark good looks back to Sorrento. The Mermaid Bar sign is missing a couple of letters, shuffled away by the wind. Beach shingle bombards the terrace; seaweed drapes promenade rails; trelliswork weeps tears of rust. The storm rages and there is no one to listen.

Living on the sea and by the sea, Yarmouth is not sea-*faring*, if you will allow the distinction. Her menfolk do not fish for profit, nor put to sea in merchant style; they are boat-builders, designers, chandlers, carpenters, caretakers. The harbour is Yarmouth's bread and butter, not the ocean; a harbour-nursery for rich men's playthings. Yet island races need more than this; they are not a contemplative breed, thirsting for trial as they do. There must be combat; it is in their blood, Norman blood, Breton blood, some of it. In Yarmouth there is only one villain: the sea. The lifeboat is there to meet the challenge.

Such a challenge occurred on 3 July 1978, as the cross-channel ferry *Viking Venturer* entered the Needles Channel at 20.02 hrs, sighting a capsized yacht five cables south of Bridge Buoy. There was no sign of life aboard. A helicopter was scrambled and at 20.06 hrs Needles Coastguard requested the launch of Yarmouth lifeboat. At 20.15 hrs the 52 ft Arun, *Joy and John Wade*, launched, with Coxswain David Kennett in command. There was a strong breeze to near gale, force six to seven, blowing from the southwest, sea moderate to rough, tide flooding. Visibility was reduced to fair in rain squalls.

While the lifeboat was on her way, the helicopter, locating the 17 ft yacht *Turpina*, put a diver aboard who, searching the cabin, reported no sign of life. Arriving on the scene at 20.38 hrs, the lifeboat began a box search of the area until dusk but, finding nothing, decided to abandon the hunt, taking the yacht in tow. Coxswain Kennett manoeuvred close to *Turpina* which was lying with her stern only out of the water, showing a freeboard of some twelve inches. A grapnel was thrown aboard and the yacht taken in tow, but in moments the line broke. The tow was again made fast and, as the lifeboat got under way, the yacht's bow was lifted clear of the water – at which macabre stage it was seen that a body was lashed to the rigging. As speed was reduced the bow sunk again and in the gale now mounting from west by south, it was impossible to recover the victim. Another attempt to put a helicopter crew member aboard failed and, for the second time, the tow wire broke as the lifeboat edged into a slight lee around the Needles.

The 'Y'-class powered inflatable was manned to take a line to the yacht, securing this line at second shot to one of her cleats; the cleat sheared. Finally, the lifeboat, using its anchor as a jury grapnel, managed to wedge it into *Turpina*'s cabin and the tow started, the lifeboat heading back to station at 2½ knots to enter harbour at 01.30 hrs. *Turpina* was brought alongside the jetty, righted, the body of Richard Sinclair extricated, before the lifeboat returned to her moorings to be made ready for service again by 03.00 hrs.

On another occasion, 'In recognition of the courage, excellent seamanship and determination displayed by him when the lifeboat under his command rescued the crew of five of the yacht *Chayka of Ardgour* . . .' Coxswain Kennett was awarded the Silver Medal of the Royal National Lifeboat Institution. The inscription reads: 'Let not the deep swallow me up.'

Dave Kennett was appointed Coxswain of Yarmouth lifeboat in October 1971 when he was thirty-two, inheriting *The Earl and Countess Howe* which, during her thirteen years' service, was launched 168 times, rescuing ninety-two lives. On a July Sunday six years later, at a service of dedication, the Duke of Kent named her successor *Joy and John Wade*, a fifty-two foot monster capable of eighteen knots – twice the speed of the previous boat – with buoyance to initiate self-righting in six seconds in the event of a capsize. The congregation sang 'O God, our help in ages past'; the Minister intoned, 'The waves of the sea are mighty and rage terribly', to which the faithful responded, 'But yet the Lord who dwelleth on high is mightier.' 'O hear us when we cry to Thee, for those in peril on the sea', – and the boat was blessed, named, slipped her moorings.

Although full-time Coxswain, Dave Kennett runs the local garage in Mill Road; he loathes cars, he says, preferring the outboard-motor business he has built up with his assistant Doughnut, so named because his vocation had been putting holes in doughnuts down at the Galley Coffee Lounge. Then he wanted to better himself, so he joined Dave in a more advanced mechanical enterprise. Dave lives round the corner from the garage, at Lindum in Station Road, a 1930-ish house, not big, not small, about right for a man, woman and dog. There is a patch of garden at the back, grass and a few bare sprout stalks. It looks as if locusts have been at those sprouts. Dick Barton is on television but Ange, Dave's girlfriend for nine years, turns down the volume. Dave refers to the screen now and then, as if expecting an important personal communication. About the house are mementoes of the sea: a polished copper lantern, photographs, sextant. In the hall, stacked beneath the red emergency telephone, are oilskins, sea boots.

Dave is chunkily built, more serviceably so than Adonis, designed for endurance. He is barrel-chested, his fingers spatulate, with the stigma of oil and scar-tissue upon them. His massive left forearm is tattooed. He is easy going, unsuspicious; but it wouldn't do to make a fool of him. He wears a heavy-knit seaman's jersey, moccasins on his feet. About his achievements, his citations for

bravery, he is matter of fact, neither modest, nor immodest; so that it is surprising to note his pleasure at being invited to an 'At Home' given by the High Sheriff at the Royal Yacht Squadron. He handles the embossed invitation card reverently, as one would a piece of Sèvres; yet it is not easy to imagine him making small talk, cocktail in one hand, canapé impaled on a little stick in the other.

He was born, one of two children, in a house called Pen-y-Bryn at Freshwater Bay, attending local Secondary Modern, conscious always of the sea and that it meant something to be near it. 'Mum and dad split up then, and I stayed with Mum until I joined the Merchant Navy. Dad frightened me, I couldn't do anything to please him, so he used to hit me. I hated him . . . he's a nice old boy now, a carpenter by trade. We made it up, he comes round here with veg from his garden – and we took him to Le Havre on a day trip once, only he wouldn't go ashore, said he wouldn't care for France. He's all right now, married again and they suit each other . . . it's just that Dad never climbed over the wall into the outside world.

'They've got this old dog, great long-haired thing, diabetic into the bargain . . . Dad walks that animal along the beach every morning at half-past four. We see quite a lot of him these days. My sister? No, not much. She's perfect – you know? Everything in the house perfect, so you don't like to sit down in case it squashes a cushion. I'm a bit mucky, see?'

He looks sheepish for a moment; then offers hospitality, pouring an industrial quantity of gin into a tumbler. He does not take a drink himself. Every now and again he is confused by the chronological order of events in his life: 'What year was that, Ange?' he asks. 'How long have we been together?'

Ange, a gentle, placid person, fills in the blanks. 'No,' he continues, 'we've never got round to marrying . . . it's better in this life to live with someone you want to rather than marry someone you don't . . . it's only a bit of paper. People can take it or leave it. I got married once, when I was twenty, but she was a London girl, couldn't stand the sea, so it only lasted a year.'

Dave Kennett left school at thirteen to take a job on Totland Bay pier to be near the sea – helping with the boats in season, maintenance in winter. At sixteen he joined the merchant service, circumnavigating the globe six times before returning to the island to work for himself, buying a harbour launch to ply under contract to the Ministry of Works, weekend fishing trips, towing, salvage. Eventually he took over the garage whose trade had been running down: 'I like being my own boss, couldn't take a nine to five job – I want to work more than eight hours a day, more like fourteen, six or seven days a week. Then came yacht maintenance, delivery and so on . . . that'd be about fifteen years ago, Ange? Joined the lifeboat crew, made up to second coxswain quickly. Why did I volunteer?' Confusion once more. 'Well – it's the excitement, isn't it?' Ask a silly question . . .

For the lifeboat crew excitement comes in all shapes and sizes, from single-handed dinghies to ocean-going steamers; it can come on a balmy July midday or a demoniac January midnight. The seeds of this excitement are planted when a vessel is endangered: a Mayday is transmitted or a red distress signal fired, such signals being monitored by the Coordination Centre at the Needles coastguard station, four miles from Yarmouth. Perched on chalk cliffs high above the Needles teeth, all calls for help within the station's area are intercepted. The coastguard Duty Officer, it may be John Asprey, telephones his report to Dolphin Cottage, a pace or two from the Bugle in Yarmouth.

At the alert, perhaps reading one of his books, *Great Sea Battles*, is the lifeboat honorary secretary, Leslie Noton, whose responsibility it is to decide whether to launch. It is not invariably a foregone conclusion: 'The coastguards give me the facts and I weigh them up to see whether to press the button . . . we're in the business of saving life. We're not a salvage company, I don't believe in going out to tow a boat in. At the end of it all I have to make a report answering every question you can think of – so Dave Kennett knows he can't do a damn thing without me. You should see him at sea, he's a different man – handles that boat outstandingly. Much of the trouble at sea is simply thoughtlessness; if you take a car on the road without a jack, it's a nuisance that's all . . . it's not the case at sea. Tragic case once. A competent yachtsman had a heart attack, but his wife and children hadn't the faintest idea about navigation . . . lot of people think the Solent's a lake, but there's a tidal stream four to five knots in spring.'

If Leslie Noton decides on a launching, he reaches for his telephone and Dave Kennett must be at the other end; if he is not at his usual number, he leaves an alternative with the secretary. A brief is exchanged: position and description of the 'casualty'. Two maroons are fired then, you can hear the report three miles away: ' . . . and everyone moves like hell,' says Dave. 'If it's at night I get dressed, jump in the car, blasting the horn all the way to the lifeboat house. You should see the men, running down the street pulling their trousers on. I pick my crew then – they can't all come. It might be Keith Hopkins, Nick Chandler, Alan Howard, Stewart Pimm – we put to sea with about eight. David Lemonius, he's my number two, comes; and Bob Cooke, the mechanic.

'Everyone's in oils and life-jackets – to the quay then, into the boarding boat and out to the lifeboat moorings. Bob starts the engine, one lad calls up the coastguard to say we're on our way, radar's switched on, mooring ropes let go and we proceed to sea.'

It sounds smooth enough, a well-rehearsed routine – but a routine put in perspective when you learn that the operation, from the moment the secretary telephones the coxswain to the time the lifeboat puts to sea, takes nine minutes at night, four minutes by day. On average there are twenty-five launchings a year, the crew receiving £2.25 for a call-out and 70p an hour at sea – about a third of a London shorthand typist's hourly rate.

The crew are not seamen: they are dairymen, mechanics, plumbers. Dave

refers to them as 'land-sailors', keen as mustard, disappointed to be left behind – despite the fact that they prefer facing fifty-foot seas to the warm cabin below; they suffer less sickness above. If they experience fear, they do not show it, realizing fear's contagion. In Yarmouth they are known as 'our boys'; they are folk-heroes in the way of footballers and television personalities.

Many launchings could be avoided: 'You get the show-off,' says Dave. 'The bloke with a fancy braid cap and blazer wants to impress his secretary – they have a few drinks, wind gets up, sails start flapping, suddenly the boat's uncontrollable. They panic and put up a red flare.

'No, it's funny but it doesn't make me angry. I can understand because the sea's one of the last free places today . . .'

Between Yarmouth and the lifeboat is a bond, a blood-brotherhood. A man is daring for many reasons: to prove himself, vainglory, as an addiction like any other stimulant, because he fears the cowardice in his own heart. Acts of daring give a man the assurance of his own worth; and when the assurance passes away he will turn to other things. There is not enough within a man himself; without courage, love, faith, he may as well not exist.

Of a lifeboat Sir Winston Churchill said: 'It drives on with a mercy which does not quail in the presence of death; it drives on as a proof, a symbol, a testimony, that man is created in the image of God, and that valour and virtue have not perished in the British race.'

The Builder

CHAPTER IV

THE BUILDER

Frank Axe

'Where did we go wrong, do you suppose?' muses Hugo Groom, the schoolmaster. 'When I came to Chalfont St Giles as a teacher in 1911 my salary was £95 a year, passing rich I was . . . now I hear they start at £3,000. Jolly good luck, but I'll guarantee I wouldn't change places with them for happiness. They're all joining marches and so on, and they don't look well washed, some of them. It's all greed and envy . . . what went wrong? I suppose we went from too little to too much too quickly, that's the trouble – all came too fast for us to cope with.'

The schoolmaster who became headmaster, remaining head for thirty-four years, sits in his study doing the *Daily Telegraph* crossword. On the wall is a signed Munnings print, on the desk an old Imperial typewriter – 'British Right Through', it reads on the carriage. The headmaster has been retired twenty-four years; add it all up, it comes to a tidy sum. 'If I last another five weeks, as I've every confidence of so doing, I shall be ninety,' he declares. Except that he never will declare; he'll just go on until he is clean bowled.

'It was a delightful little village in those days . . . there was a milestone telling you that London was twenty-three miles away. I imagine London is still twenty-three miles away, but it doesn't seem so. Do you know, the population was 1,762 then, 881 men and 881 women – *exactly*! At school we had 732 pupils, 366 boys and 366 girls. Now that's what I call good management. Today God knows what it is.

'Chalfont was an agricultural area, big houses – a lad went into the garden for five bob a week, on to the farm for 12s. 6d., pleased to get it. Young gents went off to the City in spats for £3 a week. What's happened to the big houses today? I'll tell you: Mrs Bashall-Dawson of The Vache, that's the manor house, she went off to live in San Francisco. Now the Coal Board's taken over . . . long way from any coalfields, eh? They waste millions of our money up there. The Grove was a huge estate – the Army Kinema Corporation have it, making some kind of films I shouldn't wonder. The Stow, where Colonel Phipps lived, turned into a maternity home.

'No tarmac roads then, just flint from the stone pickers in the fields . . . poor old chaps broke up the flints. I had a bike with solid tyres, not the pneumatic sort, they'd be punctured, you see? Hedges and trees met overhead, it was something to see. Great droves of sheep and cattle came down the lane, loads of hay passed through to Uxbridge and on to London. Now it's all trucks, fumes and noise, London's nearly here . . . I've held a driving licence since 1908 and still have a car, but I've a mind not to renew that licence.'

How reassuring it sounds, this demi-paradise of 1911 in the Buckinghamshire village of Chalfont St Giles; but for Hugo Groom, schoolmaster, the enchantment was short-lived . . . In June 1914 Austria declared war on Serbia; in July Germany declared war on Russia; and in August Great Britain declared war on Germany. Hugo Groom responded to the call to arms and for his pains was machine gunned in the bloody trenches of Passchendaele. He has never been quite the same man since.

In his study blue eyes peer over half-moon spectacles, while his hands shake uncontrollably. He apologizes for this, resenting the impediment. In his plum-coloured smoking jacket he is something of a dandy, sartorially dashing for a retired schoolmaster in his ninetieth year. He dismisses Passchendaele, it is something he does not wish to discuss, more comforted by pre-war memories when cattle were driven past his door and buntings decorated the village street in times of national rejoicing. Still he stands erect as the soldier he once was – 'British Right Through', it reads on his carriage.

'I see in the *Telegraph*,' he says, 'that certain city schools employ security guards to keep order . . . something must be dreadfully wrong. There's little peace in the world today.'

From Chalfont and Latimer Underground Station it is thirty minutes to Baker Street; by road, well by road it's a different matter because the moment a new stretch is open, they dig up the one before. From the gladiatorial arena of Marble Arch, it can take minutes or hours, houses, shops, factories, faceless shopping precincts blurring into each other all the way. Then suddenly, at a pub called the Pheasant, you turn left down a hill, into eighteenth-century Merrie England, Fielding's England, village green, pond, pump and all. Why, Esme Osborne, still alive and nicely, thank you, remembers being told from memory of the last culprit to sit in the stocks for stealing a chicken – Lofty was his name, a solid name hereabouts.

Chalfont St Giles rests in a bowl, hemmed in by fields all round, cattle lowing at Saturday morning shoppers queueing for crusty home-made loaves from Stratton Tea Rooms. It is a village of mellow red brick, timber, studwork and plaster; the age of aluminium, like that of the steam railway, has by-passed the place, leaving it cheerfully petrified, virtually as it was when craftsmen made their marks on building cornerstones. No wonder the pride, the sense of exclusivity, what with the Preservation Society, the Conservationists, the undisguised hostility towards the mildest hint of reform. Emotionally, Chalfont St Giles is forbidden to outsiders, as Lhasa was to Tibetans.

In a way Chalfont is under siege, outflanked and outmanoeuvred by alien

49

forces determined to colonize her every remaining inch of soil. Development and speculation are the martial arts which Chalfont is sworn to resist. Odd as it may seem, it is this very threat which conspires to keep village spirit alive – and alive it is, vociferously so. You find in Chalfont, beleaguered by opportunists, as much village ethos as survives in remote rural communities. 'Suburban' is an indelicate word to use in Chalfont.

'There's a certain amount of self-created strife about,' says Colonel Douglas Clark, curator of Milton's Cottage. 'I try to drum up visitors for the museum, but the village don't care for tourists – except the shops, of course.'

A pretty cottage it is too, this retreat of John Milton's from where he fled the Plague of 1665, from where he completed *Paradise Lost* – as cynics will have it, upon the event of his third marriage. It was probably built near the end of the sixteenth century by the Fleetwoods, Lords of the Manor of The Vache, long before the Coal Board acquired the title deeds. Only the briefest stroll from the church too, which must have been a blessing to the devout, blind poet.

Near this church, just beyond the graveyard, is the course of the River Misbourne, about which legend decrees that when the river dries, so will disaster strike Chalfont St Giles – which was precisely the state of affairs in 1963 when the present Rector, the Reverend Anthony Johnson, was inducted. It is a story he tells against himself with shy relish.

Entering through a lych-gate, you pass between a pair of yew trees; a few yards on is a pair of non-yew trees and then you are at the porch, recently stripped of lead by vandals so that the church is constantly under lock and key. But Mrs Johnson might show you the fourteenth-century wall paintings so remarkably preserved, pointing out the thirteenth-century piscina, the tomb of William Gardiner and his wife Ann Newdigate who departed this life 400 years ago, and the grave of Bertram Mills of circus fame. There are snowdrops in the grass, the very, very first sign that this winter will pass as all others.

'People are our commodity, by jingo,' says Mrs Johnson, going on to explain how her husband rings the church bell daily at 9.30 am to let the village know he is praying for them: 'Every day is somebody's bad day . . . we all need prayers said for us.' She is more circumspect on the subject of Nightingales Lane, Chalfont's millionaires' row where on the seventh day the devil created heated swimming pools and saw that they were good. 'When my husband visits, he sometimes sits by those pools,' says Mrs Johnson, explaining the Rector's temptation in the wilderness.

Sodom and Gomorrah is on a hill above the village, a tasteful arrangement of nineteenth-century Gothic mansions, twentieth-century Tudor palaces, twenty-first-century Hollywood estates. 'Beware – Guard Dogs Loose' warn signs; and there is a rash of burgler alarms on every pillar and post. It is a known fact that millionaires like to live cheek by jowl because you get a better class of neighbour that way. At one house, marginally smaller than Hampton Court, live Arabs whose security floodlights burn night and day.

Wonderful for trade, these Arabs, with the orders they turn in to A. Warner, family butcher: ten chickens, twenty-four steaks, two rolls of beef, four legs of lamb, twelve veal escallops, are about the average weekend needs. When Harry Warner came into his father's business those years ago . . . 'I used to sit under the village elm waiting for customers, trade was £40 a week . . . today it's £4,000 and there's no time for a cup of tea.' Times change and the old elm came down on 15 August 1932; customers who were addressed as 'Madam' are now addressed by first name or 'dear', and 'love' . . . and there are 'no poor people in Chalfont today – you can't afford to be poor in this village'.

Warners do a fine line in sausages: Bucks Bangers, Pre-Wars, Regency, Chilton – about 1,000 lbs. a week, that's 8,000 sausages. They are spicy, made up not so long ago from their own secret recipe; but that has changed too now that seasoning can be bought from the manufacturer in bulk. It all has to do with that magical phrase 'cost control' – and convenience, of course.

'Sunday lunch – roast beef and Yorkshire pudding is a thing of the past for most families . . . in the same way that Monday is no longer washing day. How often do you see washing hanging on a line? Everyone's got washing machines, tumble dryers. A cold slice on Monday with the wash, that's how it was. Now it's set the dial and open a packet of frozen fish fingers and chips.

'We started delivering by horse and cart, calling at the back door, sending out monthly accounts . . . it's cash and carry business today. We don't see many customers from Nightingales Lane, they buy in bulk for their freezers – they probably go to Harrods.

'Another thing, the butcher, baker, grocer . . . we used to be people of standing in the village, looked up to, respected. All that's gone. There isn't even a proper grocer in Chalfont now – the supermarket saw to that. But we try not to change too much in ourselves – we still treat the blue-bloods as blue-bloods and the peasants as peasants . . . that's our little joke.'

Another Chalfont man, born and bred, who can share a joke is Sid Hearne, eighty-five, still spitting venom from yellow fangs: 'Always told I was born in a snowdrift,' he announces proudly. 'So I'm rough and ready, see? They call me an old rascal – it's just that I'm up against a lot of things and only went to this little old school here. Never mind, too much learning's no good to anyone. Bloody education, there's too much education . . . it'll ruin their careers. I told Sir Norman Birkett – he's an old friend of mine,' he confides slyly, 'I said to him, "You split them long words in half and someone'll understand what you're on about." '

Sid coughs a lot, more of an angry splutter really; he enjoys being angry, it's good for him, his daily tonic. He moves at a little trot, darting in and out of sheds behind his bungalow, hissing with rage at chickens because they haven't laid. He wears a discarded Green Line bus driver's uniform he bought from Oxfam, a red spotted handkerchief in the breast pocket. Upon his head he wears a Cossack hat, like a mangy sleeping tom.

'My dad put waterworks through this village. Before that there was just a pump. We're in well-boring and sinking, and tree felling, see? I topped that old elm that came down. Axes we used, no chain saws, just hand saws. Sank wells all over, felled trees for building sites and roads . . . people are sentimental about trees. A tree comes before a person's life today – all this preservation, they're bloody useless. What happens if a tree falls on someone? Used to be called an act of God – that's all finished . . . it's an act of stupidity for not felling it. You can love trees, but trees is trees and people is people.'

In his sitting room he rubs grizzled head with his hands, veins tumescent, writhing, cobras ready to strike. His boot laces are undone. A television lies face down in a corner, innards gaping, disembowelled as a Tyburn traitor. On a dresser is a row of First World War campaign medals.

'Royal Field Artillery I was in . . . Loos, Ypres, we smashed them two places up. Frozen feet – you took your boots off, cor! The stink.' He grimaces, fangs bared in a rictus of memory. 'We ate frogs fried in Dubbin – stuff you cleaned horse leather with – frogs and dog biscuits, or we'd starve. Shaved in tea leaves, washed every few weeks, never saw a bed for four years . . . had malaria, scabies, dysentery

. . .' he rummages through an inventory of ailment and disease. 'Had three horses shot under me – and I've shot a few Huns in my time.

'Came home then to get on with my job – trees and water . . . only the council . . .,' he pauses, darkly malevolent against an enemy who replaced the Hun. He gives the Jack Russell at his feet a prod with his boot. 'Water . . . call it water with all that fluoride stuff – bad for your stomach, I can tell you. Bloody council . . . live and let live, that's what they should learn. Still, I'm one of the happiest men in old England and they can't take that away.'

No, they can't take that away, not the council, MI5, or little green men from Mars – all as bad as each other in Sid's opinion. Yet whatever their shortcomings – council, preservationists, conservationists – there is a certain achievement. Chalfont St Giles remains marvellously intact, a living breathing village, full of gossip, a measure of spite, abundant neighbourliness. Transgress the unwritten book of rules and you will suffer, exiled to heaven knows what emotional tundra. Accept the ethic and you will be cocooned; the village looks after its own – particularly when they did their best.

Frank Axe did his best; he never failed the village, but in a way the village failed him. Perhaps his best was simply too good, perfection being an uncomfortable bedfellow. He was the village builder, who built houses to last: endurance was his criterion, short-cuts did not come into his reckoning. He never learned the subversive art of compromise.

Frank Axe builds houses no more. A. J. Axe & Sons Ltd, Builders and Contractors, is still there of course; business continues beneath those three gables put up at some time in the sixteenth century. It is just that somehow the heart has gone out of things; the shop has become a general builders' supplier, run by one of Frank's three sons, Will. You can buy nails and glass and wood for joinery . . . and you can buy Surf and Suttons Seeds, teddy bears, sherbet, candy lipsticks and Sherbo Dabs. And no doubt there is nothing wrong in this; it just seems a let down for a firm that once built homes which would stand for years and years and years.

'Father came from North Wales,' says Frank. 'My grandparents were in the mineral water business at Towyn . . . grandpa retired and died within a week.

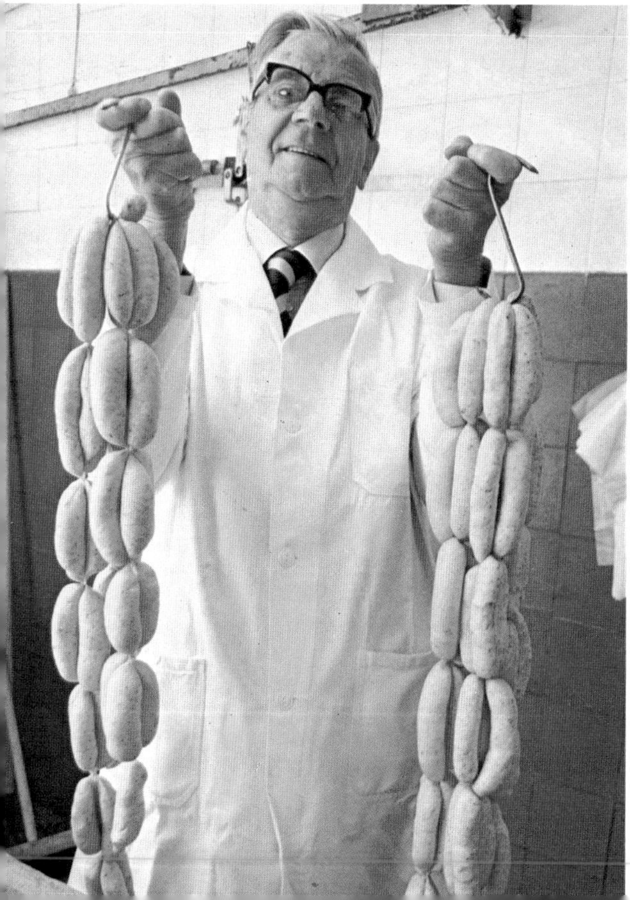

Not working killed him, he hated not working. So father set off south to look for work, stopped for a while at Chester, helping with the Town Hall. There'd been a fire there and they needed a carpenter joiner. Then he came on and put up for the night at The Feathers in Chalfont St Giles, heard that they were building a home for epileptics, went up to the site and landed the job as foreman . . . that's how we came to Chalfont.

'He soon met mother, a local girl, one of thirteen children – grandpa Tripp was in trade here and the sons, Lowing, Harry and William, were at the blacksmith's – that's now Forge Garage. Mother and father never spoke a cross word between them – three children they had, two boys and a girl. I came along in 1912, went to the Primary School when Mr Groom came back from the war . . . a good, strict teacher he was. Left school at fourteen to join father. We made joinery, window frames, staircases and so on. But it didn't work out too well, too many people went bankrupt on us.'

His face creases at the recollection; it is an india-rubber face, resilient. If it were re-moulded, by disillusion, betrayal, it would spring back to its natural expression, of trust. He is nature's gift to the confidence trickster; you could sell him shares in a Surrey uranium mine. His eyes are bland as a new born babe's and you may be sure that their view of the world will never alter.

'I trained as a joiner, so I went out on the buildings – woodwork, bricklaying, it was all experience, but I really wanted to build houses, good houses. So that's what I did – I can count up to seventy houses I built, and two rectories. The William Shakman project I'm most proud of, eight houses we finished in 1969 on Silver Hill. Couldn't do it now . . . Chalfont started building down to a price instead of to a character. There's all this cedar boarding, jerry building, economizing . . . take a roof, a normal roof is constructed with rafters at twelve-inch centres, cut either of four-by-two inches or five-by-two – it's changed now to prefabricated trusses three-by-one-and-a-half with metal dogs to hold them together, inadequate timbers, insecure. They can blow off in a gale, and have done.

'It's all official, nothing dishonest about it – just a lowering of standards so that safety as well as permanence are at risk. It's all short-cuts for time and money . . . I couldn't accept that, so we went out of business, forced out by those smart fellows, the speculators. When I started you built a house for ever – today it's for twenty years. I look around, you know what I see? Owners who'll be reaching into their pockets for huge maintenance bills long before the mortgage is paid. That's what it's come to.

'If you're going to be a successful builder, you can't be a successful businessman – it's not possible to wear a name you'll walk both sides of the street in. You do a job whether you win or lose; but to be successful as a businessman, profit is your first consideration. This is the age of the labourer, not the craftsman.'

He excuses himself, leaving the office above the shop to chaos and the sound

of passing traffic. Files and ring binders are haphazard, cheques, loose change, bank notes, a medieval adding machine, chocolate bars and half-drunk coffee mugs are in glorious disarray – it looks as if a company of poltergeists held their Annual General Meeting here.

Minutes later he returns, gingerly clutching a cardboard box which he places on the desk. He sits back, his three layers of woolly jersey lapping like waves against his equator. 'We found these', he says, 'when we were working on the Methodist church.' Lowering his hand into the box, the lucky dip retrieves a bottle, opaque, exquisitely shaped. 'How old would that be?' he asks in awe. Next comes an egg shell, wafer thin . . . finally the bowl of a clay pipe. But as you look closer it is no ordinary clay pipe; it is shaped like a lady's slipper, each tiny button-hole perfectly formed. He holds it tenderly: 'Now talk to me of craftsmanship . . . my son Will says he'll never let this leave the family.' His voice is full of wonder.

'Reminds me of my brother,' he continues '. . . A few years ago be bought two 1928 Rolls Royces, from a man in the film world. He loved those cars, rebuilt the bodywork from a plank of yew wood – the Rolls Royce Club in London said they didn't know such craftsmanship was still alive. He's still doing them up, he'll never finish that job.

'We restore, you see, not renovate – there's a difference to my mind. We restored Anthony Cottage, Rose Cottage, the Old Rectory . . . it's important to restore lovely things.

'It's funny but Chalfont St Giles still seems the village it was . . . people didn't change jobs, they stayed put, so you could never get away from the village . . . we had a resident policeman on a cycle, so you'd know the place was being looked after. Nightingales Lane used to be full of real educated people who knew how to behave . . .' He trails his sentence, reluctant to be censorious. 'But if you're born in a village you don't say to yourself, "We've become a suburb, bed and breakfast country" – it's as it always was. I still can't get away from the village.'

Hesitant at first, he now talks freely, delivering memories with added momentum, altering pitch as thoughts flood in. 'We built four-bedroom council houses for £899 a pair . . . in 1921 I completed a place in Burtons Lane for £475, sold recently for £35,000 . . . and Mrs Hollingsworth's house, she was from the Bourne and Hollingsworth family, we built in Nightingales Lane for £3,400 . . . seemed a fortune, but it sold last year for £125,000.' His lower lip pushes out, giving him a baffled, slightly petulant look. 'It all seems mad to me, can't understand it. When I was young property had no value, now it's the most valuable thing people can get hold of.

'We used to hear the King and Queen talking on the wireless about loyalty, their "loyal subjects" . . . *are* there many loyal subjects?

'Yes, I'm sad about it. Will's in the business, but the other two boys did something else, and I'm thankful. It may all come back . . . I can't believe that mass-production is the final answer . . . we've got to care more.

'I suppose I'll have to sit back now – I've had my time and on the whole I've enjoyed it. I loved building.' He looks out of the window towards the Rectory, so close that you can see Mr Johnson's outline at his desk, composing Sunday's sermon perhaps or sending up unworthy prayers for the waters of the River Misbourne to rise, giving added credence to his ministry. 'I wouldn't accept shoddy values when I built the Rectory, and I won't accept them now. That house is my pride. As I walk about the village, I see my name on bricks and mortar, and my name means something to me . . . in a hundred years' time passers-by will see my work and judge me.

'We come into the world with nothing and sure as anything that's the way we're going to leave it . . . except what we've created for others. I'd like my judges to say, "He did his best." '

58

The Lincolnshire
Gamekeeper

CHAPTER V
THE GAMEKEEPER

Stanley Elvin

As me and my companions were setting of a snare,
'Twas then we spied the game-keeper, for him we did not care.
For we can wrestle and fight, my boys, and jump out any where;
Oh, 'tis my delight on a shining night, in the season of the year.
The Lincolnshire Poacher

Had you been so minded – and of course paid your sixpence subscription – you could, on a January morning in 1932, have read Volume XXXV, No. 412 of *The Gamekeeper*, 'A journal devoted to the interests of game preservers'. There, in the leading article, you may have tut-tutted or nodded in approval at the stern words of the Editor, Mr Edgar Page: 'We refuse to believe that game will not be allowed to play its big part in feeding the country and furnishing employment, for that employment reaches very far and does not concern the countryside alone. Every pheasant, every rabbit, every pigeon, which go to market help to swell our food supply . . . we trust that what has been written will be accepted in the spirit in which it has been penned and that none will resent it as interference. If we all decided to face the year 1932 in the right way half our troubles should at once be at an end.'

How courtly it sounds, this language of the press, how well mannered and restrained in tone. The message is there, the hint of reform and self-sacrifice required to make 1932 a better year; yet the delivery is full of humility. There is no murmur of agitation in Mr Page's crusade, merely the gentlest of rebukes, as when he reminds us of our sense of duty: 'There is a tendency on the part of the wealthier classes to go abroad in these times . . .', these times presumably being the shooting season. To be abroad, the Editor implies, is un-Christian, unpatriotic, and immoral, when the alternative 'may bring new and ardent recruits to the ranks of lovers of the gun'.

So all we were required to do in order to halve our national troubles was to foresake Monte Carlo or Tangiers, those of us fortunate enough to have a choice, shooting instead at pheasants, rabbits and pigeons; while the rest of us with little choice settled down to roast, casserole or curry victims of the massacre of Yorkshire Moor and Lincolnshire Wold. What bliss if we could appeal to such a saviour as Mr Page to prescribe so sporting, so gentlemanly a panacea for the ills of today.

But Mr Page's clarion call fell upon the ears of another world; we have only to read *The Gamekeeper*'s advertising section to remind ourselves how many light years in distance separate that world from ours. 'Keeper's Breeches made to measure in 48 hours. Good roomy cut, tailored from finest quality Drills, Bedfords, Cooney Beavers, etc. 12s. 6d.' 'Watertight Boots, all rubber, laced style, 11s. 3d.', of which 'Ptarmigan' of the *Shooting Times* exclaimed with rhapsodic satisfaction: 'They keep the feet bone dry even in the softest slush.' There is the 'Nimrod' cartridge, 10s. 6d. per hundred, about which P.Y. of Horsham, Sussex, wrote, 'They kill wonderfully well.'

The Situations Vacant columns are full of jobs for the right man: *'Wanted, Keeper, singlehanded; 1,500 acres, some good woods; five-roomed cottage and garden; 27s. per week, two tons coal, suit of clothes.'* There are those seeking positions too: *'Coles, former headkeeper to the late Lord Trevor wishes to find a situation for his son (16) where he can learn the duties of a gamekeeper thoroughly.'*

'Thoroughly' – now there is a word of which Mr T. Elvin would have approved. He is the subject of 'This Month's Portrait' on page 93 of that same 1932 issue of *The Gamekeeper* beneath the photograph of a smiling man wearing a Kitchener moustache. We read that 'he comes of a typical gamekeeper family. His father was head-gamekeeper on several well-known estates in Wales, Berkshire and Lincolnshire, and he has three brothers in the same profession: Mr G. Elvin, Bedale, Yorks; Mr H. Elvin, Beau Manor, Nr Leicester; and Mr E. Elvin, Kirby Underwood, Bourne, Lincs.' After four years in the trenches with his regiment, the 21st Battalion Yeoman Rifles, Mr Elvin moved to Burn Hall New Parks, Huby, an estate of 2,700 acres, of which 200 acres were covert, good for shooting pheasants; and here, with one assistant, he set about destroying 1,700 head of vermin in his first year. 'Mr Elvin,' the article concludes, 'is a married man with three children, one boy twelve years and two girls ten and five . . . and we sincerely trust that good fortune may be with him and his family all their days.'

The good fortune ran its course another twenty-two years when, at the age of 65, Mr Elvin put up his guns, patted his dogs for the last time and quietly died. We never knew his first name; gamekeepers did not have first names, they were known as 'keeper' or by surname. They were much respected and a little feared in the field, by guns, loaders and beaters alike. They knew their country and their birds, knew the weather conditions and how the birds would fly. They could tell a novice, a nervous gun, a duffer at a glance; they could pick out the guest who might take his neighbour's bird, and the one who might fire down the line. They were never wrong; and this much has not changed.

'The late Mr T. Elvin,' reads the obituary in the January 1954 number of *The Gamekeeper,* of a man who was never late in his life. He was a stickler who left a widow, son and two daughters to whom the Editor, no longer the inestimable Edgar Page, conveyed his sympathy in their tragic loss . . . the son being Head Gamekeeper to Colonel Beale at Londesborough Hall, Market Weighton in Yorkshire.

'Father liked things just right,' recalls that son, Stanley Elvin. 'I remember times when even in the worst weather he'd remix feed prepared by an under-keeper, when others wouldn't have given it another thought – it was just that he knew the dangers of improperly mixed feed and he knew a correct job would show returns when shooting got under way. When I left Huby village school at fourteen I joined him as an assistant for two years, but he was too strict, I had to get away so I left to become kennel boy at Ripley Castle under Sir William Ingleby before heading for Lincolnshire as a beat-keeper.

'Then war came and I joined up, Royal Scots Fusiliers were my lot, but about half of us got wiped out at Dunkirk time trying to fight tanks with rifles. Went to Scotland then, spent most of the war putting up barbed wire; we thought the invasion would be up there. Got sick of barbed wire. Then it was our turn to invade and I remember crossing to France with all the Red Cross boats coming back, and I thought I could come back that way, wounded or something . . . we lost a lot of men in that war. There was a German gun we called Moaning Minnie used to shell our position, once it hit a wall I was behind . . . I was buried alive, but I'm here, I'm lucky.'

Stanley Elvin was lucky enough. He survived to return to the job he liked best, that of 'keepering'; he spent eleven good years at Londesborough Hall with Colonel Beale, a man he appears to idolize, whose photograph holds place of honour in his sitting room, whose widow he returns to visit annually for tea. He was lucky also in his time at Londesborough to meet Eileen, daughter of farming people; the daughter he courted eight years before they could find a place to live. Eight years of holding hands at the local flicks on Saturday evening, and long cycle rides on Sunday: 'We thought nothing of cycling twenty miles,' says Eileen. 'Always in the country, we're not keen on towns, townspeople don't talk to you, they look down on country folk, they think they're that much smarter – probably are too. We've always lived in the wilds, and no thank you I've never been to London and I reckon I've missed nothing. No, I don't want to see Piccadilly Circus or the Tower of London – they've been there a while and they won't go away, will they?'

She laughs. She laughs all the time, the slightest thing sending her off into paroxysms. She is making Yorkshire pudding, so scurries in and out of the kitchen, leaving the door open so that she will miss nothing, squealing with merriment as her husband recalls their wedding at St Mary's Church, Beverley, in 1954 and the honeymoon in Scotland. The eight years of courting had not been wasted; they were the years of saving, of putting something by each week – so that when eventually they wed they had £365, a fortune in those days. They spent it all, every penny, furnishing their cottage from top to bottom. 'It wouldn't buy a three-piece suite today,' muses Stanley. 'Everyone buys on the never-never nowadays, but we've always been against having things we couldn't afford to pay for. You could wear out a stout pair of shoes walking back and forth to the HP people.'

Stanley Elvin, in his sixtieth year, is Head Gamekeeper to Mrs Lea of Revesby Abbey in Lincolnshire, a post he has held for ten years and one he hopes to fill until his retirement in six years' time. He has two under-keepers, Noel Williams and David Brown. Noel's father was Head Keeper at Revesby for forty-one years, then one day not long ago they lowered him into the ground next to his wife Edith Mary, who had gone before him. Long before his death Mr Williams had to vacate the Head Keeper's cottage, after all those years; but such is the practice, understood and accepted: the house goes with the job and when the job is done the next man moves in. When Stanley Elvin's work is completed, he and his wife will pack their belongings and leave.

When they were young there was all the time in the world; now they are getting on, retirement seems close, and Stanley relishes the prospect not at all.

'I shall hate it. I'll miss the shooting, going through the woods . . . I suppose I live for it. We used to save a little, about a pound a week, it seemed a lot then, but it's nothing today – we've saved nothing, keepering's never been a job to make money. We've never owned our own home and never will . . . we could be homeless.

Oh, we think about it. Unfair? Bless you, if I had my time, I'd do it again. My wife would too – it's what we've been brought to, it's our way and that's it.'

If the rule of the land is despotic, it is more often than not benevolent despotism; when Mr Williams retired, Mrs Lea found him a cottage and it is unlikely that she would see the Elvins without a roof. Country people, rich or poor, tend to look after their own; the bonds between them surpass class and creed. The traffic in loyalty is no one-way system; the day it becomes so will be the end of husbandry as we know it.

'Privilege?' Stanley Elvin is baffled by imponderables, discomforted by words and situations he cannot grasp. 'If you mean rich people – well, if there were no rich people none of us at Revesby would have a job. Nobody's equal, there's no such thing – I'd like to be a landowner, but I was born a keeper's son. My position is to provide sport, not to have a gun in a shoot . . . and I bet being a landowner is a headache, the government and the times are against them.'

Mrs Elvin bustles about in her pinafore; cheerfully she lays the table, puts out a bottle of orange squash, her spectacles misting with exertion. She does everything cheerfully, nothing is too much trouble; it is impossible to imagine her complaining. They wanted children, waiting patiently through the seasons and through the years; but it was not to be and now too many seasons have passed. They mention that it is a disappointment, glancing at each other for consolation as the mantlepiece clock chimes away another hour. They would have been proud parents, very giving; and their children would never have inherited the ways of envy. Instead, they have each other, two against the world – only they do not see it thus because they do not ask for much, just their daily bread, and so their world is good. It would never occur to them that they have made it so.

'I'm lucky,' says Stanley Elvin again. 'It's all gone the right way – you can't take a university degree in keepering, it's just years of experience and word of mouth. Out shooting it's all left to me, and in the closed season the guns come to see me . . . I know where every bird's gone since coming here, every bird reared and every bird shot. It's big business these days, but I don't know about that – the sport's the thing.'

You could not mistake Mr Elvin for an astronaut or a dance band leader; he could be nothing but a gamekeeper, from the cut of his plus-fours to the broken veins of his weather punished face. He is very nearly pear-shaped, round of

64

girth, tapering to the top of his head. He would make a caricaturist's delight: deft strokes on a sketch pad would reveal him as John Bull, his straining waistcoat a Union Jack . . . or perhaps as Humpty Dumpty, atop his wall, feet dangling towards all the King's Men. On Eileen's cooking he looks packed with nutrition, solid as a pork pie. And solid he stands, legs apart, boots planted on to the land. Shotgun under arm, dogs at heel, the sight of him would make a poacher quail.

He is a shy man, not given to expressing views, to holding forth; with strangers he is uneasy, not wary or suspicious, merely happier with nature than with human kind. He is not adept with words, polemics confuse him: there is black and white, right and wrong, the shooting season and the closed season, nothing else matters and debate will alter nothing. He was born to service, to do his duty, not to question or analyse. He has done what he was told to do, knowing his station; he went to war and he came home. When his time comes he will die as he has lived, without fuss. He is an innocent.

The Head Keeper's cottage is up a pitted drive in need of darning. It is a nineteenth-century utilitarian place, with outside kennels for Mr Elvin's labrador pup, Rodger, twelve-year-old black labrador, Bracken, and fourteen-year-old terrier, Billy. In this chill April a coal fire burns in the sitting room; there is an ornament of a gundog retrieving a pheasant; plates with pheasant designs hang on the wall. From a vase Eileen shakes out three vicious pellets from a SS9 cartridge that went adrift from a deer culler's gun, passing through Stanley's leg. He demonstrates his 1884 hammer gun, his Spanish twelve-bore, and the sixteen-bore he bought thirty-five years ago for £30; he explains that a pair of Purdys, Churchills, or Holland and Holland would cost £5,000 today.

April is the important time on a shooting estate; and 7,000 acre Revesby is considered one of the finest shoots in Lincolnshire. The rearing programme starts in April; by the end of February so many surviving birds are penned for eggs, one cock to ten hens in wire aviaries. Laying begins in April; late this year because of the treacherous winter and only now, the day after Palm Sunday, are daffodils showing gold. Each hen, fed twice a day on breeders' pellets and wheat mixture, lays thirty to forty eggs, which the keeper brings back for incubation, twenty-one days at a constant 99°F. Once hatched the chicks are boxed, transferred to the brooder house and put under electric hens, 125 chicks under each hen for six weeks. Revesby uses Westerns, but Stanley Elvin is sceptical: 'They're egg wasters – these particular ones are as good as you'll get, but they don't compare with a broody hen, she'll give you eighteen chicks from twenty eggs compared to ten or twelve.'

At six weeks chicks are moved to release pens in the woods, half a dozen wing feathers are taken to prevent flying; and there they remain, fed twice daily, until July or August when they are released. Even then they are fed, straw is scattered;

and on 1 October the pheasant shooting season opens.

There are twenty days' shooting until the season closes on 1 February; twenty days and eight guns paying up to £100 a day for the privilege, hoping for decent weather with the birds flying well. 'Sun is a gun's day, rain a keeper's', is the saying. Then who said that a keeper is only a poacher turned outside in, and a poacher a keeper turned inside out?

If an accident of birth made Stanley Elvin gamekeeper rather than landowner, by the same token he might have become a poacher; but such is idle speculation, it is the realities that count. And even they, the realities of here and now, are perplexing enough: 'We don't feel part of today's world, we lead a very isolated life here – the papers and television keep us in touch, but it's all second-hand somehow . . . wars everywhere, women and children massacred . . . I'm afraid we don't think it's all true. And if it is, then we're well out of it – we live the way we have to, getting on with it, spinning the money out.

'It doesn't suit some . . . an under-keeper's wife a while ago couldn't take it, she wanted a gay life, bingo and such, so they went to the city – to better themselves, I dare say. But I wonder if it made them happy, I wonder if they still use their eyes – most townpeople are blind to nature, they just see buildings and products they're meant to buy, and price tags. I like to see pheasants, I like them coming towards me, high at about seventy yards . . . wouldn't do to all be the same.'

Eileen serves lunch. Stanley takes off his tweed coat, hanging it over the back of his chair; it is good sturdy tweed, hard wearing: 'Father said a keeper's job wasn't worth going to if you didn't get a suit . . . used to get a suit a year, now it's every two years.' They pour gravy into the hollow of the Yorkshire pudding; it is a man-size meal, with roast beef to follow, three vegetables, then cake and tea.

Eileen and Stanley are solicitous of each other, a childless couple who have grown up together, through the courting years, through war and peace, not having much and not wanting much. They say a cross word has never passed between them. They have been sheltered, isolated as they admit; they do not fully believe that women and children are massacred in other places beyond the Lincolnshire Wolds. Their faith is in nature, their trust in the squirearchical foundation of their existence, in relation to which the news on ITV is taken with a grain of salt.

This is their life and this their kind of loving; but oh, how the days are passing: 'Time always passed quickly, but it passes quicker now there's so little of it,' says

68

Stanley Elvin. 'I'm not getting younger – the brakes are coming on, I can feel them. But they'll never leave me walking in the shoot, I'm still up front . . . I've got to be.'

Boston is the nearest sizeable town to Revesby, and there stands St Botolph's octagonal tower, rising 272 feet beside the River Witham – the Boston Stump as it is known, visible for miles across the Fens and even from parts of Norfolk. Another Boston, in Massachusetts, owes its name to emigrants from the town who set off for the New World under John Winthrop in 1630.

Those first New Englanders were an austere band, bleak of countenance, fearing God as well they should. The Fen country shaped them, made them different, gave them a stubborn streak; they were born of a breed that raised Hereward the Wake, born to respect the flat silent Fen marshes, the bitter winds from the east. The Winthrops were looking for something England could not provide, so they went elsewhere; the Dutch on the other hand found all that they desired in the Fen lowlands – and so they settled, trailing their piety after them, bequeathing to their adopted country a style of architecture which marks these parts as slightly 'foreign' to this day.

Foreign too are Lincolnshire tulips, Prussian prim with straightback stalk and helmeted flower: battalions of them drawn up for review, not a stem out of line. If tulips could sing, *Deutschland Über Alles* would be their anthem; and then they would march into battle. Tulips are not the flowers of lovers.

How flat it is, remorselessly so; the soil crumbling, darkly rich as Dundee cake. The sky is all, you can make castles in these clouds, mountains too; the land is nothing, mile upon mile, an occasional house stranded by a dike like a boat on a sandbank. The soil is good; they say a family can do well on forty acres of Fenland . . . Tumby Woodside, Stickney, New Bolingbroke.

Then Revesby and it is here that Fen meets Wold, and what a blessed meeting: hedgerow and hummock, orchard and wood . . . and, at the end of a long drive, Revesby Abbey.

Mrs Lea lives in the new house, leaving the Abbey to the elements, neglected, decaying. Weeds have choked the gardens, ivy and moss have taken hold; one day the old place will fall down. And no one will care.

'It's a monster,' declares Mrs Lea, secure in the house she built in 1964. 'Burns the architect should have been shot. I applied to the Ministry to have it demolished, but they said no – some rubbish about it being a unique example of its period. Unique rubbish! If it burnt to the ground I'd be supremely relieved.

'I can't tell you how miserable I was as a child there – despite the horses and the hunt balls. You had to be fearfully ill to be allowed a fire in your bedroom – and the kitchen was four minutes' walk to the dining room, so food was always cold. We needed six indoor staff; here I have none.'

Ann Lea, a widow, inherited Revesby in 1957, her brother having been killed

69

in the RAF during the war. Her son Gavin farms part of the estate and will succeed to the property. She is a woman of presence, she has kept her looks and her figure; she would turn heads still. She has a semi-detached air about her, aloof; you would need to know her a long while before repeating a *risqué* story. She looks composed, well bred; she thaws slowly and then it is worth the patience.

'I'm glad you got on well with Elvin – he's a shy man, one of the old school – still calls me "madam", whereas the young ones call me nothing. The older men touch their caps . . . old Williams could never get used to a woman inheriting, always called me "Miss Ann" until I took over – then he called me "sir".

'We're living through a social revolution, ever since the war – you can't turn the clock back but neither can you have a one class society, quite impossible. It saddens me to see youngsters leave the land to "better" themselves, for material betterment only – you can't replace the country here . . . no commuters, no traffic, we're cut off with sky and space, with the odd village to keep the weather out. But you can't change their minds, they're not farm boys with straw in their hair – if they want to go, they'll go. They're "clunch" – that's local for "bloody-minded".'

She pours a couple of gins powerful as a twelve-bore kick. Sun floods the drawing room; daffodils will open if this goes on. The park slopes towards a distant road, magnificent; the Abbey chimneys reach above silver birches, abandoned, sinister. The memories must be painful to merit such a vengeance; to watch a house die is a curious act of purification.

'I couldn't leave here,' Mrs Lea continues, 'despite the dreadful climate – I've no flat in London, haven't been there for over a year. They're all on Valium, city women – "it's me nerves", they say.

'No, I don't shoot, myself. I was brought up to believe that men shoot – besides, I can't bear killing things. But I take a great interest in the estate . . . I'm not sure how many cottages we have without checking, they're mostly nineteenth century and we're renovating all the time . . . except the almshouses, they're going derelict, impossible to convert.

'Church? I'm always talking to the vicar . . . but no, I can't bring myself to attend. It's such a miserable religion, there's no cheerfulness; it's boring and I'm never bored. I don't see many people either, but I'm not lonely – perhaps I don't need people . . . what I should really like is to be invisible.'

70

She seems intrigued by the idea, as though it had not occurred to her before; but she will not elaborate. 'Perhaps I said it because you're a stranger and we'll never meet again,' she suggests. And when she says goodbye it is as if she is locking a door and throwing away the key. By this act does she place herself in protective custody.

When, in 1939, men of Revesby went to war, Fritz-the-enemy was also packing his kitbag in a small town in Germany. Güstrow was the town and Fritz really was Fritz – Fritz Wolter, youthful, blond, apprenticed to a blacksmith. He knew nothing of killing and was in no hurry to learn; but he was a country boy and wars are designed for the slaughter of country boys.

At Le Mans the Americans captured Fritz and for the next three years he was harried from one internment centre to the next, some rough, some 'cushy billets'. Eventually he was moved to Moorsby Prisoner of War Camp – which was on the Revesby estate. The huts, tower, perimeter fence are there still; and wind rattles broken glass panes, stirs dust upon concrete floors. Initials bite into the walls, and there are echoes, ghosts perhaps for those who believe in such; but nothing else.

There was no fraternization in those days; Fritz was a 'Gerry', approximate equivalent of being a warthog. He peeled potatoes, cooked, worked the land, when all he really wanted was to be in the smithy. Then one day someone said how badly Revesby needed a blacksmith, so Fritz said what about me – and got the job.

Peace came and Gerry was repatriated. But Fritz did not want to go home; the Russians were there, and anyway he had come to like Revesby. The odd part was that Revesby came to like him, Gwen Bridges in particular. Of course they married and Fritz never did return to that small town in Germany. He settled down as village blacksmith, a man of Revesby.

The
Nature Warden

CHAPTER VI

THE NATURE WARDEN

Malcolm Guyatt

'Umbrellas . . . yes, I really think it was umbrellas that made me realize I wasn't cut out to be a city gent. You've never thought about umbrellas? Well, you should. I used to study umbrellas on the London Underground. You can tell a lot about a man from the way he treats his umbrella – some people neglect their umbrellas, let them get tatty, let the spines snap, others roll them slim as pencils; extroverts swing them, introverts hug them . . . and when the umbrella brigade gets off the escalator into the street, they all look up . . . and if it's raining, they open their umbrellas. From a distance it's like the sudden blossoming of a bed of huge black lilies, they're bursting into flower to be watered.

'Something else about travelling to the city . . . my office was in Milk Street, Cheapside, which meant taking the tube to London Bridge, then walking across the bridge. All the blind mice came up the steps to be corraled into the east pedestrian way by barriers – so that the pavement was jammed solid all the way over. My daily protest was to climb the barrier, walk to the other side of the Bridge and have the pavement to myself . . . funny, no one else thought of it. Anyway, I was working one day – shipping and forwarding was what the firm was about – and I just felt I couldn't go on looking at the sky through windows for the next forty years . . . there had to be something else.'

There was something else. There was the Antarctic. Malcolm Guyatt, twenty-two years old at the time, read an advertisement for a general assistant to join the British Antarctic Survey Expedition. He was taken on, sailing from Southampton in December aboard the 3,000 ton *Perla Dan*, an ice-strengthened Danish cargo vessel . . . Montevideo, Falkland Islands, South Georgia ('An outing to see Shackleton's grave – my hero, far more so than Scott,') fetching up at base in Halley Bay.

For the next two-and-a-half years he looked after dog teams, sledges, tents, clothing, sleeping bags, in temperatures down to minus 52°. 'We used to get what we called "frost-nip", not as serious as frostbite – we used the American "buddy system", you watched your buddy's face and if you saw the signs you warned him.

'What did it teach me? It taught me to be less tolerant. If you're in close proximity for two-and-a-half years with twenty-seven blokes and no women, you tend towards irritability from time to time. If a bloke scratches his ear in a particular way, it can drive you barmy – so you say something, you tell him to experiment with different methods of ear scratching, encourage him to be versatile, ambitious . . . I mean, we were individuals cooped up together, not stereotypes. And we were stuck, you couldn't simply walk away.'

Malcolm Guyatt's parents met at Brixton roller skating rink, a rendezvous of such apparent refinement that the romance flourished – until 'that German corporal with a moustache' intervened. But the course of true love was not to be diverted and a marriage was arranged. The only child was born in 1944, a year or so before Malcolm's father returned from the Royal Artillery to resume life as an electrician. They settled a short distance from the roller skating rink, in the London borough of Peckham Rye.

'Father took time with me, that's important,' recalls Malcolm Guyatt. 'He taught me to use my hands, introduced me to hand tools, and I'm grateful for that because I understand craftsmen, I know what bricklayers are doing. He thought it essential that I should have a craft, so when I left primary school to go to Strand Grammar in Brixton I think he was disappointed . . . but I turned out to be the original "could do better", so I left school at sixteen and went to work in Halford's bicycle shop in Peckham.'

Despite his name, deriving from the Huguenot, Malcolm Guyatt has the look of a Viking: he is broad-shouldered, fair of beard, blue eyed; his even teeth sparkle with the ring of confidence. He has the permanent tan of a South American playboy, the bouncy exuberance of an Alsatian puppy. If he had a tail it would wag all the time, indiscriminately; he is completely trusting, finding it inconceivable that the world could play him a dirty trick. He is nature's boy scout. He is never without the sort of pocket knife that bristles with armaments for disposing of bottle tops, extracting flints from the hoofs of sheep. He uses it for excavating the bowl of his Meerschaum pipe. He smokes a brand of tobacco which would induce immediate cardiac arrest among the less robust.

'Father was in the scouting movement, a scoutmaster, mother was interested too, so we always had camping holidays. No, it wasn't a case of roughing it. Good campers don't get cold and wet, they know how to compete – although mother didn't particularly enjoy ants in her tea.

'One thing led to another and soon I began to explore Wales, camping in Snowdonia, the Ogwen Valley, the pull being the rugged countryside. I used to shout, "I'm free! I'm free on this pinnacle of rock." Then I'd ask myself what sort of rock it was, what sort of terrain, what's this, what's that – and when I got home I'd look it up at the library and read *Climber and Rambler* magazine. Some of it rubbed off and I became competent as a mountaineer – navigation, the skills of moving on rough ground, assessing weather conditions. Then I went on a two weeks' scouting expedition with Woodford Green United Free Church Rover Crew (he recites it

slowly, rolling his tongue over the title like a Gilbert and Sullivan opera) to an ice-cap called Eyjafjalla Jokull in Iceland – and came back knowing I'd found something worth pursuing.'

By then he had graduated from the Peckham cycle shop to Cheapside, and thence to Antarctica. On his return he took a job with the Holiday Fellowship and was sent to assist at Coniston in the Lake District. There he met Helen, a farmer's daughter from Somerset; that was in 1970. Two years later they married and Malcolm, accepting the deplorable truth that he did not have what it took to wield an umbrella with distinction, applied to the Lake District Planning Board. From 300 applicants he was selected and in the spring of 1972 became National Parks Ranger responsible for an area of 100 square miles.

'In a way I wanted to be more adventurous,' he says, 'but I wasn't a bold enough spirit . . . I'm a Second Field Rabbit. Remember in *Watership Down* – First Field Rabbits stayed safely near their burrows, feeding with all the others and the pickings weren't too exciting. Third Field Rabbits took the chance of exploring the distance where crops were more succulent but the risks higher . . . well, I'm a Second Field Rabbit.'

Malcolm and Helen Guyatt moved into a rented cottage in Boot, at the heart of Eskdale Valley and there they were happy; as well they should have been because it is a place of yesterday's dreams: a mill race at the bottom of the garden, mountains beyond, times unchanged for a hundred years at least. But they wanted to buy, to become home-owners, so they moved to Lonning End Cottage at Waberthwaite, on the coast near Ravenglass. They have three-quarters of an acre and when sea mists clear they can see the Isle of Man. There are not many neighbours, but the Guyatts have become accepted, Malcolm and Helen, young Conrad who is three and baby Sara who is really little more than a damp, gurgling bundle admitted very recently to this planet.

Cam, a large unsuitable dog of suspect ancestry, completes the circle; Cam and half a dozen sheep shearing away at lush spring grass. Cam barks, sheep baa, and baby Sara yells most professionally for one of such limited experience. Radio Two is on most of the time and Malcolm whistles between his teeth, so one would not select Lonning End as the ideal retreat after a nervous breakdown.

Helen is the quiet one; you would hardly know she is there. She is rather a beautiful young woman, her face unlined, unmarked in the way of a Madonna;

there is a serenity about her, an acceptance that all is well. Whether she is cooking, holding her baby, clearing the table, she draws silence about her. She does not say much, and when she speaks it is to the point, as if she knows the answer already. She seems remote. In the garden she sits on the grass by a pile of bricks, by a ladder, cradling Sara and smiling at some wondrous secret. Malcolm says she is old-fashioned and he is glad that she is not interested in a career, only wishing to raise her children. Counting Malcolm, Helen has three children.

The cottage is about a hundred years old, but they are building on a larger kitchen, another bedroom, a study. They have been building on for some while; it was going to be finished last Christmas, but Christmases come and go so fast when you dress four tons of slate yourself, dig foundations, lay concrete, put in window frames and roof felt, put the bedroom floor down . . . to say nothing of establishing a garden, converting barns to 'holiday units', restoring a motor cycle, repairing a Shetland boat, building Conrad a model farmyard, shaping a spinning wheel for Helen. Then there are *Goody Two Shoes* rehearsals at the village hall, making elderberry wine, the Saturday evening outing to the Brown Cow for a sing-song.

The Guyatts also want to be self-sufficient: 'If it's said that four acres will support a family, we're having a go with a bit less than one acre . . . and as for the

77

building being a bit behind – well, everyone's saying that Malcolm's Five Year Plan is slipping.' He laughs, he doesn't mind at all; it will be done when it is done, and very likely there will be a lot of half-finished projects when they are all ninety years old. It is hard to imagine Malcolm pulling on his slippers and thinking: It's complete, now I can rest.

They live in preposterous disarray, their chaos being on a grand scale: it is all a majestic heap of Wellington boots and oilskins, baby pots and Weetabix packets, breadcrumbs and tepid tea. The guest room wardrobe is full of homemade marmalade and pickled onions, wire coat-hangers grapple with each other like stags locking antlers . . . but this is home where there is much love and much security, where never words of betrayal will be uttered, where Conrad and Sara will grow up with straight limbs and honesty.

The morning sun of May is bright and daffodils are poised, prayerful almost, like monks in saffron-yellow cowls. Malcolm Guyatt's Ford Escort van REO 604S rattles along the lanes towards Eskmeals Nature Reserve where sand-dunes are scooped high, fringed and pelmeted with Marram Grass, Lyme Grass, Creeping Willow, Marsh Pennywort, Adder's Tongue and Dune Centaury. Oystercatchers pick delicately along the shore and if you are sharp you may spot Black-headed gulls, Ring Plover, Shelduck, Sandwich, Common, Arctic and Little Tern. Ravenglass is across this estuary where Esk, Irt and Mite flush into the sea; Ravenglass which remains unsullied, bereft of boutique and discotheque, so that fashion is far behind the times and music made by moaning wind and screeching gull. No one has tarted up Ravenglass; no one has given her a lick of paint and the kiss of death.

'Lambing Time! Keep dogs under proper control.' So instruct the signs the moment you turn inland towards Eskdale Valley; and there are the lambs, everywhere, frisky as puppets on strings, making olympic skips and jumps, all four legs off the ground at once. Where on earth do they learn it all? They are safe enough so early in the year; there are only climbers now, and serious walkers – the cars and coaches will come later, in the season Malcolm favours least: 'Spring, autumn, winter, I like them all. It's hard sometimes to follow tourists' routes in summer when they've been spreading litter – it's hard to love one's fellow humans then. Sometimes they get angry and frightened, they're not used to a single-track road with gradients of one in three like on Hardknott and Wrynose Pass, with hairpin bends and drops all the way . . . they get nervous, clutches burn, there are breakdowns. Last year a man got so windy, he rolled down his window and threw away his keys, said someone could tow the car away – I swear.

'Then you get the walkers who set off ill-prepared, without listening to the weather forecast – you know, in plimsolls and open neck shirts. Mist comes down and they're lost – scared as well, and when they panic it's dangerous. These mountains can be *killers*. They should set off in boots with nails or moulded rubber soles, waterproof, warm jersey and trousers – not shorts or jeans – a rucksack for food, map, compass, whistle, spare clothes and a polythene bag to climb into in case they have to shelter all night. Mittens, torch and flares are useful too, and in winter an ice-axe is essential – first-aid kit as well. It's not being fussy and faint-hearted, it's being selfish *not* to bother because you involve others, put other lives at risk – that's what they don't understand . . . the number of times I'm called out on rescue operations . . .'

This countryside of lake, gorse and daffodil, where Wordsworth wandered lonely as a cloud – as well he deserved for putting his name to such verse – can be treacherous in the high fell. Lingmoor Fell, Ulpha Fell, Troutal Fell have all taken their toll; but none can match the challenge of England's highest mountain, Sca Fell.

From Eskdale Green, passing the George IV pub (known prior to 1914 as the King of Prussia, when local sensitivities rebelled), the road turns towards Strands before dropping to Wast Water, deep as hell, 258 feet in places, with great screes falling vertiginously to the very surface, screening the lake from sun most hours of the day. There are those for whom one visit is enough, who find this eerie corner of Cumbria too haunting, daunting, mindful of death; others are hypnotized, compelled to gather up the gauntlet the gods throw down. And gods surely do inhabit this desolation, tempting gods, vengeful, lusting for sacrifice.

Young Colin Paice was offered to appease their mood, on 1 January 1976, and he was consumed. 'Colin Michael Paice', reads his headstone in St Olaf's Churchyard. 'Born 13th Feb. 1957. Fell Asleep on Scafell Pike 1st. Jan 1976. He lived and died happily on his beloved mountain.'

'Moving?' considers Malcolm Guyatt. 'No, I don't find it moving. I tend to see it more as a statistic in the records of mountain rescue operations – and you've got to remember what that night was like, atrocious. He was a brave lad, but should he have gone out on a night like that, with the snow blinding down?'

There are other victims: 'A. P. Rossiter – climber in these Hills 1903–1957'; 'Max Philipp Gunter Franz – our only son killed on Buttress Scafell 1953' – and so on, the death roll of the few who needed to go forth, to stand closer to the gods than most of us, the rabbits of the third field.

Wasdale Head is a scattering of four farms, and an inn, the Wastwater; the place is isolated, a dead-end in the road, electricity came only in 1978. St Olaf's, originally the chapelry of St. Bees Priory, is 450 years old, a long time to be in the dark. Pace the church out beneath the wooden beams: ten paces from altar rail to font, five from side to side, so its claim to be England's smallest church may have merit. Turn your head to the right at the end of one pew, look up and there framed in leaded glass is Scafell; and there inscribed on the same pane is:'*I will lift up mine eyes unto the hills from whence cometh my strength.*'

So Wasdale has the highest mountain, the deepest lake, the smallest church in the land; and if that is not enough, it also claims the biggest liar. Will Ritson, landlord of the inn a hundred years ago, was a teller of tall stories and his memory is

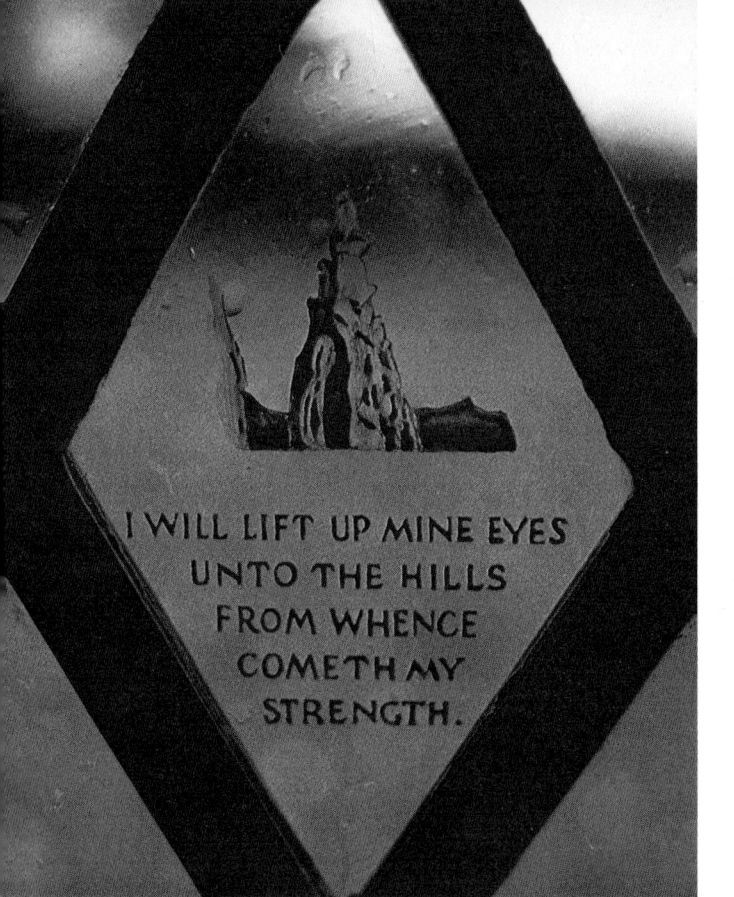

I WILL LIFT UP MINE EYES
UNTO THE HILLS
FROM WHENCE
COMETH MY
STRENGTH.

commemorated each year with a competition for the biggest liar. Wasdale has 't'deepest lake, t' laalest Kirk and t' girtest li'er,' it is said.

There are practices more strange than lying: such as 'gurning through a braffin' – grimacing or pulling faces through a horse collar; or 'tekin hod', a form of wrestling whose combatants attire themselves in long drawers tucked into stockings, and velvet trunks finely embroidered with flower motifs; then there is fell running, an extreme in masochism if ever there was, of which Joss Naylor, who farms at Wasdale, is acknowledged champion. And the dialect itself is quite a game, unintelligible to the novice when spoken by natives like sheep farmer Willie Greenup, over eighty and going stronger than ever. Malcolm Guyatt converses freely with Willie because they have become friends; Malcolm carved a crook for Willie and took the trouble to learn the dialect of the dells of his adoption. Which almost makes him one of the family.

Another popular sport is taking sides about the weather: oh yes, it does rain; oh no, it doesn't. Her Majesty's Stationery Office avows that '. . .a popular fallacy must be quickly corrected. For it does not always rain in the Lake District. In fact, rain is little more prevalent in the fell country than in most parts . . . ' Yet facts are facts, one such being that the fells have an average of 225 'rain days' each year, Grasmere receiving 83 inches, Ambleside 72, Scathwaite 129. Perhaps it would be kindest to say that it usually rains twice a week, the first time for two days, the second for three.

And when it rains it is very wetting stuff, no matter what Her Majesty's Stationery Office has to say. Let them stand around in it a few hours, they would soon be back in the High Holborn office with a revised set of attitudes. But when it clears, the air sparkles, effervescent as one of Bollinger's more august vintages; you could serve this air in crystal goblets, get drunk on it but never morose. Air comes no fresher and no better than in these stark, forbidding hills and valleys.

Still, there are threats, as no one can deny. Today probably the biggest influence on vegetation is farming, although housing, road building, quarrying and afforestation have profound effects. Cultivation of the land, control and intensity of grazing animals as well as widespread use of insecticides, herbicides, fertilizers, has far-reaching effects. Some insecticides based on chlorinated hydrocarbons do not break down after application, remaining in the soil to accumulate in the tissues of animals until fatal levels are achieved; beneficial insects are destroyed by spraying; fertilizers may accumulate in lakes through drainage from the land into rivers . . . the search for a mythical Golden Age of plenty is having disturbing results, as ecologists will tell you.

Malcolm Guyatt, concerned as few others, makes light of it: 'Frank Muir was asked to define ecology and he said we're getting so short of essentials that we had to be careful, eke out the petrol, electricity – so it came to be known as eke-ology. It's difficult, I'm against legislation for matters of common sense – like seat belts and whether we should be allowed to poison the environment, there're too many people who know what's best for us . . .' He trails off, unable to contribute a balanced solution, too tender to appreciate that ultimate solutions are never balanced.

The Ford dances over pot-holes, with picks, shovels, chains, barbed wire, buckets, boots and maps in unholy disorder, making the van seem like home. Brake, accelerator and clutch are scarcely visible beneath a detritus of chocolate wrappers, sandwich bags, burnt-out Swan Vestas. It has been a day of checking footpaths, assessing litter and vandalism, communicating with the RSPB about the golden eagle nesting at Blengdale. The grave of Tommy Dobson, who followed the hounds and is better fêted here than John Peel, is spruce and tidy; no damage has been done by cattle roaming through gates left open by tourists. Malcolm has chatted to Mary Postlethwaite who runs Fell View Guest House, and he has checked that route and trail signs, designed and lettered in his own workshop, are in order. He has watched youngsters from the Outward Bound School, swopping notes with the instructors. It begins to rain again, more of a misty vapour of the kind through which Dracula appears in horror films.

At the foot of Hardknott, Malcolm pulls off the narrow track, above a stream. He whistles through his teeth, tunelessly, though somehow excitedly; he has been keeping something up his sleeve, saving the best till last: 'I was chairman of Eskdale Jubilee Committee,

we wanted to mark the occasion,' he explains. 'So I said what about a packhorse bridge, there's not all that many left – a good one at Wasdale . . . anyway, we agreed to go ahead. I designed it and two or three of us did the work, it took about six months of weekends.'

He stands on a boulder mid-stream, then moves from rock to rock, closing distance between him and his pride, this lasting object of his creation. It is a small bridge crossing a small stream, three or four steps and you are over. It is hidden from the road, so few passers-by will ever see it; but it is there, and at its centre is a plaque: 'Jubilee Year 1977'. Malcolm looks at his bridge with a kind of awe, lays hands on it as if in blessing. 'It will last,' he says anxiously. 'It must last.'

Back in the van he dips into his lunch-box; there is one sandwich left, built like Hadrian's Wall. He eats it thoughtfully, showering a confetti of breadcrumbs, tomato pips on to his lap. 'The plane is my favourite tool,' he says, 'or perhaps the turning chisel, you can watch the shape coming . . . I hope it won't be a case of "clogs to clogs in three generations" with me – I mean, I hope Conrad won't want to go back to the city. Father wanted me to do something. When I bought my MG, he was pleased, said it was what he'd always wanted himself. He's not very well nowadays and we're trying to find him a bungalow so that he can be near – and see all this. I respect him . . . I'd like to be respected myself, but I'm not sure it will be possible in a world whose fashions change so quickly, whose criteria I suspect. That spinning wheel I'm making Helen, I'd like Sara to treasure it . . . and her daughter too.'

He finishes the sandwich, lighting his terrible pipe. His eyes never leave the Jubilee Bridge. It is very different from the one he crossed, as another person, on his way to Cheapside.

The
Lock-keeper

CHAPTER VII
THE LOCK-KEEPER

Roy Dunstan

They are picturesque little spots, these locks. The stout old lock-keeper, or his cheerful-looking wife, or bright-eyed daughter, are pleasant folk to have a passing chat with or rather were. *The Conservancy of late seems to have constituted itself into a society for the employment of idiots. A good many of the new lock-keepers, especially in more crowded portions of the river, are excitable, nervous old men quite unfitted for their post.*

Jerome K. Jerome – Three Men in a Boat.

We are entitled to our opinions, and such was the opinion of the author and his companions George and Harris – to say nothing of the dog Montmorency – during the course of their episodic punting expedition along the Thames those many years ago. You will find the indictment, neatly pasted upon a board, in the Abingdon lock office. It was put there by the lock-keeper, Selwood Roy Dunstan.

'My bosses on the Thames Conservancy weren't too keen on that,' says Mr Dunstan, 'but I've never been one to do what was expected . . . when I was a lad I was known as Nick, like Old Nick-the-devil – we had this black mongrel Bonzo and when people saw him they'd say, "Trouble – meaning me – can't be far behind." I suppose I can't deny it, me and my brother Richard could always look after ourselves, I suppose we *were* trouble makers in a way.

'I don't know why – maybe it was being let off the leash, things were very ordered at home. Father was strict enough, but mother was the disciplinarian . . . she was six inches taller than father, a strong woman she was, so the three of us youngsters, me, Richard and Mary, were brought up to speak when we were spoken to and not to speak at all at mealtimes. That was in the thirties, there wasn't much money about – not that we went hungry, but mother was frugal, she made broth from pearl-barley and she'd make a joint last a week. They married in 1930 and I came along five years later when father was a fitter at Falmouth docks. Oh, yes, I'm a Cornishman, couldn't you tell my accent?

'Anyway, war came then and father went to work building airfields for Coastal Command, he was a Jack of all trades really, like me . . . he was lodging in a house in Bristol when it got a direct hit in the blitz, took the ARP thirty-six hours to dig him out, but he'd been shouting for help so long he'd lost his voice – didn't come

86

back for over a year and then it was always high pitched . . . odd that, he'd always had a deep voice. All that time while he was moving around from airfield to airfield mother was taking in London evacuees. She only had places for three at a pinch, but when they arrived by train from the East End there was no room for them all, so she took in the ones no one else wanted . . . probably because she guessed what it was like up there, that's where she'd come from herself, she came to Cornwall nursing.'

It is easy to imagine Roy Dunstan's mother, this tall, raw-boned woman who ruled with iron, stretched a joint until the bones made soup, but would never turn away a snot-nosed kid from the London bombing. You can see her as dry, humourless, reared to drudgery in a world before Ford Cortinas and the Costa del Sol. If her boys told a lie she would tan the hide off them and they would never guess in a month of Sundays how much she cared, how often she wept; and 'month of Sundays' would be one of her expressions for, as Roy recalls, she had a saying for every occasion: ' "It's a long lane without a turning," she'd tell us. "The Lord will provide," was another – and "Count your blessings." '

The father remains a shadowy figure, diminutive: he was only five feet four inches and his falsetto voice would not have increased his stature. But they were bound together, they had made their vows: 'I think they loved each other and anyway it wouldn't have made much difference if they hadn't. You didn't divorce in those days, you took your vows in church and you feared them as sacred – divorce was a scandal in Cornwall, if you were unhappy you kept it to yourself until the end.' It seems unlikely that these parents felt no love for one another because when the mother went, father followed a few days later, dying of grief, as Roy puts it.

Roy is shortish too, there being five feet six inches of him, sinewy, wiry every inch. There is no spare flesh, no tell-tale signs that he eats three cooked meals a day, enjoys a pint of beer. His face has taken on some lines, a couple of crevices deep as sabre cuts; outdoors his eyes screw into slits in the way of men who sail before the mast. He has a sailor's walk as well, a tipsy gait; on his left forearm is a tattoo, rather inexpertly done in India – it is an anchor, let into the curlicues of which is 'Mother'.

So it is unsurprising to learn that, having failed his scholarship, he went to sea at fifteen: brother Richard joined the Royal Navy, Roy went into the merchant service, coasting at first around the British Isles, then sailing the deep sea – Canada, Egypt, the Indian Ocean, the Far East. After picking up a tropical skin rash he returned to coasting when, at the age of twenty-two he met Pat, a friend of his sister Mary, later one of her bridesmaids. It was at Mary's wedding that they first noticed each other.

'It was a whirlwind courtship,' says the lock-keeper's wife. 'I was nursing nights, Roy was at sea, so we wrote . . . we didn't go out a dozen times, we never went to a dance, he don't like dancing. We went to the pictures, *Indiscreet* was one of our favourites, it had Ingrid Bergman . . . six months and we were married. I

87

knew I was going to marry him long before he did.'

'Well, I'd been engaged three times already,' Roy says arithmetically. 'I used to drink quite a drop . . . used to duck into a pub on the way to meet a girl, forget I'd got a date and meet another in the bar . . . everyone was amazed when Pat tied me down, my skipper couldn't believe it.'

He sounds a pushy young fellow, cocky with it, not altogether tamed today despite responsibility and two sons, Andrew who is a swimming pool lifeguard and Martin who makes rocking horses.

He is chirpy, bushy sideburns adding to the bantam effect; he is as good as the next man and no one is going to patronize him. 'We're all working class today,' he is fond of saying. 'Anyone who works – farm labourer, doctor, judge – is working class.' Pat agrees with him, nodding emphatically as he makes his point. She still does night duty as a nurse twice a week for United Oxford Hospitals and stands in occasionally as District Nurse: 'It's not right to be together twenty-four hours a day, 365 days a year – you'd grow like carbon copies of each other.'

Even so, their attitudes are not hugely at odds. They agree about most things, as they did when Roy took a land job with the Electricity Board for £9 a week in 1961 after earning £21 as a mate at sea. As they again agreed when he recognized the warning signs among his elder electricity linesmen: 'Father always said you learn by your mistakes, but I think you learn by other people's mistakes. A linesman's job takes toll on nerves and physique – I saw men put out to grass at forty, old and broken, and I said that's not for me.'

For some while they had spent their holidays exploring the Thames, hiring a cabin cruiser; on one visit they struck up friendship with the St John's lock-keeper and his wife who subsequently came to stay with them in Cornwall. One day the job of relief lock-keeper turned up and the two families discussed the pros and cons to see whether Roy might apply. After renting a house for years, they had recently bought their own for £1,100; it was something that needed thinking about.

Pat: 'We weighed it all up, there was real heart-searching – a move from Cornwall to Abingdon was like emigrating, like going to another country. It meant leaving our roots.' But decide they did and, after a spell of relief work, Roy was appointed lock-keeper of Abingdon. The uniform suits him: peaked nautical cap, black tie, white shirt, navy blazer with crested buttons – it gives him status, as good as any man's. The lock-keeper's lodge suits Pat: red-brick 1928, wistaria-and honeysuckle-clad, trim lawns and roses lining the Lock.

There are flood marks beside the house, showing how perilously the water rose in 1875, 1894 and then again in 1947. A notice lists the keeper's working hours: now, in May, they are 9 am until 6.30 pm with a Sunday extension to 8 pm; at other times the public may operate, at their own risk, the lock-gates without supervision. In the lodge's sitting room is a gaily patterned carpet, a painting of the Atlantic pulverizing Cornwall's coast and a print by a policeman friend, looking along the Thames towards St Helen's Church, Abingdon; on the sideboard is a miner's lamp, and a fireman's brass helmet belonging to Pat's father who was awarded the British Empire Medal for saving a child's life. On the table are home-made Cornish pasties. During lunch two Doberman Pinschers, Abby and Zara, and a black cat Buster III, range about the carpet as if it were a safari park; to add to the authenticity Zara has been equipped with a rubber toy which emits predatory squeals. You take your life in your hands when patting the Dobermans.

Someone else who took a chance was John de Salter, Abbot of Abingdon, who in 1316 so raised the weir that both banks flooded. John kept his head above water; his successor, Richard de Clyve, was less proficient – or perhaps his guardian angel was otherwise engaged at the time, for as Matthew of Westminster relates: 'Unhappy fate that the Abbot, with certain monks and seculars, through the kicking and plunging of their horses, at a certain river swollen with land water near their monastery, which he was disposed to cross with the said company: by some fell handling and the steerman's unwise management of the fragile craft were all at one stroke drowned, oh pity! in midstream.' The king's officers later invited complaints against the late abbot, but: 'The tenants found not them selfs greved wt said abbot concerneng anye matter.'

By 1576 the situation was getting out of hand when it was discovered that elm trees lay in the water ' . . . with flakes stakes earth and gravel stopping the course of the water and letting both boates and fysh to pass and repass.' But patience, patience! In no time at all a benefactor was found, as we may read upon a tablet to this day, let into the left wall of the midmost weir: 'This Locke was bvilded by Sr George Stonehovse and Richard Adams Ann. 1649.' Those medieval stonemasons could never get their u's right.

Since when three men in a boat, together with their dogs, cats, budgerigars, kitchen stoves and Elsans may pass Abingdon lock with impunity: *Laguna Rosa*, *Reading Consort*, *Fairhaven*, *Hydra Star*, puttering through the first set of gates to be discharged, after a suitable period of gestation, through the second, bound for the Elysian pastures of Bray, Cookham and Mapledurham. Roy Dunstan is there to open the sluices, to chat, to dispense his philosophy on life; then to send craft and crew steering a sometimes erratic course, propelled by diesel and a valedictory wave of his hand.

He likes chatting, he is in his element: 'I talk the hind leg off a donkey. It was

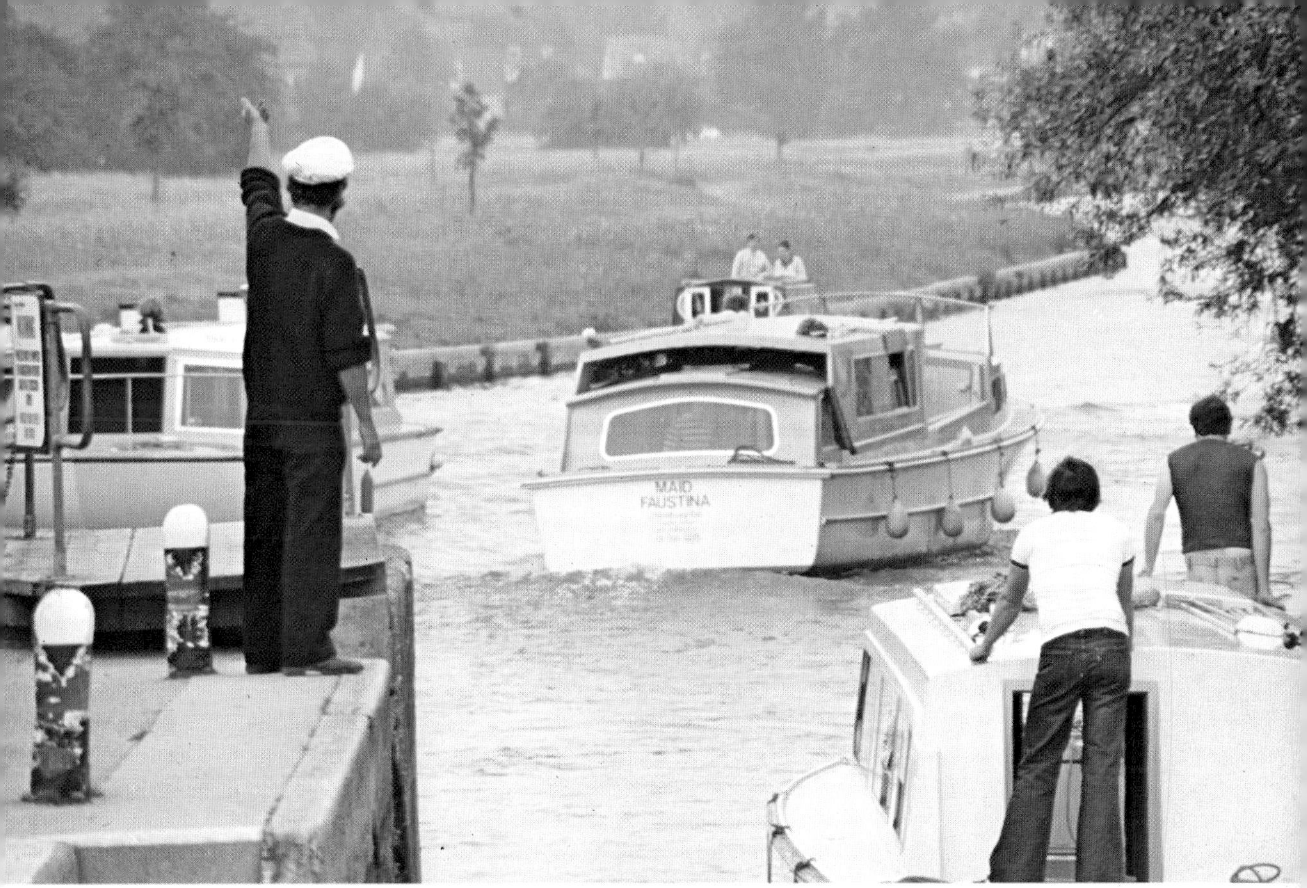
MAID
FAUSTINA

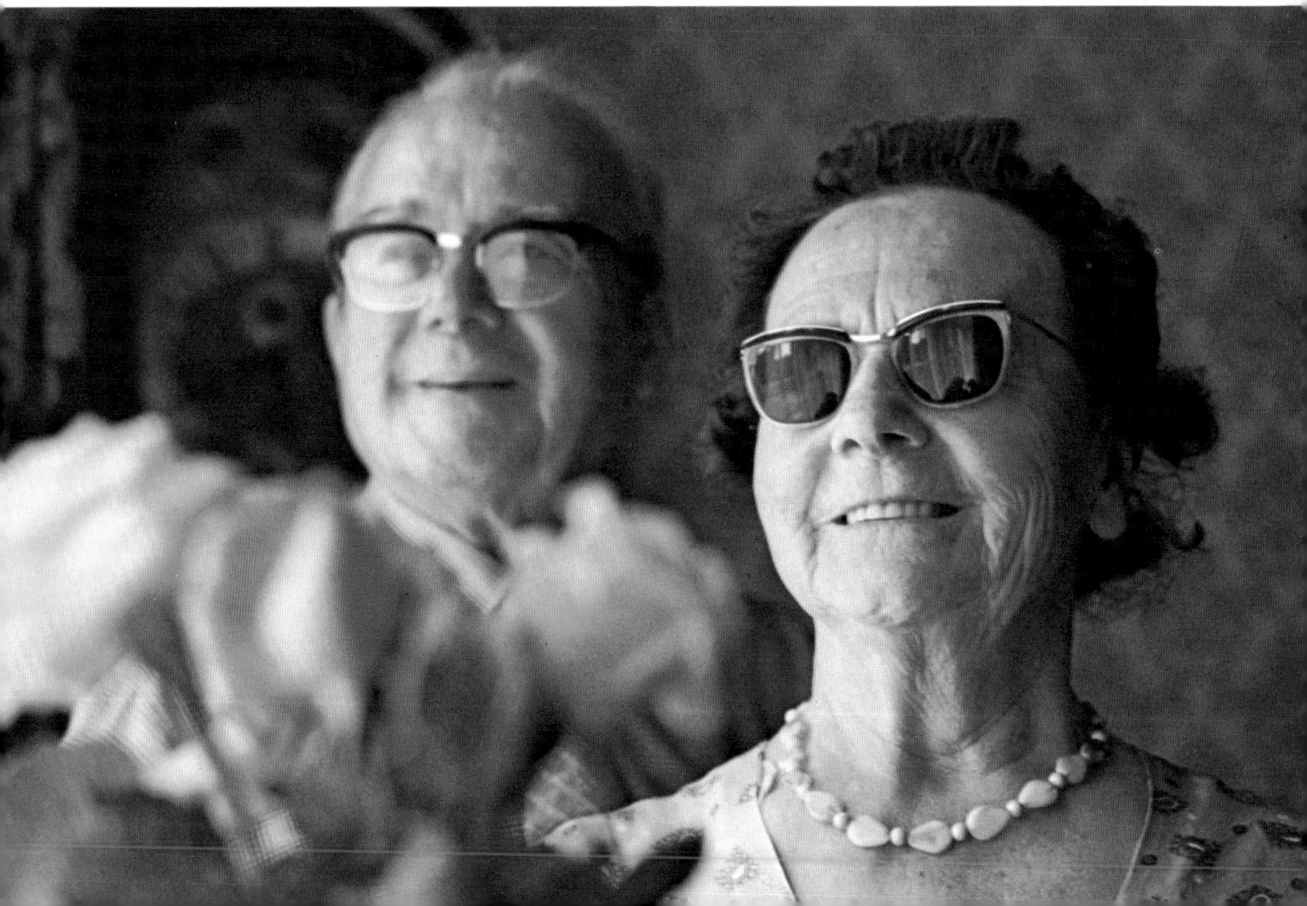

different in Cornwall, they're insular . . . here I tell them about the swans, where chub are rising, where grebe are nesting, safe places to swim, decent pubs like the Nag's Head in Abingdon or the Barley Mow at Clifton Hampden – they're *real* pubs. Some pubs get spoilt by these stockbroker types who look down their noses at muddy boots and dogs . . . the landlord knows which side his bread's buttered and sticks up a sign "No muddy boots or dogs".

'It's change all the time. The river used to be a place for gentlefolk, snobbish – you could tell the ones who didn't belong by the way their fenders were always out. Today no one notices, there are far more hire-boats than private – it's a great leveller, the Thames. There are very few cowboys, they're not sure of themselves, not competent at boat handling; that makes them a bit subdued, they're afraid of making fools of themselves.

'People think lock-keepers lead a life of Riley, a cushy number – I don't mind, I'm a bit thick, I don't know much about much, I admit that . . . I just talk and smile even when it's chucking down and everyone else is miserable. Well, you're a long time dead . . . if I didn't laugh I'd cry.'

There is something indomitable about the lock-keeper; he inherited this from his mother, along with the clichés which kept her going in bad times. Like when she said there was no hell when you died; hell was here, so when you died things could only get better. Her clichés were the aspirin of the times.

Roy is a survivor, he has an instinct for it. If he had been buried alive in the blitz, he would have scrabbled his way out in no time. If Abingdon was struck by a nuclear weapon, with one life spared, the survivor would be Roy. He would climb out of the hole, dust himself down and start looking for someone to chat to. There is little erudition in the output, but he would score highly for persistence. If you preceded him through a revolving door, he would still emerge first.

There is also his feeling for nature, which even the ebb and flow of verbiage have not suppressed. His walks, morning and evening, along the riverside towards Nuneham Deer Park, are perhaps his pockets of retreat. Stepping as he does between the cow pats, it is his hour for observation, for introspection: for this is late May, summer is not far away, nor autumn far behind. The meadow is dew drenched, lush, spread with daisy, buttercup and dandelion; it is the day of the cuckoo, of laburnum, lilac and larch. One moment the sun is out, then the sky bruises and showers fall so that you turn up your collar, lengthen your stride. Rain stops, leaving the earth miraculously scented – if only one could bottle such fragrance.

Abby and Zara are making a nuisance, rooting about in riverbank rushes, too near the nesting grebes for comfort. There is a consternation, a flapping as they put up a pair of disgruntled mallard; next, in long grass, they put up a pair of courting teenagers.

Roy points to a bend in the river: 'Seems that long ago this was a popular place for drowning,' he says. 'One bank was in Berkshire then, the other in Oxfordshire – well, one of the county constabularies, I can't remember which, paid more for a body . . . so if a stiff was found floating on the less rewarding side, someone would get in and tow it across before yelling for the police. They'd make a bob or two that way. Money? I don't know – I wouldn't turn down another fifty quid a week, but if I won a £10,000 premium bond, it'd bother me, I wouldn't know what to do. It might make me greedy, people are greedier today . . . the change in money is incredible, that's why we went metric, so's people wouldn't understand how prices kept going up. If I'd told dad beer was six bob a pint he'd tremble in his grave, if we hadn't cremated him. When he was dying he asked me for a drink and a cigarette, he knew it was time to go – so I propped him up and he sipped a couple of drops of brandy and gave one puff at the fag, then he went, just like that.'

Pat: 'I see a lot of dying, it doesn't worry me at all – the only thing I fear is going blind, I couldn't cope with that.'

'Old Father Thames . . .' hums Roy, polishing another cliché. 'It's all about people is the river. There was this old lock-keeper, proper bugger he was – that's how I'd like to be remembered. I may have moved, but I haven't changed, I'm still a Cornishman. I was John Dunstan's younger son and that's who I am today – my wife is Mrs Lock-keeper, that's who she's known as.'

93

If time and tide wait for no man, they do not appear to force the issue along this reach of the Thames. The pace is that of some faerie postal service, promising eventual delivery; but not yet. The river meanders; it dallies and it flirts, provocative and pure as a virgin. You may look and you may sigh, but never shall you touch. You may travel hopefully, and end up where you started – for rivers hold their secrets, more jealously than forests or mountains. There is a wilful quality in rivers, a madness which communicates with the mad. Rivers are hypnotic, beguiling, enticing and lethal. Suicides do not fling themselves off mountains; they offer themselves to rivers, slipping quietly into a bed of reeds, drawing water comfortably about them like sheets. Sweet Ophelia embraced a river:

Till that her garments, heavy with their drink,
Pull'd the poor wretch from her melodious lay
To muddy death.

Yet how serene it seems, looking from the lock, across the water meadows towards Abingdon Bridge, the spire of St Helen's Church pointing like a finger of admonishment against the vulgarities of the twentieth century. You do not come across many boutiques, discotheques and laundrettes in patrician Abingdon. In Market Place, where the Queen's Hotel stands, shops carry an air of refinement, as if you would have to persuade reluctant owners to part with their wares. The Pantry sells jam, bread and naughty but nice cream-oozing cakes; The Chocolate House handles humbugs and brittle treacle toffee; Messrs Savory & Moore do a line in hot water bottles and enemas. A thoughtful hostelry has set out chairs and tables upon the cobbles; and striped umbrellas protect patrons from sunstroke.

The town's most munificent gift to the sensibilities is County Hall, an aesthetic feast, the only lamentable part being that Abingdon cannot recall the architect's name. The 'undertaker' of the work was Christopher Kempster, one of

Sir Christopher Wren's masons on St Paul's, but that is hardly the same. You would scarcely believe that so illustrious a name as whoever, could simply get mislaid; dear, dear, someone has been awfully careless. It is a superb building, completed in 1682, severe, classical, with the grace and elegance of an age which understood such virtues, which showed little taste for the rococo. It was designed to serve a three-fold purpose: cellars as a warehouse, ground floor as covered market, first floor as courtroom.

Announcements are made from the balconies, while on special occasions buns are thrown to hungry Abingdon burghers in a custom traced to George IV's accession. Why buns rather than slivers of Gorgonzola or pickled gherkins is a complete and utter mystery.

Market day at County Hall is Monday and what bargains are on offer: diamond necklaces, strings of pearls, amethysts big as gulls' eggs all at 60p; china bowls inscribed 'Go aisy with tha sugar', coronation mugs, milk jugs, salts, peppers and periodicals with yellow curling covers. Mr Glyn Evans sells books, such treasures: *The Manual of Modern Radiology* by J. Scott-Taggart, *Freckles* by Gene Stratton Porter, *The Grocery Trade – Its History and Romance* by J. Aubrey Rees, in Vols I and II, which latter still carries the Metropolitan Borough of Bethnal Green's library label, surely detracting from the grocery trade's romantic image.

Abingdon is compact; you could pick the whole place up and steal away with it in a hatbox, Abbey Gateway and all, leaving behind the modern Abbey Hall, which resembles a very large refrigerator. Everywhere is in short walking distance, the Guildhall a moment or two in one direction, St Helen's Church a couple of minutes in another. St Helen's is a curious church said to be one of only two in these islands to be broader than it is long: it is 97 feet in length and 108 feet in breadth.

Long Alley Almshouses which flank three sides of St Helen's churchyard are

administered by the Master and Governors of Christ's Hospital founded in 1553, before the incorporation of the Borough, although it benefited from endowments and was itself incorporated by royal charter in 1441 when part of its mandate was to provide for 'thirteen poor sick and impotent men and women'. It has been reworded today: 'poor *or* needy men and women', emphasis being on the 'or'. 'You can be rich and needy,' reminds Joyce Tribe, the Matron.

'Remember that death will not be long in coming and that the covenant of the grave is not shewed unto thee'; 'The number of a man's days at most are an hundred years' read two jolly texts from Ecclesiasticus in the corridor, faded with age, the implication faded not at all. Matron has put up a text of her own: 'Say something nice to everyone you meet today! It'll drive them crazy.' Not Ecclesiasticus – Snoopy.

Matron looks after twenty-one residents over sixty – the youngest is seventy-five, the oldest ninety-three and they could be so much worse off than living in these warm, cosy flats with all mod. cons., a lovely garden, telly too and sage Snoopy sayings. 'Meet Mr Berry,' says Matron, 'he's marvellous with his hands, he'll make anything.' Mr Berry steps briskly, erect, turned out spruce as a sergeant-major of foot guards. Retirement is a full-time occupation for Mr Berry, so clever with his hands; he is always at his neighbours' beck and call, there's no end of jobs needing his skill. He has a workshop where he does running repairs, designs household gadgets for his wife, makes clothes pegs: you should see these pegs, each one a work of art, perfect in itself.

Mr Berry's first names are Atholl Gordon, after a Duke of Atholl, Colonel of the Gordon Highlanders. Mrs Berry says so, very proudly; she is so proud of her husband, she mentions him all the time, as she slides a homemade pie into the oven, as she sets an ornament straight on the mantelpiece. Maud Berry is house-proud too, the place shines, glowing under constant attention; and where she cannot reach behind furniture, Atholl Gordon has invented a 'waggling-stick' which she has fitted with a dusting cloth. She demonstrates her latest joy, an electronic device which she places on the ground beneath the clothesline; when it rains the device reacts, giving off bleeping noises so that Maud brings in her washing.

Her bleeping machine is important because Maud had been totally blind for thirty-seven years. It was a rare disease, she cannot remember what they called it, only that it seemed sudden and that whatever it was affected her hands too; she has no nails and little feeling in her fingers. She says she is happy because she learned the 'Three A's': acceptance, adjustment, achievement. She looks happy, bustling confidently about their flat, polishing, scrubbing and cooking, listening for the door when Atholl Gordon comes home for lunch.

'No, I don't miss the flowers and sky so much,' she says. 'I remember all that, it doesn't alter. What I miss is growing old with my husband. I remember him as he was thirty-seven years ago. He can see my wrinkles,' she touches her face, drawing hands across sightless eyes, 'and he knows I'm old – but he's still young to me, he's never changed.'

Then she brightens, pats her hair which is crisply curled and neat. 'Every Sunday we go to St Helen's. I don't think we've missed a Sunday in fifty-six years of marriage – we kneel together at the altar and we thank the dear Lord for letting us be together still. Oh, we've so much to be thankful for.

'We're warm and well fed . . . my husband was putting on weight so he went on a diet. I couldn't see, but I knew it was working because when I hugged him my arms would go round him easier.' She laughs at the memory. It is a gay sound, full of love and caring.

The Lobster
Fisherman

CHAPTER VIII
THE LOBSTER FISHERMAN

Jack Jarvis

There is the photograph, showing signs of fatigue at the edges, freckled with spots of brown that mark a septuagenarian's hands. It is beginning to fade, like a memory of misspent youth in which we can clarify only momentous events, turning points that shaped us into the creatures we have become. All of which is scarcely surprising, since the camera winked on this particular tableau in the year 1905. Edward VII was trying in his way to perpetuate the magnificent follies of the Victorian era; the 'Red Sunday' massacre bloodied the streets of St Petersburg; Togo defeated remnants of the Russian fleet, capturing Admiral Rozhdestvensky in the Sea of Japan.

None of which events would have registered deeply on the persons in the photograph, for they are too young, not yet dry enough behind the ears to assimilate the vibrations of the world beyond Hope Cove. And what ears they have, these three sons of a fisherman; had they wiggled and flapped them they would have become airborne . . . something in their genes perhaps.

On the left is Percy, starched to attention in his sailor suit, lanyard about his collar, black stockings taut, boots catching reflections off the cobbles upon which he stands. He is holding in his right fist a hoop and the suggestion on his face is that he would prefer to be bowling it along the gutter than posing in this soppy get-up. In the middle, a full head taller than brother Percy, with all the insouciance of maturity, is eight-year-old Frank. He wears his nautical apparel nonchalantly, hips relaxed in the way of one who regularly attends cocktail parties; his smile is expert and his left arm drapes elegantly about the back of a high baby chair. He is protecting the infant Jack, who has been around twelve months or so and looks perplexed by the whole charade. His frock is frilly, white bootees are on his feet and his pudgy little elbows are dimpled. His hair is in ringlets and, despite the misty sepia, the indications are that he is trying to suppress a burp.

The photograph was taken outside a nameless thatched cottage, a few paces away from the Methodist Chapel in The Square at Inner Hope; not Outer Hope, which is almost a mile away and quite another matter. It was the home of a fisherman whose father had been a fisherman, whose grandfather . . . and so on. This sire of our three graces had gone afield to find a spouse, four long miles to South Milton; she was the daughter of a family in the undertaking business and agile with her fingers, having learned dressmaking at Adams of Kingsbridge. A girl of stamina too; in the blizzards of 1891 she walked to work on the crest of snow-packed hedgerows.

'Hard-working girls,' remembers Jack, the one in ringlets, a few years on. 'They were good girls, too good to waste on outsiders, so my uncle married my mother's sister. Frank and Percy came, then me . . . went to school at five, walking two-and-a-half miles to Marlborough and two-and-a-half back. Did that until I was thirteen-and-a-half – war was on then and the government let you leave school to help. Mother had taken on the post office, so I delivered telegrams to the army defending the coast from invasion. Coastguard and post office, the only two telephones in them days.

'In 1920 us youngsters built an eighteen-foot crabber with our own hands and went to sea at once. Daylight to dark we worked, three to four miles out – plenty of fish, that wasn't the problem – it was selling them that was difficult. Still, we made about £10 a week, good money – we'd get two shillings for a big three-pound lobster. There were thirty fishermen making a decent living at Hope Cove then . . . today it's down to four. John, my son's one of them, my nephew Eric is another . . . the others aren't local families, we're the only ones left. The men didn't marry and if they did their wives didn't give them sons. The few boys there were went away to better things . . . my great-nephew, young Keith, was keen all right but he never got rid of his asthma, it killed him at sixteen.

'Yes, three to four miles out we'd be – baited the pots with mackerel, skate, the lot . . . sink them well weighted to twenty-five or thirty fathoms. We'd put out sixty to eighty pots, then return to harbour for twenty-four hours. Two or three lobsters wouldn't be a bad haul, then there'd be crab – and in August you'd get pilchards. The pilchards have all gone now, but father and I would salt them for the winter, everyone did, it was our winter diet. Spring tides were best, about fourteen-foot tides – then came the neap tide, not much rise and fall, so the fish don't move.

'Today skindivers are picking up the lobsters . . . we don't make much . . . ask John, he'd get away if he could. He got himself called up by the RAF once and went wild up in Kinross somewhere . . . he'd been to Marlborough school, like me – then joined me fishing when he was fourteen. After his national service he went bulldozing in Plymouth for seven years, but like father like son . . . he came back to Hope. You ask 'ee – John will tell you,'

The next photograph in Jack's collection – stored, as all treasures should be,

in a biscuit barrel – is dated July 8th 1924. It marks the occasion of the Wesleyan Sunday School outing by charabanc to Torquay. What a smart vehicle it is, with gleaming black coachwork and solid tyres; brass lamps sparkle, as do handles to the eight doors. The driver, resplendent in long motoring coat and peaked cap, has one hand on the steering wheel, the other on a bulbous horn; and the roof has been rolled back, so it must have been a fine day. The ladies are in huge straw hats decorated with leaves and cherries, the men wear cloth caps – except for two sporting the wide-brimmed trilby favoured by Al Capone. There are twenty-one aboard and in the back row is Jack Jarvis – only you have to take his word, for at the vital moment he must have had an itch. At any rate, he moved, so that his face is reduced to a blur, as if he has donned a stocking mask. Just in front of him is a pretty girl, which may have accounted for his distraction.

'It was a very nice day,' he says. 'You could get about then . . . bet you can't damn well move in Torquay these days. They weren't bad times – wasn't all that long ago they did a bit of smuggling to improve their lot . . . spirits, silk. A lugger would go to France, collect the goods, sail back and drop it overboard to rest on the sea bed in kegs; when it was safe they would raise them and cart the stuff to pubs, to Thurlestone, all over, by donkey. Nine women went to jail in Exeter once – a

102

coastguard surprised them so they tied him up and dumped him in a sack . . . they were good enough to each other in the village, but strangers needed to beware.'

Jack Jarvis, ex-Sunday School boy, fisherman retired, sits on a bench above the sea, chewing a blade of grass. His hair is white beneath the cloth cap he takes off only for bed; he wears a blue jersey and beneath his trousers white Long Johns show above his socks. He has not worn badly, for all the salt and sea spray; there is life in him yet, it is time he went courting again. A shame to waste those handsome looks just staring out to sea.

'Women . . . what would I do with a woman? They're trouble, that's all. My wife was a good 'un, but they're not trustworthy today, they only bring trouble. I've got no trouble and I want none – I'll just go on my way until I stop. They're all dead in that Sunday School outing photo – 'course I miss them, I used to go to their houses to have a talk. They've gone, that class of people . . . young John, he's always around the pubs every blessed night, drinking and yapping, I never know where he is. He had a girl once, asked if he could bring her home to tea, so I said yes she can come and cook us a decent meal for a change. Could she cook? Could she hell . . . pretty, oh pretty enough, but only fit to put in a glass case. She had to go,' he adds darkly.

He was not always a misogynist. In 1934 he went a-courting, crossing the social frontiers from Inner to Outer Hope to escort the daughter of masons – a scarcely acceptable trade it is true, but she came from fisherman stock on her grandfather's side. In 1935 they married at Kingsbridge registry office, honeymooning with fishermen friends in Penzance. John was born two years later and life was sweet enough in this part of Devonshire known as the South Hams, where green schists, hornblende and grey and pink quartz that form the cliffs provide some of the grandest coastal scenery in England; and rich red sandstone and tawny limestone inland break down into lush pasture.

It lasted for thirty years this marital union of Inner and Outer Hope; there was fishing from March until the end of November, then repairing and making good through the winter, lobster pots to make as well. They built boats too, seven or eight in total, all solid; it was a tidy little business with one thing and another, enough to put something aside for the bungalow they put up for £600: 'There was hardly a house in sight then, now look.' He jabs a finger at a neat colony clinging to the hillside like an impending avalanche of bricks and mortar. '£6,000 they cost to put up three or four years ago. Last time one sold it went for £30,000. Look at them . . . cowsheds.' He is contemptuous.

'She died then,' he says simply. 'Funny thing, we didn't smoke or drink, as much clean air as you could swallow and she died at fifty-five of cancer of the bowel . . . same age as mother, same illness, mother had all the pain in the world, they'd discovered pills by the time my wife got it. The pills she took, pills, pills and more pills . . . it was terrible nursing her for six months. She was opened up at Plymouth Hospital – riddled like a colander. My missus was clean as a pin, a good life, never went to work . . . but she slowed up day by day, you could see it. Scientists do all these wonderful things, but they can't cure cancer. The doctor asked me if she knew – she knew right enough. She was too young to die. It crawled all over her, that cancer.'

Back indoors he is reflective, studying wallpaper patterned with an Armada of galleons sailing across the room; he fiddles with a bowl of plastic tulips, adjusts a lobster-designed plate on a shelf. He moves into the kitchen to see how the roast mutton and boiling cabbage are doing. As he raises a saucepan lid a greenish vapour hovers above the stove like a genie awaiting his master's command.

'I'll turn it low,' he says with Escoffier confidence. 'We can walk down to the lifeboat house. The station closed in 1930 . . . sailing and pulling lifeboats went out, so we were wiped out.' There is another photograph, taken in 1879, showing fourteen men and fourteen moustaches lined up by their boat. At the centre is Coxswain James Thornton – who died at the age of eighty-six in the first war – flanked by Jack's father and five others from the Jarvis family.

The lifeboat house was erected in 1877 by the Grand Lodge of Freemasons of England as a thanks offering for the recovery of the Prince of Wales from a dangerous illness. Two shields adorn the seaward-facing wall, one bearing the Masons' emblems, the other the feathers of the Prince of Wales and the motto '*Ich Dien*'. Now it is deserted, storage for rope, spars, tarpaulin and nets; it smells of tar. No one goes there, except Jack Jarvis. He has the key and a favourite chair. He goes there sometimes and sits. He doesn't coil ropes or start the winch or tidy the place up. He sits. And maybe thinks a little . . . and when he has had enough he gets up and goes away.

The fishermen's reading room – the Appleton Reading Room, as it is more importantly called – would be a more comfortable place for sitting, and it is only a few yards away. Jack has the key to that door too. More photographs there, more names: Legassick, Thornton, Jarvis, Partridge, Steve Hurrell . . . 'Damn me, if a sniper didn't get him in France in 1916, knew him well as a boy . . . they're all dead, all gone. There's old George Legassick, ninety-eight when that was taken, always said he'd make a hundred, but he couldn't quite get there.'

The Reading Room was opened on 18 May 1908. It was a formal occasion and Inner Hope was justly made conscious of its fortune in having such a benefactor. In his speech Major Miles Halton Tristram eulogized: 'Let every member try to live the straight clean life which he, William Appleton, lived – a fine pattern of an English gentleman in its highest sense, and nowhere more plainly defended than in the Fifteenth Psalm which, though written thousands of years ago, is as applicable as ever in England today.'

Mr J. C. Carter then rose to his feet: 'As a youth he [the exemplary William Appleton] was keen on cricket, always fond of riding, and a good man with hounds. Later he was a really first-rate shot, and many a time I have seen him drop his right and left at driven partridges in a high wind. Of fishing was he particularly fond, fishing with a dry fly for trout . . . he was a master of the beautiful game of billiards . . . he loved the sea, rowing and sailing . . . he was imbued with the same spirit as those old British sea-dogs whose exploits you delight to hear out, and whose doings you yarn about over the winter fire. Of his kindness of heart, extreme generosity, unfailing courtesy to women without any regard to their position in life . . . his many other personal qualities you will not expect me to speak of more fully, nor could I trust myself to do so.'

What a man indeed. The very sort one wouldn't mind one's sister marrying. We can only hope that in the Valhalla to which he was summoned the wicket is firm, the birds flying well, the trout rising, and the women to whom he addresses his unfailing courtesy not too lowly of birth.

Across the lane is The Square in which Jack Jarvis first saw the light of day; and there stands the cottage, nameless still, with low thatch hugging the cob-walls like a tea-cosy. Jack is silent, deep in reverie, lost in some rhapsodic memory of times past, when he could doff his cap at a true gentleman like Mr Appleton. 'Bugger,' he says. 'That cabbage will be boiled dry.'

In Outer Hope flaming June is doing its best, not that it is warm enough for swimming yet; but the enclosed beach is a microcosm of beside-the-seaside behaviour. Little girls turn cartwheels and little boys build castles of sand, Golden Wonder crisps are munched and ice-cream cornets licked, Rover-the dof lifts his leg against a deckchair and all the babies look like Boris Karloff. There are shrimping nets and men in braces and spray leaps over the breakwater and there is an after-lunch torpor, which goes to show that the barmaid at the Hope and Anchor is earning her keep. There are pig-tails, Batman T-shirts, plastic wind-breaks, empty packets of Rizla roll-your-owns, and grandma has fallen asleep, snoring rhythmically, her thighs ajar a fraction too wide for delicacy.

A crowd gathers around David Brooker who is landing his haul, dragging the catch of crab, lobster, spider crab on to the beach. He is one of the four still fishing at Hope Cove and good humouredly he answers questions as he works: yes, you nick the crabs, cutting the claw tendon or they fight and tear each other apart; yes, a crab claw can crush your finger to the bone; and yes, those are rubber bands about the lobsters' claws because if you nick a lobster it will discolour him. He packs his catch tight into wooden crates, a seething, squirming, ugly sight; it cannot be much fun being born a crab, ending up with brown bread and butter for tea.

Girl Jean II, John Jarvis' boat, is nowhere to be seen; his pots laid this morning, he is taking trippers around the bay and will be back only when they have had enough. It brings in a few quid, Jack tells . . . which is the only reason why he ever puts to sea again at his age: 'I don't get much pleasure in looking at the sea, I've looked at it all my life and it doesn't change much – not like it does ashore. But I'll go out for a few quid, it helps the pension.'

He turns his face inland, towards the bungalows and guest-houses, an

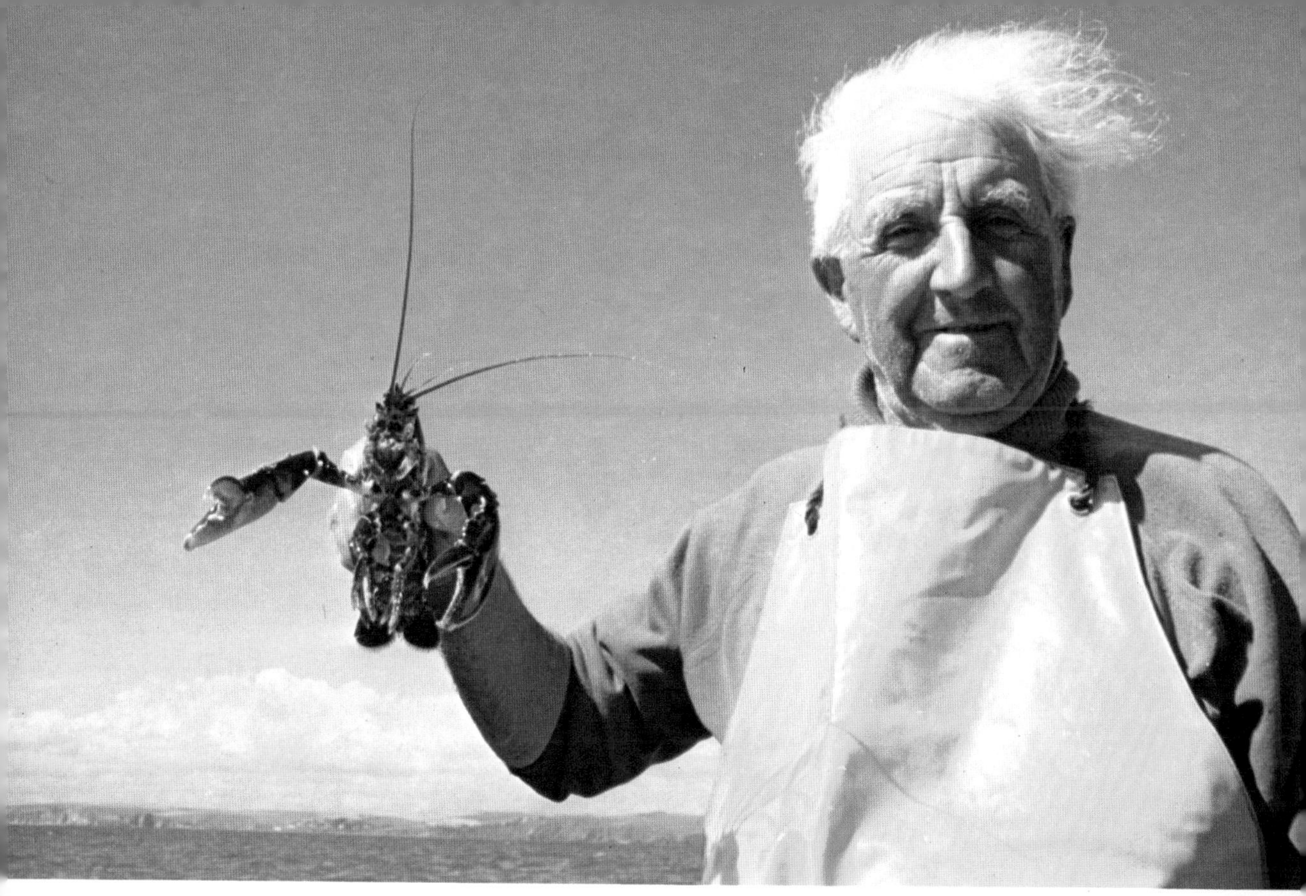

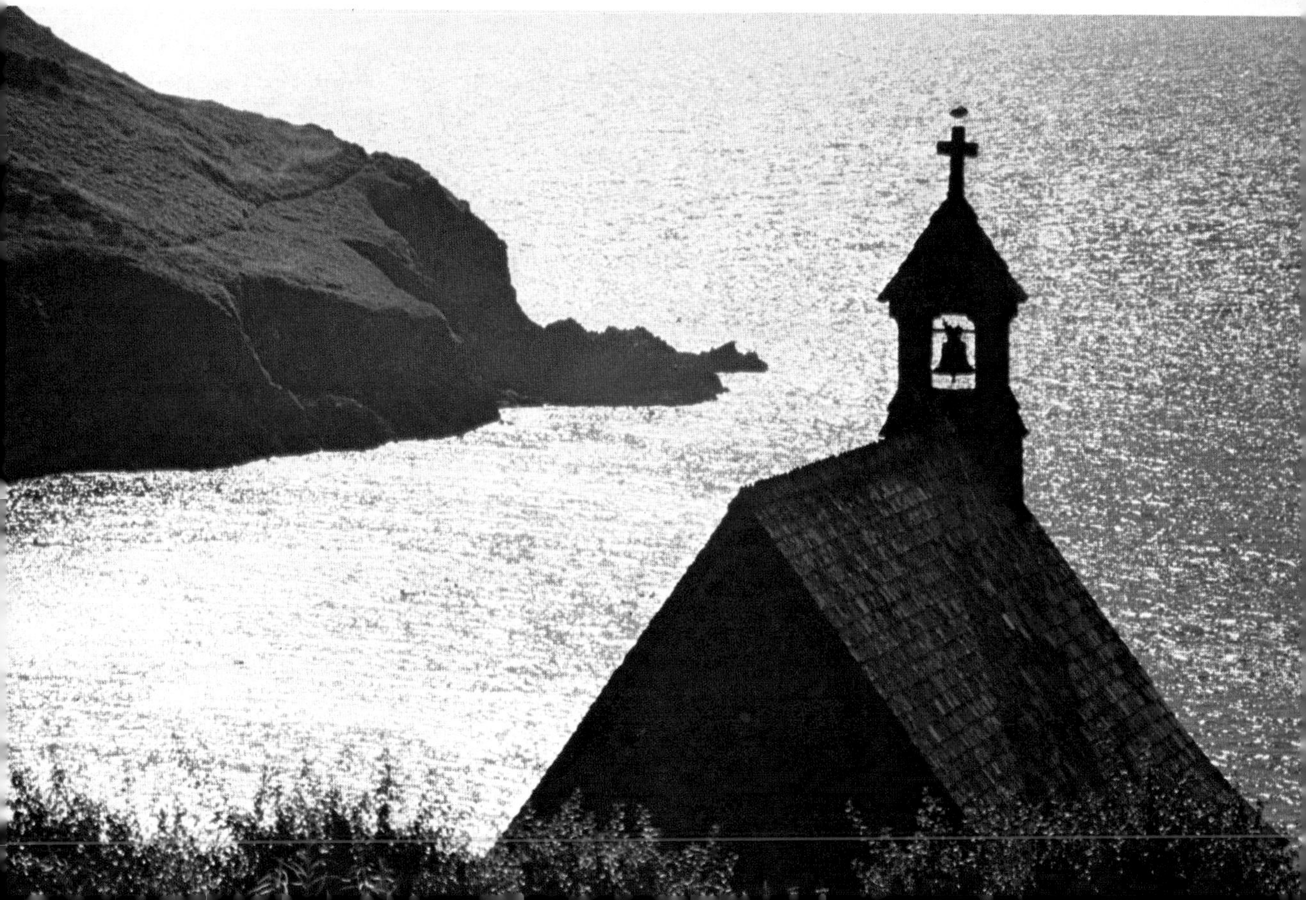

epidemic for which there is no known cure: 'We were bred here and it don't seem that long ago . . . we were bred in these cliffs, we'd go bird-nesting, knew every rock and cranny . . . Greystone Rock was a coastguard look-out, they painted the rocks white so they could see their way at night . . . it's all wishful thinking, this looking back. You can't go back to the old ways. I was talking to the parson the other day and I said, "Don't you know, it's useless all you parsons praying for peace when all the world's building up for the next war." It was the same in 1939, we prayed for peace in our time, as Chamberlain called it . . . well, the Germans were praying for peace too and they prayed to the same God. I pulled a fistful of money out of my pocket and said, "That's the god of today" – he had no answer to that. It's ruined England. Do anybody know the answer . . . does the Prime Minister? I don't know if I'd like to be young again, I don't know . . . I think you can have it.'

There was a time for pride and patriotism; and for valour too. In the biscuit barrel is an envelope, cream coloured with black edging and a seal: 'Central Chancery of the Orders of Knighthood'. In the letter Jack Jarvis is instructed to attend an investiture at Buckingham Palace so that King George V could present him with the Bronze Medal for Gallantry for his part in saving life when the *Joffre* went ashore on the rocks at Bolt Head at 2 am on 27 May 1925 during a gale.

'He was a little bit of a fellow,' he remembers. 'King Teddy, he was known as . . . and in an awful hurry too, he shook my hand, moved on and I hardly knew a thing. I must give that medal a clean sometime.'

Bigbury Bay, where Hope Cove is situated, was always a wicked place for sailors, a formidable reach where rocks are meaner than sharks' teeth. 'Terrifick to the mariner', wrote Abraham Hawkins; and terrific it is as portrayed by Turner when he painted the Revenge of Polyphemus where the enraged and blinded giant is depicted hurling rocks from the headland of Bolt Tail upon the ships of Odysseus in the bay below.

St Peter the Great of the Spanish Armada went down here. A hospital ship of 500 tons with a crew of thirty and carrying 100 soldiers, she was laden with 6,000 ducats' worth of drugs and 'potecary stuff'. In November 1588 she was driven on the rocks, becoming a total wreck; her plate and treasure were plundered before the arrival of George Cary, a Deputy Lieutenant of Plymouth. No doubt the local donkeys had a strenuous night humping the spoils over the hills to Thurlestone . . . which might not be too far from the truth since numerous beams and rafters of the prestigious Thurlestone Hotel are shaped from timbers of the ill-fated ship.

Ramillies Cove, one of the chasms on the Tail, is named after HMS *Ramillies* which, under the command of Admiral Boscawen, carrying seventy-four guns and 734 men, mistook Bolt Tail for Rame Head in a storm on 15 February 1760. One report states that all lives were lost except for one midshipman; another that twenty-six hands were saved by climbing the cliffs.

At Jack Jarvis' *alma mater* Marlborough is a memorial recording the wreck of the homeward-bound London–West Indies *Dragon* at Cathole Cliff in 1757. It marks the grave of three boys and a girl, children of Edward Chambers of Jamaica, taken by the sea.

Between 1806 and 1817 Bigbury Bay was the scene of at least eighteen wrecks, this being the total mentioned in *Lloyd's List*, so that when a sea mist closes in on Hope Cove, and *Girl Jean II* is overdue, with young John and nephew Eric aboard, small wonder that Jack is anxious to be down by the harbour.

'They're all right,' insists Jack. 'They know what they're about . . . they'll set the pots and John will come in on his compass. Blindfold, he could make it.' And blindfold he may as well be as the mist turns to fog, fifty or sixty yards visibility, no more; and not a breath of wind.

The trippers have retreated, deserting their moated castles of sand, scampered all the way to their home-from-home at 'Tarqua', where Mrs Sullivan offers bed and breakfast. Along Devon lanes they flee, through tunnels of green gloom, with bluebells and cow parsley dappling hedgerows; it is marvellously untidy, this hap-hazard landscape, not crimped and trimmed with the forensic passion of stockbroker territory. There are few signs telling us to do this, to do that, to keep off the grass.

It is a long wait at the harbour, the air salt-sticky, opaque. Jack chats away the quarter-hours, his eyes straining: 'The Ministry told us to throw back spawn lobsters, but the fishermen scrubbed them hard and sold them . . . so today we're reaping the benefit of our own greed . . . a plague of octopus wiped out lobsters and crabs another year, they'd even get them in the pots . . . what can they do, the visitors in bad weather? Nothing, that's what they do – except be miserable . . . hah! the glass fell again last night.'

At last there is a muffled sound from out of the fog, the pulse-beat of pistons, regular, steady, coming nearer; and there she is, *Girl Jean*, parting the clammy curtain that drapes the sea wall. You can see John's yellow oilskins, his shock of hair, once blond as a Viking's, now streaked with grey. Eric is next to him, passive, taciturn; there is nothing new to men who live by the sea. One day it could take them; then they would choke and vomit on brine – but not for long, it is an easeful death, those who have been close say.

'Come in on your compass, then?' asks Jack. It is a rhetorical question; he knows the answer, expects no reply and receives none. 'Eaten nothing since five this morning and I'm not hungry,' says John. He is a big man and there is a bitterness about him, an impatience. For whatever reason he returns to sea, it is not for love; that went long ago, together with ambition and hope. 'I'd go inland,' he says. 'But what would I do? I'm stuck.'

'I'm stuck too,' says Eric. 'I'm fifty-six years old and I'm stuck. The sea's overfished, we've taken too much out . . . there's no real job here. You call your chapter *Fisherman's Ruination* . . . they don't want to know nothing about us.'

For a big man, with so many years ahead, John's stoop is too pronounced. The bitterness shows. He wears it like a scar. He is trapped; very nearly is he defeated.

Jack gets to his feet. 'I'll see you when I see you,' he tells his son. 'I'll be getting back.' He takes the path that climbs the cliff towards the cowshed bungalows, towards the home he built for the wife who died of cancer, towards the galleons that sail across the walls, towards the smell of boiled cabbage. He has come in from the cold, turned his back on the sea.

'Didn't tell you about Ellen, did I?' He muses. 'We were brought up pretty strict, chapel was part of life . . . you feared the Lord. Mother died . . . father went on alone. Perhaps he couldn't take too much of that. He got to seventy then he married Ellen – she was thirty-five, a Lancashire girl . . .they're different people up there. She's still here, but we don't visit.'

It is the first time he has mentioned Ellen, the Lancashire lass who became one of the family. He has not pointed out her cottage; yet Inner Hope is a small place, so she cannot be far away. 'We don't visit,' he has said. Nothing more; just three words of excommunication, spoken with Christian feeling.

There are questions one cannot ask, areas of privacy that should not be invaded; there are secrets which are best kept secret. But how does she live, this Ellen from a different people; how old is she today and does she live with regret that she vowed to love, cherish and obey a man who was old when she was young? What manner of person is she, and are there mottoes on her wall? Does she watch her window, hoping for a visit; or does she live apart from memory and pain?

There is more to the riddle: 'Father was a deeply religious man. After he married Ellen he went off alone to the Holy Land, said he wanted to prove the Bible to himself. He went to where Christ was crucified – he went to where they put His body, wanted to see if anyone could roll the stone away from the tomb. He told us it was all commercialized, postcards and souvenirs, priests holding their hands out for money.

'So he went to the Sea of Galilee, thought he'd understand it more than the city. When he got there he told us he'd sit watching the fishermen cast their nets.

110

After a bit he went up and started talking, asked if he could go out with them as Christ did. He didn't speak the language, but he said it didn't matter because they understood each other by making signs. And they took him out. He was impressed by that, said it showed we were all really the same . . . they were fishermen from Galilee and he was a fisherman from Hope Cove, so they were like brothers.'

The
Landowner

CHAPTER IX

THE LANDOWNER

The Marquess of Tavistock

TAVISTOCK, *Marquess of: Henry Robin Ian Russell; a Director, Trafalgar House, since 1977; b. 21 Jan. 1940; s. and heir of 13th Duke of Bedford qv; m. 1961, Henrietta Joan, d. of Henry F. Tiarks, qv; three sons. Education: Le Rosey, Switzerland; Harvard University. Chairman, Cedar Investment Trust, 1977–; Director, Touche, Remnant & Co, 1977 –; Heir: s. Lord Howland, qv. Address: Woburn Abbey, Woburn, Bedfordshire. Telephone: Woburn 666; 3 Clarenden Place, W2. Telephone: 01 262 5588. Clubs: White's, Buck's, Jockey Club Rooms, The Brook (New York).*

It is all there, in this extract from *Who's Who*, the impeccable pedigree of a blue-blooded aristocrat. Not to the finest detail, of course: it does not divulge the shade of pyjamas favoured by Lord Tavistock, nor that he breakfasts off one boiled egg and freshly squeezed orange juice, neither does it relay the distinction of his inclusion among the world's ten best dressed men.

Who's Who is surely in further dereliction of its duty in failing to mention Lord Tavistock's addiction to the American beverage Coca-Cola, his habit of smoking American Chesterfield cigarettes, of addressing his secretary, 'Hi!'. No reference is made to an ancestor, William, Lord Russell, beheaded at Lincoln's Inn Fields in 1683 for his involvement in the Rye House Plot against Charles II's Roman Catholic leanings; shortly prior to his fatal indiscretion he had contracted marriage with Rachel, daughter of Lord Southampton, and heiress to his Bloomsbury property, and it was due to her tireless quest to prove her husband's innocence that he was declared 'the ornament of his age' and posthumously pardoned. Since there were obstacles in the way of commuting the sentence, William's father was created Duke of Bedford as a gesture of apology.

There are countless snippets of ducal gossip with which the eclectic *Who's Who* could regale its readers: how, for instance, the third Duke so dissipated family fortunes that sighs of relief at his death, at the age of twenty-four, stir branches of the family tree to this day. The tenth Duke and his Duchess found each other's company so unrewarding that they never spoke, unavoidable conversation at meals being conducted through an intermediary. The eleventh Duke is noteworthy because he kept fifty indoor servants and lived in 'moderate comfort'; shy of personal contact he resorted, when cornered, to one of two rejoinders, 'Indeed' or 'So I have been led to believe', and there the matter would rest. It is his wife Mary, known as The Flying Duchess, who catches our admiration: isolated by deafness, she started taking flying lessons when she was sixty-two; two years later she flew single-handed to the Cape and back in seventeen days; then, on Monday, 22 March 1937, at the age of seventy-one, she took off in her de Havilland Gypsy from the Woburn hanger – and was never seen again. Both she and the aeroplane vanished.

Where did they come from, these Russells who for centuries have made more than a glancing contribution to the fortunes of the realm? Only once has their fealty been in question; it is ironic that this aberration should have earned them a dukedom when usually such falls from grace led to ignominy. Lord Southampton's daughter must have been a determined lass indeed.

'Much nonsense has been written about our origins,' states the present Duke, Lord Tavistock's father. 'The plain fact is that we are of good lower-middle-class origin, although we did at least start on our way up five hundred years ago. The first Russell in the direct line of which there is indisputable evidence was a Henry Russell, who lived in Dorset and was returned as Burgess for Weymouth in the Parliament of 1425. The family was engaged in the wine trade and had close connections with Bordeaux, whence their ancestors doubtless came. He made a good marriage, prospered, owned a few parcels of land round Shaftesbury, Stour Provost and Compton Abbas, and in 1440 was appointed the Royal Customs Commissioner for part of Dorset and a couple of Devon ports. It was probably a case of setting a thief to catch a thief . . .'

His grace seems to have small regard for some of his predecessors: of Sir John Russell, first Earl of Bedford (1486-1555) – 'To this one-eyed old man I owe Woburn . . .'; the fourth Earl – 'He was the author of several religious works which he required to be read by his descendants. One at least has not done so . . .'; the eighth Duke – 'A bachelor of promiscuous and inconstant taste for women . . .'; the ninth – 'Convinced that people liked him for his money. This is possible . . .'; his great-grandmother, Elizabeth, bought 'a lot of hideous carpets with which we still have to live . . .'; great-aunt Adeline was 'coerced into marriage with a homosexual . . .'; grandfather Hebrand was 'a selfish and forbidding man . . .'; while his own father, the twelfth Duke, was 'the loneliest man I ever knew, incapable of giving or receiving love, utterly self-centred and opinionated.'

The bonds between father and son were never exactly cordial; far from it, there was an underlying bitterness which came to a head when, in 1939, the present Duke announced his engagement to Clare Hollway. The fact that his fiancée was thirteen years his senior and divorced appears to have stunned society in general and his father in particular less than the acknowledgement that he was marrying 'out of his class'. Nevertheless the marriage took place at Caxton Hall: 'A singularly unromantic procedure, rather like buying a dog licence.'

In a letter of justification for cutting his son off without a penny the father began:

> *Dear Ian*
> *I told you that I did not feel it expedient to tell you my reason for discontinuing the allowance if you marry because it might divert my purpose – the promotion of your own welfare.*

A state of emotional armistice existed between them for three years when, with all the piety of a self-appointed apostle, the father took up his pen once more: 'As far as I can judge,' he wrote, 'we now live in quite distinct worlds and there is hardly any point of real contact between the two.' The recipient's comment was both wry and, endorsing the thesis that blood is thicker than water, contained similar strains of holier-than-thou: 'There seemed indeed nothing I could do to save him from himself.'

In any event the marriage, first of the Duke's three, ended tragically when Clare died of an overdose of sleeping pills. It was in 1953, while living in South Africa with his second wife Lydia, that he was called to the telephone to receive the news that his father was 'missing', subsequently translated into death from a shooting accident on the Tavistock estate in the West Country. The twelfth Duke, introverted, querulous, lonely, was no more; the thirteenth Duke returned to England, to £4½ million death duties, to Woburn Abbey looking 'as if a bomb had fallen on it'.

The rest is common knowledge: Woburn was restored and opened to the public, many of whom paid 2s. 6d. for the privilege of shaking the Duke's hand; in 1970 the Duke, with Jimmy Chipperfield, launched the Woburn Wild Animal Kingdom. The World Nudist Convention was held . . . and the Duke's fellow peers were mortified: 'I have been accused of being undignified. That is quite true, I am. If you take your dignity to the pawnbroker he won't give you much for it.'

The thirteenth Duke of Bedford was not the first to open his gates to the charabanc trade, but he became the pioneer of the Stately Home Industry. 'Showman' was an epithet that stuck; but the Duke remained unrepentant, unflinching – because it *worked* and was seen to work. It became known as the 'Woburn Way' and other peers in the Stately Homes market place were not above a little aristocratic industrial espionage: if Woburn held a pop-festival, then dammit, Viscount Y would have a pop-festival.

The Duke installed espresso coffee machines, a juke-box; he appeared on the Hughie Green Show, played the wash-board in a skiffle group, even invited Marilyn Monroe to spend the weekend and sleep in Queen Victoria's bed . . . and then he did something unpredictable. He decided that he had had enough.

That was in 1974 when he was fifty-seven; his eldest son Robin, the Marquess of Tavistock, was thirty-four: 'My father built up Woburn, but there were enormous pressures, he's a great showman but he was tired, he needed a rest – he said it was a young man's job. To me a sense of inevitability became a reality in a way I felt would never happen.

'Luckily I'd failed to get into Eton, I might easily have been more snobbish had I gone there. Instead I went to Le Rosey in Switzerland where I met people from all over the world and this persuaded me to go to Harvard. I was married by then – we'd had a long honeymoon exploring the chateaux of the Loire, then took the *Queen Mary* to New York on the way to Round Hill in Jamaica. We took a small flat in Boston, Henrietta cooked, we had to watch the dollars and cents. I was studying economics . . . Kennedy was president and he drew from Harvard for his administration, so one was taught by Galbraith, Schlesinger . . . my tutor was Kennedy's personal adviser on African economic affairs.'

The Tavistocks met at Claridges when they were both two years old; the Marquess is six weeks older than Lady Tavistock and this she finds 'psychologically important'. They married in 1961 at St Clement Dane's, to vehement parental disapproval: the Duke, whose own experience made him none the more charitable, objected on grounds of the couple's youth; Lady Tavistock's banker father was concerned about his future son-in-law's ability to make his only daughter happy.

'We were making our own world,' says Lord Tavistock. 'I knew my life had been cast for me, I realized that Woburn had been created for us by the people of this country – but after America there was a sense of unreality about it. At Harvard I was Robin Tavistock, strings of titles were meaningless. We'd bought Chevington, where we were happy – we had time for the children, for horses, for each other . . . we were free and we were happy.'

Chevington is the Tavistock's Suffolk house, not far from Newmarket and Lady Tavistock's passion, racing. At Chevington the Tavistocks are a different couple: the house embraces them and their guests, it is a loving house and this you feel instantly. At Chevington there is time – to look at roses and walk, to play records and talk aimlessly with friends after dinner. It is a house that makes no demands, a house that gives; the giving is reciprocal and it would be perverse to be unresponsive to Chevington. The Tavistocks' three sons, Andrew, Robbie and Jamie, said recently that at Woburn their parents do not belong to them as they do at Chevington.

'When my father said he wanted me to take over Woburn I motored to Chevington and told Henrietta to have a large whisky because I had to talk to her . . . she burst into tears when she heard. We knew it would happen one day – I mean, I just didn't wake up one day and say "Gosh, I'm a Marquess." But we didn't expect it so soon.'

Lady Tavistock: 'It actively distresses me to talk about it. I live at

Woburn because I love Robin, that's the only reason. Every time I go out I have to ring a bell and someone comes with a bunch of keys – the same thing to get in. It's as if I'm my own gaoler. I have time to walk the dogs perhaps once a month, to ride once or twice a year. I don't see enough of the children . . . everything is for Woburn. Beautiful houses, beautiful pictures, objects, take a lot of looking after. I find it shocking that I know so little to appreciate it all. We have an indoor staff of six when there used to be fifty or sixty. Robin's grandfather only saw the butler – when he went riding a smoke signal went round to clear people out of his sight.

'This sort of life isn't real. I'm paying for the thirteen years before we came here. You have to pay for happiness, for times you've enjoyed – I believe that. Our *real* home is Chevington, it's our privacy.'

The *unreal* home, Woburn was founded as an Abbey by the Cistercian brotherhood in 1145, remaining a thriving establishment until the sixteenth century when a fire extensively damaged the buildings prior to the Dissolution. When Sir John Russell was granted the property, under the terms of Henry VIII's will in 1547, there was little to recommend it to this already wealthy man, as he owned far larger estates in the west. For about twenty years Woburn remained in the background while the Earls of Bedford continued to live in the Manor at Chenies in Buckinghamshire. In 1572, however, Queen Elizabeth I chose to stay at Woburn, causing the second Earl to rush to the Heals of the period to acquire furniture and plate for the Royal visit.

But it was left to the fourth Duke to rebuild the entire mansion from about 1750 onwards. Sarah, Duchess of Marlborough, who was his first wife's grandmother, had an influence on the shape of things to come. The rotunda and giant order of pilasters were designed by John Sanderson; the main house, Stable Courts, State Rooms bear the signature of Henry Flitcroft, a protégé of Palladio, so it is unsurprising that Woburn reflects many Palladian elements.

The fifth Duke was only five when he inherited and barely in his twenties when he returned from Italy to spend £65,000 on remodelling Woburn. Henry Holland, who worked for the Prince Regent at Brighton, was his architect; it was he who designed the finest rooms in the house, hanging them with pictures by Rembrandt, Van Dyck, Cuyp.

Wyatville was the last architect to make substantial improvements to the Abbey; he designed the Camelia House and a heathery for the seventh Duke during the 1820s, adding a temple to the Sculpture Gallery.

Over the centuries Woburn has become a great and noble house. The Park of 3,000 acres, surrounded by eleven miles of brick wall, is merely part of the 18,000 acre estate. In the eighteenth and nineteenth centuries Woburn became the social fulcrum of some of the most gracious living in the land . . . and yet it is a house which has inspired awe rather than love. Walpole, who stayed there in 1751, said he 'admired it, rather than liked it'. Which, curiously, is about the gist and sum of it. Lady Tavistock has said, 'It's as if I'm my own gaoler.'

If, on the other hand, Woburn does have a soul – and there is a case for believing that centuries of life, death, prayer, connivance, goodwill leave an imprint upon a building's fabric – perhaps Woburn sacrificed its soul when the thirteenth Duke turned it into a magnificent peepshow rather than a home. There was little alternative, it is true; it was the unavoidable solution: we, the nation, enjoy Woburn, the Russells are caretakers – and when their time runs out they will leave with the rest of us. And there is the sadness.

So . . . the thirteenth Duke had enough and went to live in Monte Carlo with his third wife, detailing his son to manipulate the affairs of Woburn. But this son received his adult education in the States as Robin Tavistock, and it has made of him another person, a man with two sets of standards, dual terms of reference. He says of himself, 'I'm a man of today rather than yesterday, my need is to contribute to the present more than rely on the past.' This is the American idiom speaking through him, the Robin Tavistock; yet he is still the Marquess, custodian of a heritage and an artefact the like of which will never be seen again – so not only does he have dual terms of reference, he has twin responsibilities as well. Which must be perplexing and burdensome; in the end it could be sorrowful.

Unlike his father, Robin Tavistock has not succumbed to the temptation of censoring his own line; it is as if his memory retains that which was worthwhile, rejecting the insipid and the mean. Of his grandfather, the 'utterly self-centred and opinionated' twelfth Duke, he recalls: 'One day he said to me, "We're going to London." We set off in the car, with two chauffeurs – you always had two in those days, one to drive, the other to open the door. We went into Churchill's gunsmiths and he said, "I want you to fit my grandson out with a decent gun" . . . which I'm still very fond of. It was a spontaneous gesture. We used to walk in the Park at six in the morning and he'd tell me all about the deer. He'd ring the bell at the Chinese Dairy and the Japanese carp would rise from the lake to eat from his hand. He had a bird hospital and tamed budgies to "home". If an animal was ill, he'd have it in his study – even deer would eat from his hand. Perhaps he had an affinity with animals he never had with his fellows . . .

'Mother was beautiful, daunting, impatient with children – the morning she died we were in the country, father came to us and said, "Mummy's gone away in a big ship." When he married Lydia, I called her "Mummy" – being a step-mother must be one of the most difficult things in life. When we came back from South Africa, she turned Woburn from a junk shop into a home.

'No, I don't share father's acidity towards the past – some of my ancestors made hideous mistakes, like great-grandfather selling Covent Garden for two million pounds he didn't even need, like the third Duke gambling away Streatham and his shareholding in the East India Company . . . father sees their weaknesses rather than their strengths. He can always spot a weakness at once . . . if he was with us now he wouldn't take into account the good points about you, but he'd know every weakness within minutes.

'Really he's a person of his upbringing, it made him remote and this remoteness made it difficult for him to get close to us. I love him very much, but there's a communication barrier which we both admit. I don't have that with my children . . . one good thing came of moving to Woburn – I promised Henrietta that if ever we had to come here she could have another child, we'd decided that two boys were enough. Jamie was born nine and a half months after we moved in and he's given Woburn its character to us – he knows everyone by Christian name. He's the first baby here for over 100 years, he *is* Woburn. He loves Woburn more than anyone here for centuries.'

Being invited to stay at Woburn in the time of Robin Tavistock's great-grandfather was a palaver: it was necessary to report to one of the Duke's two London houses where four cars and eight chauffeurs were maintained. You would travel as far as Hendon, where you changed cars to the one which had been sent from Woburn. You never travelled with your suitcase because it was not considered the thing to do; it travelled in another car, so you had a chauffeur and a footman with yourself and a chauffeur and footman with the suitcase, with another four at the Hendon immigration control. Eight people involved in moving one guest from London to Woburn. This régime continued until 1940.

Once in the house you would be allocated a personal footman, who stood behind your chair at meals, while a further sixty servants kept the household going, including seeing to the eighty wood fires throughout the Abbey. On the Duke's insistence all housemaids were required to be five feet ten inches tall. Food was reputedly good, even if the Duke was served special delicacies not offered to his guests; and one was not expected to dawdle – no meal lasted longer than half an hour.

Today the procedure is marginally less formal: you arrive in your own transport, to be greeted by Mr Seal, the butler. Antonio, the footman, escorts you to a guest room, perhaps Chenies, where he unpacks and runs your bath. The telephone number of Chenies is 227; Queen Victoria's bedroom is 202, the fourth Duke's 252, should you feel lonely in the night. There are seventy-four internal numbers on the card by your bed together with a bottle of Malvern water and a bottle of Perrier. Above the bed is a portrait of Anne Carr, Countess of Bedford, who died in 1694, an elongated woman with a fringe on top and a froth of lace at her not inconsiderable bosom. There are seventeen paintings in the dressing room and bathroom, including several sensitive animal watercolours by The Flying Duchess . . . how much one would have liked to know her. You may open your window, but if you lean out an 'electric-eye' will set the alarm off; there are two full-time security guards in the house.

The Tavistocks are in their sitting room, seemingly a quarter of an hour's walk away. Unless there is a dinner party, dress is informal, jeans if you wish; Henrietta Tavistock pours the drinks; Pam Jimson, the Nanny, brings young Jamie in to say goodnight, he gives you a lovely wet affectionate kiss. At 8 o'clock Mr Seal announces, 'Dinner is served, my Lady', and you move into the Canaletto Room, perhaps one of the most famous rooms in the world, where twenty-one views of Canaletto's Venice hang. The food is excellent, the wine too – a pleasure the host denies himself, preferring Coca-Cola which he drinks from a crested silver goblet.

It is agreeable; it is relaxed. The Marquess grumbles: 'Wherever we go people recognize Henrietta – "that's Henrietta Tiarks," they say . . . no one ever knows who I am. She's never changed.' He is right: she looks the same today as when she was

eighteen; she was beautiful then, and she was direct then, if she liked you it was apparent, if she disliked you it was apparent also. Nothing has changed. She says: 'I was doing the flowers in the library and overheard some people drawling on about me, pretending they knew me – it was so unbearable I went up to them as they were leaving and asked if they'd enjoyed their visit. Some other ghastly people said to me, "We're dying to see Woburn", so I said that we're open to the public every day.'

Robin Tavistock is in one of his withdrawn, mournful moods; he wears a hangdog expression: 'I remember asking father once if he was happy . . . he said it was a question he never allowed himself.' He drinks his Coca-Cola; all alcohol, he comments, tastes like medicine; Henrietta says he is marvellous when he has a very occasional drink because it goes straight to his head. 'Come on,' chivies Robin, 'let's have coffee upstairs.' Like his great-grandfather, he does not encourage dawdling at the table.

It is an agreeable evening; it is relaxed. But it is a Woburn evening, not a Chevington evening. There is a world of difference.

Three years ago, in the same Canaletto Room, the conversation ran something like this: 'You're giving me the choice,' considered Lord Tavistock, 'of choosing between Woburn or my wife? . . . Undoubtedly Henrietta would have to go!' 'The worst thing that could happen to me?' considered Lady Tavistock. 'That Robin or one of the children should be killed or badly injured.'

Since that conversation, Robin Tavistock gives the impression that his priorities are shifting; he has even said that there are moments when he cannot see himself living at Woburn as the fourteenth Duke of Bedford. Since that conversation Andrew, their eldest son, has been severely injured in a car crash; he is lucky to have survived the many operations to piece him together; he will always walk with a limp.

In the morning there is a 7.30 start. Each day he is at Woburn Lord Tavistock drives his Range Rover 1 DOB about the estate, listening to the day's work allocation, calling at a farmhouse for coffee, making tentative suggestions, 'tentative' because he admits to knowing little about farming: 'All I do is ask, and ask again and the men are prepared to help me, so that I know more today than I did six months ago. They're very loyal – we really need a farm manager, but they said, "You learn to farm and we'll manage." '

At 9.30 am Pam Jimson serves breakfast in the nursery; it takes about two-

and-a-half minutes – then Lord Tavistock is in his office to be briefed by Mrs Hall-Garner, his secretary. The Marchioness has left for London until the afternoon, there is a meeting at the estate office, one of the dolphins has lacerations the keeper would like his Lordship to see . . .

The day passes in the company of dolphins, lions, tigers, bongos and bears, giraffes, camels, zebras, sea lions . . . and *homo sapiens*, many hundreds of the species who have paid their money to see as much as they can: the Animal Kingdom, the Sèvres dinner service which was worth £18,374 in 1763, the Duke's Corridor, the State Saloon, the Reynolds Room, the Grotto. The Marquess trails round with a group, holds a door open for a visitor: 'Thank you, dear,' she says.

'When I took over Woburn, I was terrified,' confesses Robin Tavistock. 'I thought what on earth could I do that's better than history . . . then one day an old lady came up to me with her friends and said, "We'd hate to live here, but please keep it going for others to share." It's that sort of debt I'm trying to repay. It looks easy but it's not; Woburn runs on exact management. In Jubilee Year we had a Neil Diamond pop-concert that took nine months to organize . . . 56,000 people came and there wasn't a single unruly incident, the sunset was the best I've seen in my life and afterwards we said, "We've done it" – and we had.'

'Let me tell you about the very rich,' wrote Scott Fitzgerald. 'They are different from you and me. They possess and enjoy early, and it does something to them, makes them soft where we are hard, cynical where we are trustful, in a way that, unless you were born rich, it is difficult to understand. They think, deep in their hearts, that they are better than we are . . .'

The same could be said of landed aristocracy. If you have walked with kings and queens, and held the seal of life and death in your palm, then you are different; not better, different. You have been raised, rewarded highly; and thus your debt is greater, you have more to lose. For what is given may be taken. That which was the king's Divine Right to decree, may now by common consent be repealed. The balance is finite and precarious; but never be foolish enough to imagine the rich and powerful to be our playthings, disposed of easily when we have tired. The last laugh will be theirs, as sure as night follows day. For all their power and all their glory, and all their arrogance, they are a resourceful breed and fateful – more so when, in the case of the Dukes of Bedford, the family motto is '*Che Sarà Sarà*'.

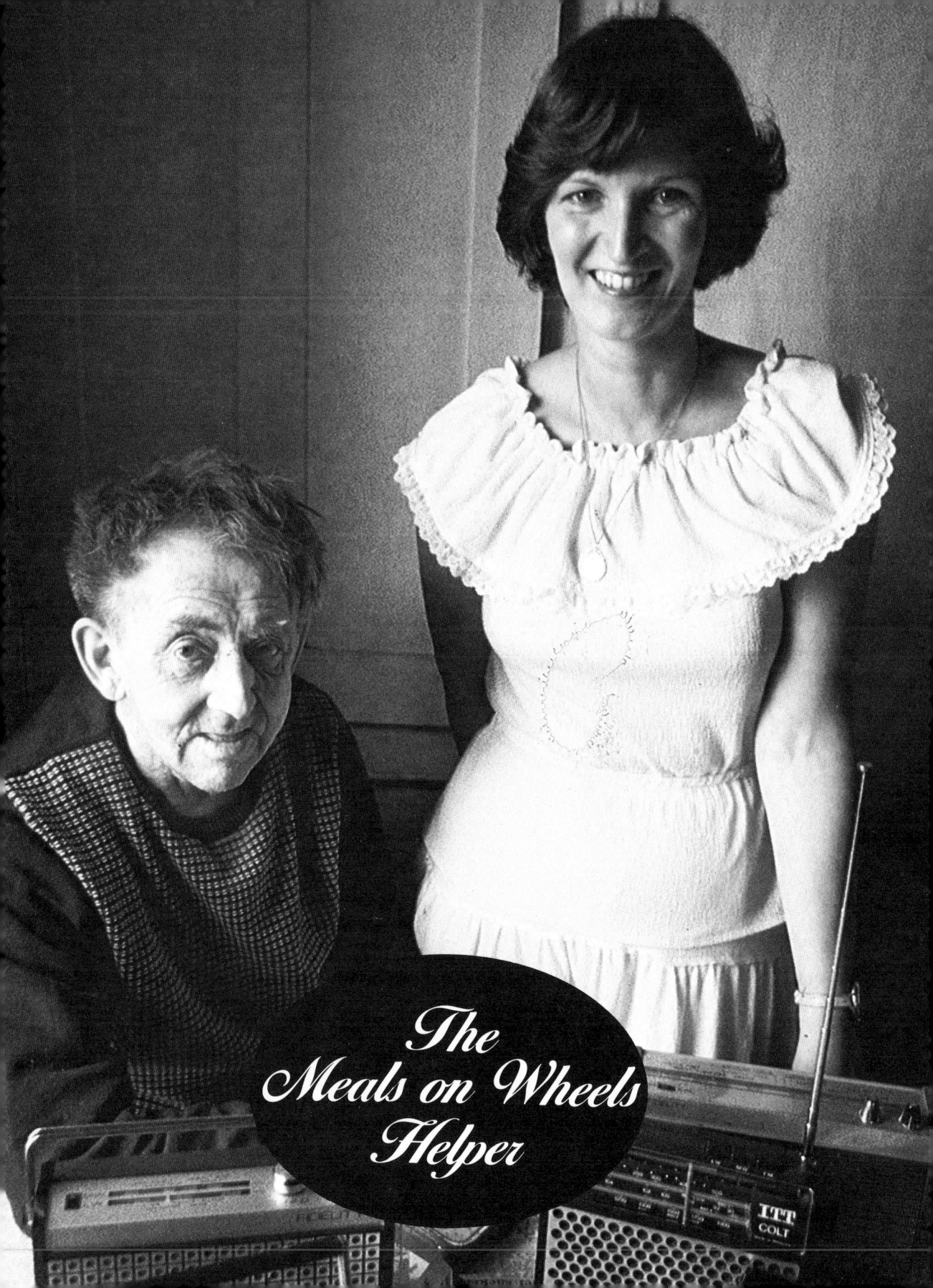

The
Meals on Wheels
Helper

CHAPTER X

THE MEALS ON WHEELS HELPER

Annette Warren

15 April 1836: *Upon the advice of his neighbours, who attributed their friend's recent misfortune to witchcraft, a local farmer burnt a calf alive as a method of breaking the spell.*

23 February 1838: *After the vicar of Newlyn had refused to bury a child on the grounds that it had not been baptized, the father was obliged to inter his child outside the cemetery with his own hands.*

3 December 1841: *A witch-finder visiting Tywardreath traced local deaths to a witch's incantations . . . the manner of her initiation, he reported, was by attending the sacrament, reciting the Lord's prayer thrice backwards, partaking of the wine, but securing the bread and giving it to a toad.*

17 March 1843: *Cornwall Easter Sessions sentenced Simon Jury. aged 12, to seven years' transportation for stealing six currant cakes and twenty walnuts.*

26 August 1844: *Matthew Weeks, a 22-year-old servant, 'lame in the right leg and missing most of his teeth', was hanged at Bodmin before a crowd of 20,000 spectators.*

16 January 1846: *In the open market at Callington a man sold his wife for the sum of 2s.6d.*

These and other such events were reported in *The West Briton*, a newspaper which faithfully mirrored the life and times of a county out of step and out of tune with the nation at large. For most Cornishmen emancipation and reform came to a grinding halt on the east bank of the Tamar. Cornwall was Celtic still, isolated, superstitious, suspicious. Conditions in workhouse or prison were not necessarily worse than those outside, where houses were small, dark, damp and squalid. Cesspits were by the door, six persons shared a bed with perhaps two or three times that number to a room. Measles, influenza, typhus, scarlatina, small-pox were killers; killing too, quite literally, were conditions in quarry and tin mine. Cholera was rife.

Deliverance lay in death or emigration and, by the middle of the century, thousands were leaving the creeks and hillsides of Cornwall for the Australian diggings, round the Horn for Chile or California. Few Cornishmen, however, left their homes without misgiving. Many returned, their fortunes made; some returned broken.

Those long absent came back to a county of innovation and paradox: witches had abandoned their broomsticks, but travelled on the Great Western Railway; a miner's leg might be amputated by anaesthetic, but his whooping cough cured by a spell; mermaids were little in evidence, but piskies were seen and long-legged beasties still went bump in the night. Monolithic hotels were built so that Victorians could gulp the bracing ozone of Newquay; and by the 1920s and '30s the Austin Seven and bull-nosed Morris were making sight-seeing safaris from all over England.

Cornwall was being dragged into the twentieth century, and not responding with unqualified enthusiasm. There are still partisans who shoot at the tyres of Jaguars. But the gold-mines of the holiday business have richer veins than tin mines; so tourism is at its zenith. Its attendant pollution is tolerated because the money is right and because it is too late to put the clocks back. Progress is irreversible.

The old order had yielded to the new; where there was poverty there is now affluence. Fishing and mining are on the decline, mechanized farming on the increase; and summer roads from Penzance to Land's End, all the way round to St Ives, are punctuated with number plates from Birmingham, Warwickshire to Birmingham, Alabama. The average wage is up, the mortality rate down; shops are full of fancy goods, doctors' surgeries are full of patients with fancy-sounding complaints. But there is no starvation and children do not go barefoot; so the sociologist would have a difficult case proving that change is for the worse.

Cornwall has become the 'Cornish Riviera'; and there are palm trees, sea, sun, sand, and sedation – the ingredients needed to soothe away the cares of factory and office, of mortgage, maintenance and mothers-in-law. The climate is mild and it is soft; the scenery, once sombre Camborne and Hayle are over your shoulder, is Arthurian. The legends, myth and magic spread far beyond King Arthur's court at Tintagel; they engulf the entire peninsula, impregnating the land with mystery still unsolved.

Clever modern men deride Camelot; they state categorically that the Round Table is a fable, that Merlin could not produce a rabbit from a hat, that any softy could draw Excalibur from its sheath of granite. They question too that men from the parishes of Breage and Germoe lured ships on to their rocks, armed themselves with axes, ready to plunder, maim and murder when doomed vessels struck shore. Such sceptics miss so much . . . do they never consult the Small People?

'Give a gnome a home', entreats a sales notice in a St Ives shop. Has it really come to this? Gnomes, cheap ashtrays, plastic lighthouses, made not in Helston or Looe, but in – would you believe it? – Hong Kong. Teetotal festivals, wrestling matches, fairground, market, the obscenity of a public hanging, have been re-placed by bingo halls. Where tambourine, hurdy-gurdy, drum, fiddle and brass band made music, pocket transistors have taken over. There were charmers,

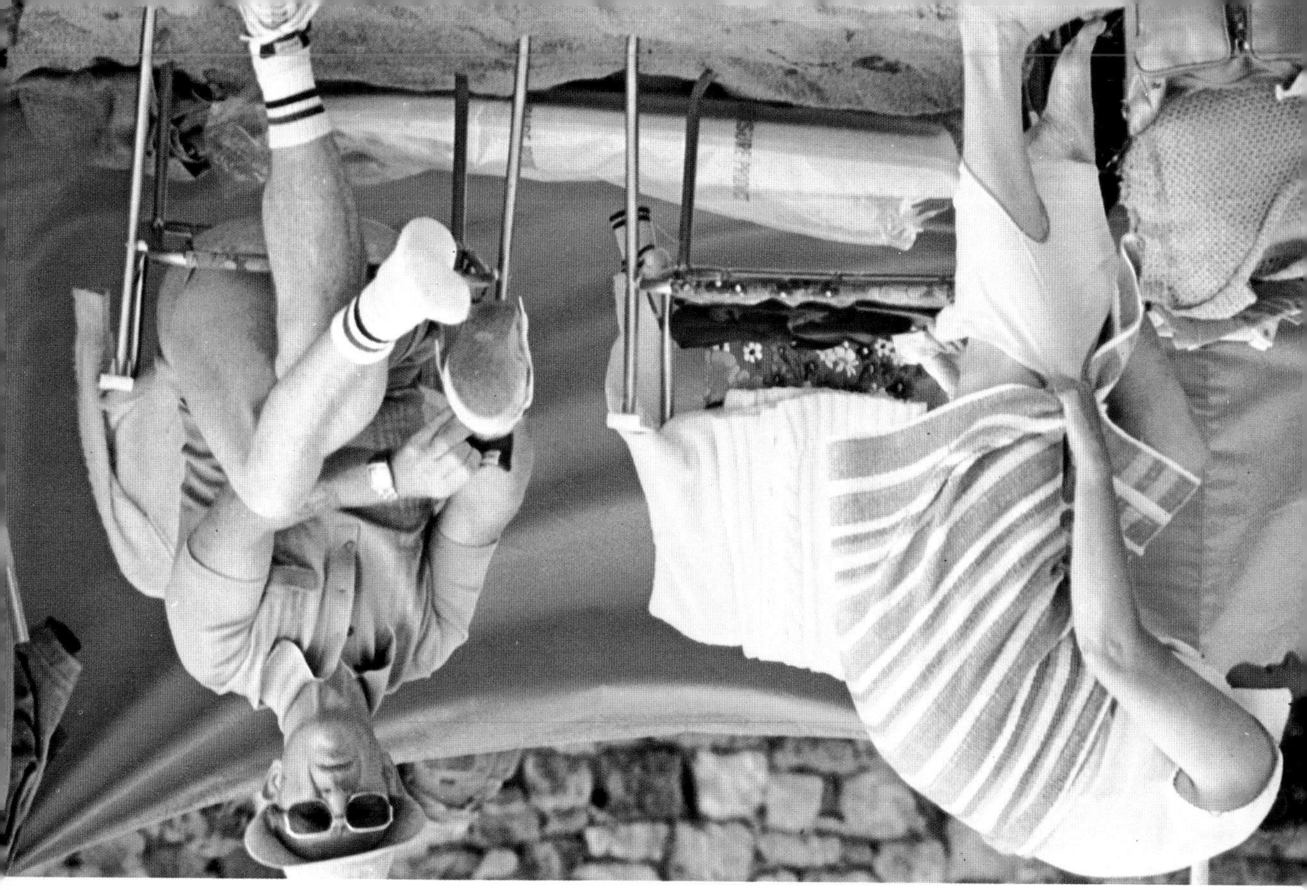

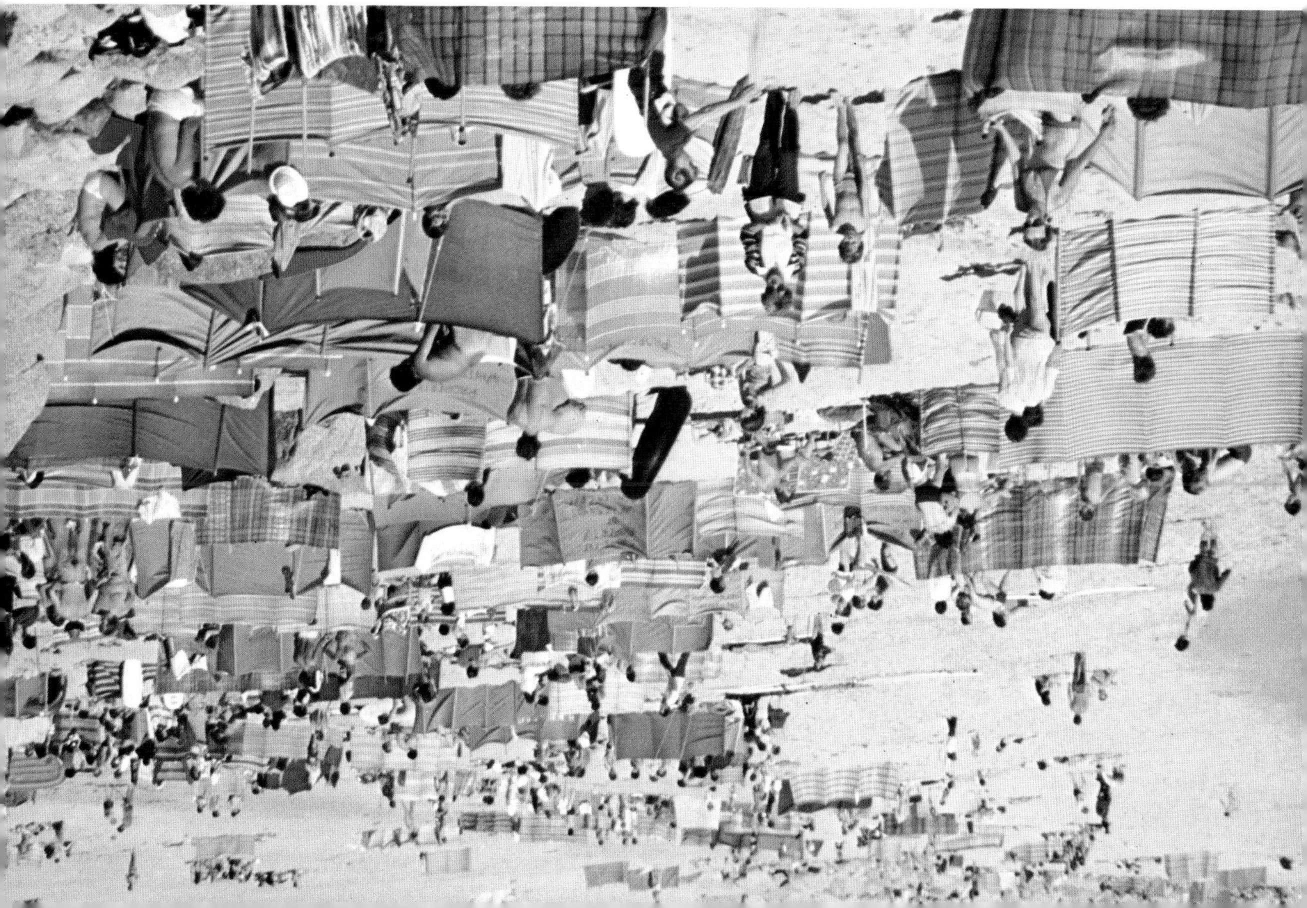

quack physicians, thimble-riggers, beggars displaying their deformities, fat women, bad girls and pickpockets . . . where there are now neatly suited trade unionists looking for a cup of tea.

Not all is lost, not every vestige and remnant that smelled of human kind and foible has been deodorized from Cornwall. The names are intact along to where the land ends, and back again: Zennor, Morvah, Bojewyan, St Just and Sennen Cove; around the tip of England lies Porthgwarra, Porthcurno, St Buryan, Newlyn, Mousehole. Lovely names, all, still naked, unadorned with postal codes in numbers. Oh, to die in Lamorna; or better still to live there, within earshot of the gulls that sound like babies crying for their mothers' milk . . . until July and August when the quayside becomes funeral parlour to the motor car, with windows raised against sea air and the *Daily Telegraph* unfurled across the Belisha-beacon forehead of dad taking a beery nap.

If you do not believe in mermaids, consider this: Mathy Trewhella, whose tenor voice sang out in the choir of Zennor church, became bewitched by a beauty who attended service three Sundays in succession, watching him and him alone. On the third Sunday Mathy followed her down to the cove and was never seen again. Years later a ship anchored off-shore and the crew were astonished to see a mermaid appear, begging them to move their anchor, which blocked the entrance to her dwelling, so that she could not get to Mathy and their children.

At Mousehole a tablet set into a cottage wall reads: 'Here lived Dolly Pentreath one of the last speakers of the Cornish language as her native tongue. Died Dec. 1777.' She lived to eighty-five, some say 102; deaf and bent, she walked six miles a day and made a living selling fish. Afraid of no man, she cursed rich and poor with impartiality: '*An cronach an hager dhu*'– 'Ugly black toad!' – she screeched at the squire who upturned her basket.

Well, well, she survived 102 winters, if we give her benefit of the doubt; and had she made it a few more she would be on Social Security, become eligible for Meals on Wheels. In which event she would have met Annette Warren from Penzance.

Annette was born at Redruth in 1940. Her father worked in a draper's shop in St Austell to where the family moved; her mother was district nurse. 'It was a fine marriage, they were happy . . . mother was devoted to nursing, and father was – well, he was a good man. He gave parties for local children, played the organ at St Austell parish church, was involved with people and their problems.'

She makes them sound nice, ordinary people; not the sort who scale Everest or holiday in Bermuda, more reliable, of the kind you would trust with postal orders and neighbours' children. The mother died though, after enjoying her daughter for a bare six months; her husband was left to cope as best he could, bringing up a young child alone, holding down his position at the draper's shop.

He seems to have done a more than adequate job: 'They were the happy years,'

132

Annette says. 'I couldn't remember mother, of course, so I turned completely to father . . . and I had a sense of vocation, even at ten I was reading books about medicine I couldn't understand . . . perhaps mother left me that. The tragedy came when father died, I was only fourteen and an orphan then . . . I grieved, really grieved, I still miss him. I went to Grandma, she lived in Stoke Newington in London, and I was sent to private school . . . but I cried a lot, I cried in bed for father, I still felt his presence. I do even now, he's spiritually with me, guiding me in decisions.

'I had this dream that I'd come back to Cornwall. London was too fast, just spinning too quickly . . . shops were huge, not like little family shops here. So when I was eighteen I came to Penzance, to the West Cornwall Hospital to do my SRN at £3. 15s. a week.'

At twenty-one she qualified as State Registered Nurse, transferred to Bristol to a premature baby unit and to paediatric work; children and the elderly have long been her passion: 'I know the sense of deprivation they can feel. Caring for them compensated perhaps for my own barriers of loneliness [an expression she uses frequently]. I have empathy with old people because I've been there myself in loneliness. When they get very old and helpless, their characters are still there, that doesn't fade.'

From Bristol she went to Tehidy Hospital in Camborne, then back to the children's ward at Penzance – where she fell in love with a rugby full-back: 'He was from St Just – it's a very closed shop there, they don't like strangers, even I was a foreigner and so was his mother for forty years. We met at the Admiral Benbow pub here in Penzance. He offered me a lift and I said no, but he followed me in his car and kept saying "Get in", so in the end I did.

'We went out to meals and I watched him play for the Penzance Pirates . . . and we married at St Just church in 1965. It was the wedding of the year, top hat and tails . . . Brian's family are the big baking firm, shops all over . . . we went to Sitges in Spain for the honeymoon.'

After nine years they divorced, Brian applying to the Court for custody of the children, Jonathan and Sarah. 'Brian has custody, I have care. I don't know why . . . Brian resented medicine, he was aggressive to medical people . . . I was on call, voluntarily, for childrens' emergency – I might suddenly have to take a child up to Great Ormond Street.

'Divorce knocked me for six, it was the second desertion to come to terms with . . . it was like being orphaned all over again. I felt empty. There's something missing being a housewoman rather than a housewife. It was my salvation going to St Michael's Hospital at Hayle, it's run by the Daughters of the Cross. Brian got married again then . . . strange what a blow it was, to me and the children. We were trying to manage in the tiny flat we had.'

They are in the tiny flat no longer. A change of fortune moved them into their present house in Penzance, a roomy, pleasant early-Victorian terrace house a minute from the promenade. The kitchen is done in pinewood and there are gadgets, buttons to push, machines buzz, whirr and foam. There is a large sitting room, lived in and used, a welcoming room and you know that children are around. The furniture is modern, Scandinavian; there are books, pictures, a game of marbles that look too perfect in their symmetry to disturb.

Annette Warren is a pretty woman, very feminine, almost too perfect in the symmetry of her poise to disturb. She looks younger than her years, her figure excellent; she is sexually appealing and you can see why Brian from the bakery would not take no for an answer. There is no wariness about her, no guile; she does not consider, reshape or rephrase the intimacies she reveals, merely hopes that they will not be reported in the same detail. There is a calm about her; at the same time there is an incandescence by which you could warm your heart or burn your fingers.

After more years of aloneness, her life is once again changing; occasionally she bumped into a married couple in church and at the art gallery, enough to say hello. A short while ago she heard that the wife died so, after church one day, she said to the husband, Travers, how sorry she was; if he felt lonely, please drop in for coffee one day. Plucking up courage, he eventually did so and a friendship has grown; they have children the same age, similar interests. Recently they went to Leicester to see his invalid mother.

Travers is ten years older; he was a producer with the BBC in London, but was losing respect for the medium and the Corporation, so came to Cornwall to make a new start, to become a potter. There is a BBC trendiness about him; Chelsea or Islington is his natural habitat, along with other rare birds of kindred plumage. And in this indictment one is only half wrong: he admits that he loves Cornwall, has settled well, but makes no claim that he will plant roots here. He is a middle-aged 'don't-know'. It is quite clear however that he knows his fondness for Annette.

Three years ago Annette became a WRVS helper, taking on a Meals on Wheels run; soon she became District Organizer, with nine helpers. Meals are cooked by Mrs Edwards at Madron Primary School, collected in insulated hampers and delivered to elderly people who have difficulty in preparing food for themselves; thus each is guaranteed two hot meals a week. A typical meal of roast chicken, two veg, treacle pudding costs 30p. Helpers usually travel in pairs, one to drive and park, the other to serve, collect the money and chat. There is never enough time to chat because food gets cold, even in insulated containers.

Which is a pity because a good chat is a relief if, like Mrs Retallack, you haven't seen a soul since the last Meals on Wheels helper. She has a council flat on the ground floor of a house in Newlyn. There is a bedroom, sitting room and kitchen. Mrs Retallack keeps mostly to the sitting room, in which there are two upright chairs; there is no other furniture, no ornaments, photographs or pictures. The floor is of lino and stone. A fire burns in the grate, as it does every day of the year. The fire is her staff of life; if it went out so would she. For about fourteen hours a day she sits in front of the fire, prodding it sometimes with her walking stick, which gets shorter as the coals devour the tip centimetre by centimetre. Not long ago Annette Warren arrived to find the stick in the fire, burning quite merrily, Mrs Retallack watching, unable to bend sufficiently to retrieve it.

She sits too near the fire, so that there are third degree burns on her bare legs; the wounds are suppurating. As a nurse Annette is concerned; has the doctor been, she asks: no, the doctor never comes, he is too busy, he just leaves tablets from time to time, tablets she will not take. And the district nurse? No, Mrs Retallack doesn't want the district nurse, she doesn't want to be a bother. Two years ago she was taken to an old people's home, but did not think much of it and discharged herself – since when she has not been out of the house.

Mrs Retallack was born in Penzance in 1889. She married a fisherman, but he died way back in 1940, since when she has been alone. She has white hair and clear blue eyes the colour of cornflowers; she reads without spectacles, her eyes are very sharp. Her National Health false teeth are ill-fitting and keep slipping as she talks; it looks as if she is eating something that won't go down. She is deaf and Annette holds her arm, shouting into her ear; she nods, pretending to hear more than she does. At her feet is *The Sun*; there must be a copy for every day of the month. Today's paper is open at an article headed: 'Hit Man Decorates Topless Models'.

Mrs Retallack is incontinent; she urinates as she sits, and Annette is anxious that her burns will become infected. Annette's hair was cut recently, so Mrs

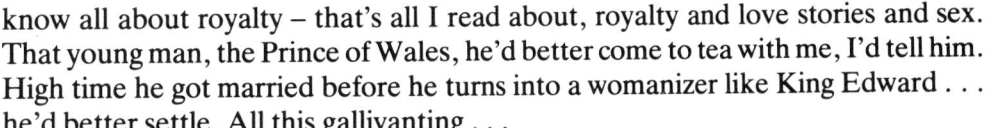

Retallack does not recognize her at first. She is further confused by a visit on a non-meals day.

Eventually she registers: 'You're the divorced one,' she announces brightly. 'What happened . . . your husband go off with a fancy woman then? You've got to keep your man. I made the best of my marriage, never lost me temper, it's not in me nature. People with tempers are no good. I can always tell by faces . . . dark people are fiery, even the gentry – fair people are better.

'I worry about that young man, the Queen's son . . . she's a lovely lady, I know all about royalty – that's all I read about, royalty and love stories and sex. That young man, the Prince of Wales, he'd better come to tea with me, I'd tell him. High time he got married before he turns into a womanizer like King Edward . . . he'd better settle. All this gallivanting . . .

'Oh, I'm happy, never been unhappy in me life. I look out of the window, watching people – you can't be lonely doing that. I have bread and jam and I'm up at eight every morning. I'm not one to lie in bed, I've got to get on. Can't sit around doing nothing.

'I feel no older than I was seventy years ago. I'm young-young . . . you'll be gone before me, young woman. Go and get that photo of me when I was twenty-one will you . . . I was a lovely girl then.'

She was too. It is a broad face, this studio portrait taken in Penzance, with the fair hair of gentleness, in which temper never flared. Mrs Retallack holds the frame, admiring herself through the decades; she has not changed, she is telling herself, just a little stiffness in the joints, but she is the same person, needing to get on.

'I've got me fire,' she says, as Annette prepares to leave. 'And don't you send the nurse, I don't need her . . . you're divorced, aren't you,' she calls gleefully. She sits back into her upright chair, staring at the fire; she will eat some bread and jam soon and later, much later, she will go to bed. Annette has never heard Mrs Retallack complain; it is a good life still.

Mrs Northey comes next. She can be strange on occasions, warns Annette; often she barricades herself in, locking the door, piling up furniture so that WRVS helpers cannot get to her. Sometimes it takes ten minutes or so of doorstep parley to convince Mrs Northey that she is opening the stockade to friend rather than foe. There is a conspiracy against Nrs Northey, tribal warfare in which she appears to favour a policy of genocide towards her enemies.

It has to do with the house they bought for her husband's retirement from the Civil Service; a large Edwardian house on a hill, with glorious views of St Michael's Mount. Mr Northey should have been well content with such a house, but a few weeks after moving in he had a sharp pain after lunch and died at the table. That was in 1949, but to his widow it is yesterday; she lives with the memory, the deeds and the cobwebs, as bitter, jilted Miss Faversham lived with the mouldering remains of her wedding feast.

'You remember Mr Sneed,' she accuses. 'No, well perhaps you wouldn't . . . they're in league against me, they swindled us over the house, do you see? I saw them . . . yesterday I think it was, all three of them. They won't get me out . . . not that I care for the place any more, but I'll die here I suppose.'

It all took place over thirty years ago; the hapless Mr Sneed has long been cold in his coffin, but the feud continues. Mrs Northey seethes, beating a table with her cane; it seems almost as if she is having a seizure.

'Who are you?' she demands of Annette suspiciously. 'How old am I? My age . . . it's 1979 isn't it, or 1980? I must be eighty then . . . and don't I look it. I was about to do my hair, but I've always got to be ready for them, you never know when they'll come. I can't leave the house – I'm waiting for the warm weather . . . June is it? Well, I never. I must be getting forgetful. Come upstairs, that's where I keep my husband's books.'

She leads the way, bent almost double with arthritis, to an upstairs sitting room. There are the books and an upright piano made by John Spencer & Co. of London. In a silver photograph frame is a picture of Cary Grant; she does not know his name, she cut the print from a newspaper because she had an empty frame. She has snapshots of an owl called Gulliver. Gulliver broke a wing, and she and Barney – her dog – nursed him back to health, so he became attached to the family. There they are, sitting down to tea; Mrs Northey is pouring, Mr Northey moodily examines a sponge cake, Barney and Gulliver stare at each other with unblinking, implacable hatred. You could fill an album with photographs of Gulliver; small wonder that Barney's nose was out of joint.

'Next time you come, send me a telegram. I'll know it's not a trick . . . I'll get dressed properly, do my hair. You'll never want to leave me then,' she says, flirting.

Mr Ellis, born on St Andrew's Day 1891, is registered blind. His wife died several years ago, but not before teaching him to cook, to look after himself. She would be proud of him if she came back on a visit: his flannel pyjamas and combinations flutter from the clothes-line, Omo bright, meticulously darned; and when a shower comes he is as fussed as any washday housewife. 'We used to get better winters than we get summers now,' he says. 'My old girl was lovely . . . I was fifty when I met a chap who said he'd thoroughly recommend marriage, so I went out and got her. Best day's work I did. Well, she's gone and I'm lonely, so that's that – but I could have missed those years same as I missed my early years.

'That was in the war, I mean . . . father and grandfather were drag-fishing for mackerel, but mother hated it, she wouldn't even look at the sea, she'd turn right away. So I went into trade until the war . . . wish I'd had more of a chance, but you didn't have a chance in them days . . . I'd like to have been in the post office, but I didn't have the proper connections. We were just thrown on the market at fourteen and took what we could.

'Then you were thrown in the army . . . my life was foiled by that war, the best years went for nothing in the trenches, it drained me of ambition. My leg was smashed by shellfire . . . my youth was in the mud and it's still there. That war killed a lot of us who survived . . . we came home and we didn't bother because we were dead really, and that's the truth.'

He brings out his exercise books marked 'Newlyn Boys Board School'. There, in bold copperplate, reads:

Church St., Newlyn, 17.2.1904
Received from Mr. Carne, Newlyn, the sum of one pound in
payment of one Quarter's rent due December 24th 1903.
Robert Ellis

Not bad for a twelve-year-old. The post office must have been slow not to take

on young Robert, capable of such a hand. But trade, you could say, was a step up from drag-fishing and at least someone in the family was pleased.

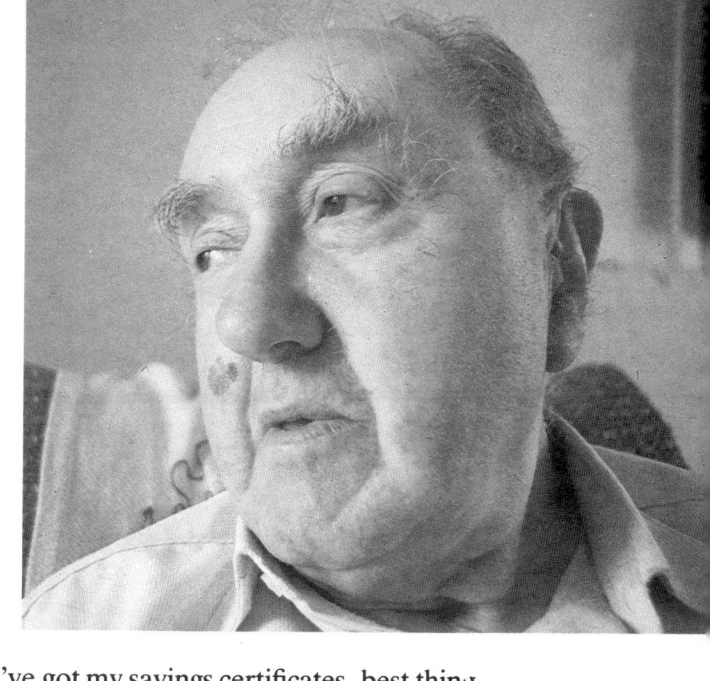

'I like a bit of company,' he says. 'I like the girls coming.' He gives Annette a squeeze and turns on his talking book, settling back to another chapter of Nevil Shute.

Not far away is Mr Wallace's room. He is dressed in dungarees and boots, a big man, muscular, with opinions of his own. He keeps himself to himself, not on the best of terms with neighbours: 'I speak out of turn, I forget myself . . . they think you're bloody mad today if you save – but I've got my savings certificates, best thing you can buy. No one crosses this porch, let 'em in you'd never get the buggers out. I'm still strong . . . boxers used to come to the country fairs and challenge anyone to six rounds . . . I'd say, "I'll take the buggers on", and they'd never floor me.'

At the quarry, Penlee Quarry, he wielded a twenty-two pound sledge-hammer for ten hours a day, seven days a week, no holidays and no 'wet weather', for 11¾d. an hour. 'Blue Elvin we sledged, hardest stone in the world, it built the Bank of England . . . I'm still known as Old Wally at the quarry. "He's all bloody work, is Old Wally," they'd say . . . my real name is Joseph Garfield Wallace, father said it was the name of an American president. After forty years they gave me that barometer.' He points to it on the wall; it must have cost a tenner or so when he retired at £11 a week basic wage in 1967.

'Father was a horseman on a farm for 13s. a week, mother was in service at £8 a year, and I started as a carpenter at fourteen in St Leven for £5 a year, so I didn't do badly. Married Winnie when I was thirty-five, I wasn't in a hurry . . . she was a huge woman, as many pounds to her as there were days in the year, 365 pounds she was. She was over sixteen stone when we were courting . . . she'd sit on your knee and you'd know it, and she was the world's best cook.

'I'd rather have a little 'un nowadays . . . why have a farm truck when a mini will do? Not that I'd marry again – what'll keep two will keep one nicely . . . no disrespect to Winnie. I miss the food, we enjoyed our food, that's why I'd have Meals on Wheels every day if I could. She was only one day in hospital before she died . . .

'A lot of dying, there is . . . those who drank tea instead of beer, they're all dead. I keep half a bottle of scotch in my bed, I have a nip when I go to sleep and one when I wake up. The doctor told me to do that and he was right, best advice I've ever had.

'There you are, you've got to live twice to learn how to live once.'

Down the hill from Old Wally is Newlyn Harbour, to which the pilchard once brought prosperity; now every kind of fish, deep water and inshore, is landed – much of it sent daily to Billingsgate. The irony of it all is that the harbour, built by Cornishmen to benefit Cornish fishermen, today more successfully lines the pockets of strangers who have taken over.

Newlyn is full of fish cellars and 'long rooms' for net-making; boats of all shapes and sizes are tied up to the quays. There is tiny *Halcyon* PZ132, without even a deckhouse; *Marie-Claire* PZ295 is rusting, she has seen action and better days; *Nereid Broadford*, registered in the Isle of Skye, is far from home. Suttons of Cornwall are selling white fish and, next to the Royal National Mission to Deep Sea Fishermen, the Gents is also signed 'Hommes', and the Ladies, 'Dames' – it gives the place a sophisticated, international flavour.

You can see it all from where Willie Trehearne lives. He lives alone because he could never quite make girls out; his brother was the same – the only woman they ever cared for was their mother, and that love sounds a gentle obsession. Willie worked on the harbour: 'No lies, when we was unloading, I wouldn't see me bed for two weeks. Mother came down at midnight to bring me tea, I *hated* that . . . it was too dark and rough for a woman. When was I born? Now, you've got me. I don't know when I was born . . . wouldn't make much difference if I did, would it?'

Willie is simple, 'not quite there', as some would say. He was born in the next door cottage and, apart from walking to the harbour to unload fishing boats, he has not done a great deal with his life. And now he is old, no one wants him; possibly he was never very desirable, being simple. He never walked a girl after church or held hands at the summer fairs, watching Punch and Judy on the sands. No girl ever traced the lines of his face with willing, eager fingers or wished him in her bed.

They would have called him Daft Willie, giggling behind his back, and spread their thighs for handsome boys who knew a thing or two. Willie missed all this and so his loins remained inert. Those pert and predatory girls of long ago who could have

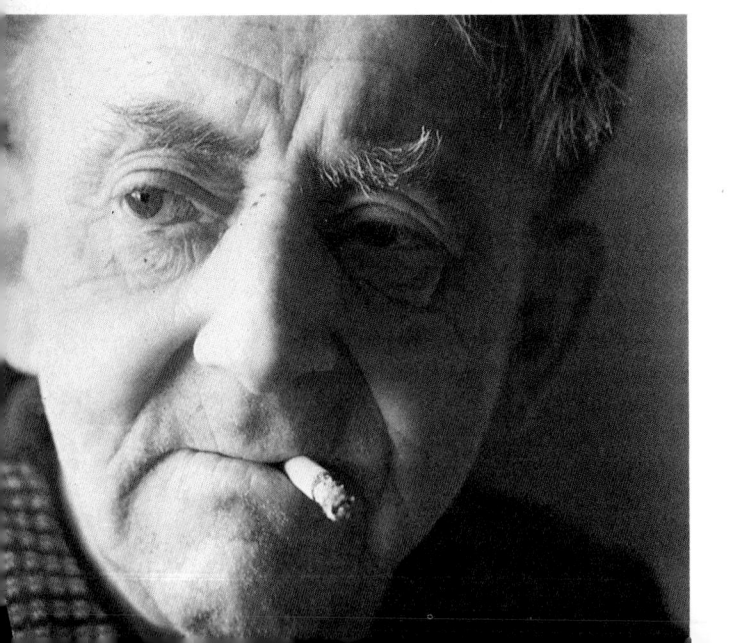

made of him a man, left him instead a eunuch; so he turned in on himself, to his own language hard to follow, and to silence.

Rarely does he wash and, smoking heavily as he does, his nostrils are stained with the ochre of nicotine. He is not too careful in the arrangement of his trousers, so that the more sensitive Meals on Wheels ladies are reluctant to visit Willie; and whichever barbers cut his hair should do penal servitude because they have shorn him into a travesty.

He is a hoarder: bread loaves, rich green with mould, partly eaten, pot-holed as a lunar surface, rest on a table, foothills before an escarpment of Cornish 'heavy' cake. He offers hospitality, a *table d'hôte* of bread and cake, Hobson's Choice in the ineluctable. There are packets of matches and unwrapped cartons of King Size Embassy cigarettes; there must be over a thousand cigarettes. He counts the packets artfully; then he counts his radios. There are six portable radios in the room, each one in working order; he tinkers with them, turns them on and off, raises and lowers the volume, adjusts them so that the variety of sounds and stations is the best he can manage. This absorbs him totally, he is the von Karajan of the wavebands, conducting for his visitors . . . who shortly go, leaving him in the joint company of Pete Murray, Roy Plomley, and Wolfgang Mozart.

'Mrs Grosvenor-Smith is the one who really makes me sad,' says Annette in the car. 'She comes from what I suppose you'd call gentlefolk, so it must be more of a shock somehow, she's not used to this sort of thing.'

Mrs Grosvenor-Smith opens the door, looks momentarily bewildered, recovers composure instantly and invites her callers in. 'How do you do?' she says formally, motioning towards chairs. It is a big house, again with superb views of Mounts Bay; every house in Newlyn seems to have this outlook, as if the town is designed as a theatre set.

'Of course it's in a dreadful state of repair. Four years ago the bath fell through the ceiling into the kitchen.' She mentions it conversationally, a mild inconvenience, like a castor coming off a sofa. There is something familiar about her, a purring, feline quality – something about those eyes. One isn't quite certain whether she is playing the scene straight or satirically. Do bathtubs really fall through kitchen ceilings in twentieth century Cornwall?

It is impossible to guess Mrs Grosvenor-Smith's age. She has taken trouble with herself: she is in blue jeans, a fetching jersey, she wears make-up and nail varnish. She smokes incessantly, she lives off biscuits, tea and cigarettes, she tells you in her droll, 'really-what-a-bore' voice. Then you know whom she reminds you of: Vivienne Leigh, of course.

She went to a girls' public school in Penzance, a gap then – of how many

years? – until the last war when she served as a WREN in Alexandria and Italy. After the war there was Rhodesia, where she met her husband, who turned out an alcoholic; there was a divorce, a spell in South Africa, then back to look after a 'dotty old aunt' in Penzance. She does not know whether her ex-husband is alive or dead. The aunt died at ninety-eight leaving the house but no funds to run it, to restore the decaying fabric.

'So I went on Social Security. I've always had appalling circulation, can't stand extremes of heat or cold – it exhausts me so that I can't walk or even stand. Friends collect my pension . . . if only I was well and strong.'

Adroit stage management has placed Mrs Grosvenor-Smith beneath a portrait of her as a young beauty. She parodies the pose the artist made her adopt, chin at the same tilt . . . surely she must have been told time and again of the resemblance. But perhaps not for a long time.

Tell her, tell her; for God's sake tell her before it is too late, before she closes the door.

'You know you're the image of Vivienne Leigh?'

Mrs Grosvenor-Smith's eyes open wide. She is about to say something, which is still-born in her throat. But she smiles – and you see that she is the girl in the picture.

The Village Schoolteacher

CHAPTER XI

THE VILLAGE SCHOOLTEACHER

Mary Bryant

They came to a pond. The children of Flagg came to a pond on a July morning, the scent of hay clinging to the breeze, new-mown, cloying. There should have been fifteen children, but there were only nine; six absentees were 'in the hay'. When your livelihood depends on it, making hay and silage take priority over books and learning and looking at ponds. Minutes are precious and many hands make light work, even when those hands are a bare five years old. Baling hay is child's play; quite literally when thunder murmurs.

The village pond at Flagg is not just any old pond; it is secret, remote as a dream, incarcerated in the region of dreams. When we were children we under-

stood as children; and when we became adult we put away such childish things as toys and teddy bears and ponds. We banished them, put them in exile, pursuing a new-found sophistication which led us to maturity, to first love and other sorrows.

Flagg has no centre as such, no war memorial or jubilee horse trough which define the heart of many villages. You climb out of Bakewell, resting, as it aptly should, in a deep pudding bowl, and continue climbing into the Derbyshire Peaks; in five miles you enter Flagg at Town Head – keep walking for a few moments and you let yourself out, by the exit known as Town End. There is Town Head Farm, Hobson Farm, The Plough pub, Ivy Farm, Ash Tree Farm, Town End Farm; there is the Post Office, Methodist Chapel, Unitarian Church, a scattering of cottages, a scattering of inhabitants, not much else. In 1891 there were 176 souls counted and you would arrive at much the same total today.

Tucked behind the Methodist Chapel, raised in the last century to the glory of God at a time when the lead mines were manufacturing wealth for Mammon, is Flagg Nursery School. Erected in 1833 from local limestone, it marks the start of the childrens' Great Trek; no journey at all when you are grown, but when you are only three, four or five it seems a very long way. Past the Hall, past Hobson Farm, up a track, through a gate, sliding steep down a meadow, clutching at buttercups and daisies; and there it is, the pond.

The children were hushed; they had never seen a pond before. They knew all about them; naturally, because for weeks they had been making a mural on a classroom wall: willow green with grasses collected by the handful, ocean deep, indigo and turquoise deep, crayon-coloured lurking depths where Mr Frog swims, pot-bellied, blown out with the majesty of self-importance. Cardboard cut-out fish dart by in suspended animation, getting nowhere energetically . . .

But this was different; this was real and a little frightening. You could fall into this pond and the water, duckweed, milfoil and all, would close in over your head, would drag you down into another world. Teacher had said to be careful, and teacher knows best. So Rachel sucked her thumb, and Shawne Marie twisted the hem of her summer frock, Andrew sniffed hard because his nose had started to run and he was too preoccupied to use his handkerchief; even Mark, Mark-the-Brave who has a go at anything, was subdued by this pond.

The surface was choked with weed, slimy green algae spread a canopy from bank to bank; an old tyre, bald as a monk's pate, floated on water the texture of consommé. An empty petrol can bobbed fussily, like a marker buoy in a regatta. The pond seemed dark and dreadful; in such water did not Childe Roland fear to set his foot upon a dead man's cheek? No wonder the water babies are apprehensive.

Then a small miracle happens. A dragonfly settles on Sarah's shoulder. 'Oh, look Sarah,' says teacher, 'a really beautiful dragonfly . . . ' And Sarah smiles a huge smile and hugs herself; the dragonfly takes off, a shimmer of silver green . . .

suddenly the pond comes alive, it stirs with microscopic life, it teems with under-water energy. A water boatman sculls by with fevered, busy strokes; pond skaters perform amazing feats, and whirligig beetles thrash round and round in giddying circles. There are frogs and minnows; water crickets move in slow motion on long legs, aquatic circus clowns on stilts.

The past, pervaded with subliminal fears, becomes an easeful present, becomes the now, this very second. It is seen in an instant by that watchful whirligig whose eyes are divided into two parts, one directed upwards, the other downwards, the better to take in events above as well as below the surface. More dragonflies skimming along, going into reverse at whim, actually flying *backwards* for short distances.

All this and more the children of Flagg witness. It is a genesis, a creation; you can see it in their eyes, hear it in their gasps, feel it in moist palms held in yours. They will remember – or will they? – this summer day when warm air was convector fanned across the High Peaks. When she is old and nearly done, her joints stiffened with rheumatics, her soft skin turned coarse, will Sarah remember when a dragonfly settled on her shoulder? Perhaps she will; it all depends on the years between. It depends whom she loves and whom she marries, and whether she will bring her own children to the pond, telling them about today so many yesterdays ago. She may forget by tomorrow.

But midnight came and went, folding the old day away and Sarah remembers, her brown eyes turn luminous when you ask, she squirms, hugging herself again, nodding the pretty head that one would like to shield from all ill grace. If only one could have a say in her future, so that one's own mistakes would show a profit. If one could ban from her vocabulary such words as 'status', and let her see that generosity of spirit means more than generosity of purse. Yet if these wishes could be granted, it would be her downfall, for Sarah must learn to be her own person, to distinguish – or not, whichever it will be – with her own eyes the worthwhile from the shoddy. She must learn in her own way that we are all alone.

'Good morning, Sarah . . . hello, Ian, what's that on your shirt? A big yellow duck . . . hello Shawne Marie.' Another day, mint new, yellow bright as Ian's duck; the thunder was a false alarm, but it is heavy still. Tractors grope about the fields, urgent, you cannot tell with the weather.

'You're seeing Flagg at its best,' says the village schoolteacher, Mrs Bryant. The wind was that cold last week, they were all in woollies, she says; Flagg is not infrequently cut off for six weeks at a time by snow. It is high in the Peaks; Flagg is a thousand feet above sea level, exposed to every vicissitude the elements care to serve. There is little protection, few trees or hedgerows shelter the village, taking the brunt of winter punishment. It is an orderly landscape, shared out in miniature parcels of two or three acres, each field enclosed by its dry-stone wall; from the school the countryside looks like a geometric jigsaw.

In other times there were three options if you lived in Flagg: the lead mines, quarrying for limestone, farming. The lead gave out – old Charlie Millington of nearby Monyash was the last of the miners; he kept his white beard trim and sucked at his clay pipe until the end, which came not long ago. So now it is one or the other, limestone or the land. Flagg keeps its own, they do not wander far; the land exerts its magnetic influence, holding families together . . . the Naylors, Needhams, Boams, Allens, Redferns, all still here, belonging, not apparently tempted much to move away.

'They're a dyed-in-the-wool people,' explains Mary Bryant. 'They're pulled more by the past than the present, the twentieth century still hasn't arrived in Flagg . . . I think modern youngsters might say to themselves, "I'd like to marry a girl from London", even Paris. But here a young man says, "I'd like to marry a girl from Flagg." Oh yes, they still say, "Teacher knows best", but the village knows better.

'I can understand this, it's second nature to me because I'm a farmer's daughter, born and raised in what I call the "panhandle" of Cheshire – you can probably pick it up in my accent. It was a 200-acre mixed farm, rough hill grazing, milking cows . . . we tried to be self-supporting and failed miserably. Father was in love with nature, you could say that, he literally *loved* animals – all our baby photographs were taken with animals on the farm. He was a simple man, honest and with faith in nature, he lived cheek by jowl with nature – he taught me all I know about flowers, trees, animals. He was looked up to by local farmers, he could calve cows, they called him in as often as they did the vet.'

Bothams Hall, where Mary was born in 1932, was farmed by grandfather Amos Booth. It was a Cheshire gritstone house, with exposed woodwork, built in 1620; here she was raised, with brothers Hamish and John . . . for Amos had by then handed down to his son, who had met a Derbyshire girl at the Mottram-in-Longdendale Agricultural Show and shortly married her.

'Mother was drawn to the country too, a quiet person, she didn't show her emotions like father, always reading, going off to the library at Hyde – I feel she would have gone far as a scholar. She was ladylike and shy, and they understood each other. She died when I was

fifteen and father married her young sister . . . I think mother had a hard life, like her own mother who was widowed early and forced into the cotton mills to provide for four daughters. Well, it's all gone now – when father died we owed money to the bank and had to sell.'

It sounds a bland statement, passive – which is at odds with the woman Mary Bryant has become. You would put her down as a fighter if the cause was just; there is a bit of the evangelist in her, a bit of the politician as she juts her jaw out, emphasizing a point. Childless herself, the children of Flagg are her charges; by proxy if you insist, but she would protect them, lead them to the Inn of the Sixth Happiness, beyond harm. She would have little time for diplomacy or hyperbole, or anything that could not be expressed in the least abstract terms. She is a teacher, and when class is out she plays tennis at the Buxton Tennis Club.

'Father had a milk round at Hyde, so we helped him deliver on the way to school there. Hyde was a cotton town then, so we were different, being country children. I adored school then, I adored it when I went on to Hyde Grammar, and nothing's changed. I loved the company, I was an outgoing child and as a family we were isolated, we didn't socialize – it was in the war and father wouldn't go in for black market petrol, so we were left to our own devices. In the holidays I longed to be back at school.

'There was no alternative to teaching. I've always loved children . . . oh dear, it sounds so simple, but I'm afraid it just worked out that way.'

From school Mary Bryant went to teachers' training college before taking up a probationary post at Buxton, in the Peak District. During her five years there she heard that a tiny village school needed a headteacher; so she applied and was accepted. The village was Flagg, the year 1957; here she has remained.

'No, I never had many boyfriends, one or two. I played hockey for Buxton Ladies and went home at weekends to be with father . . . I met my husband at a teachers' course on physical education – he's a teacher as well. We knew each other six years before marrying . . . Barry had an elderly mother, I had father, we were both concerned. Put like that it sounds terrible, but I suppose it was there.

'Barry bought a plot of land at Taddington and we built our house with its view towards the Sheffield Moors – it took us three years. Barry did most of the work, he's good with his hands. He's teaching at Chapel-en-le-Frith. I'm still mad about sports, Barry hates sport . . . he's a man of many parts, but watching *Match of the Day* isn't one of them.

'I was very surprised when no children arrived, disappointed . . . we could have gone into it more but Barry was dead against that, it's still something we feel we can't talk about. Barry said if it's not meant to be, it's not meant to be. He said we're in the business of children, that will have to satisfy us. There's no void in my life, I'm surrounded by children . . . oh dear, it's so personal talking like this. I'm fascinated by children, but I've no illusions about them – I hope I don't have a sugary attitude to them.'

148

The children of Flagg are, in truth, children from Monyash, Taddington, Chelmorton and Earl Sterndale as well, Peak villages all. They are between three and five years old, brought and collected each day by their parents. As headteacher Mrs Bryant has an aide in Elizabeth Barnett, a qualified nursery nurse. Internally, the school has been redesigned so that there is much light, an impression of space. In the garden there is grass to roll about on, a sand-pit, a slide; they are out-door children, you won't catch them in the schoolroom if there is a chance to be outside.

The pond mural has more significance today; and so, in a way, does Topsey, the lone goldfish in a bowl . . . and why has no one thought to provide her with a companion, a scaly mate to play Harlequin to her Columbine? Next to Topsey's bowl stands Rupert Bear, and there are games of Wee-Shapes, Fuzzy Felt Fairy Tales, and Fit-It! There are books called 'I Went to School One Morning', 'Andy Pandy's Kite', 'Walter Duck and Winifred'. Shawne Marie, with ferocious concentration, is glueing a Persil packet to a Birds Eye beefburger carton; she impales on to this unlikely union the cardboard centre of a lavatory roll – and what has she made? A battleship, she says scornfully. Why, of course.

Watched by Sarah, Mark-the-Brave is hanging upside down like a bat from an exercise bar. 'You don't have to do that,' Sarah says crossly, addressing knees where eyes should rightfully be. 'I'm bigger than you,' she adds superfluously,

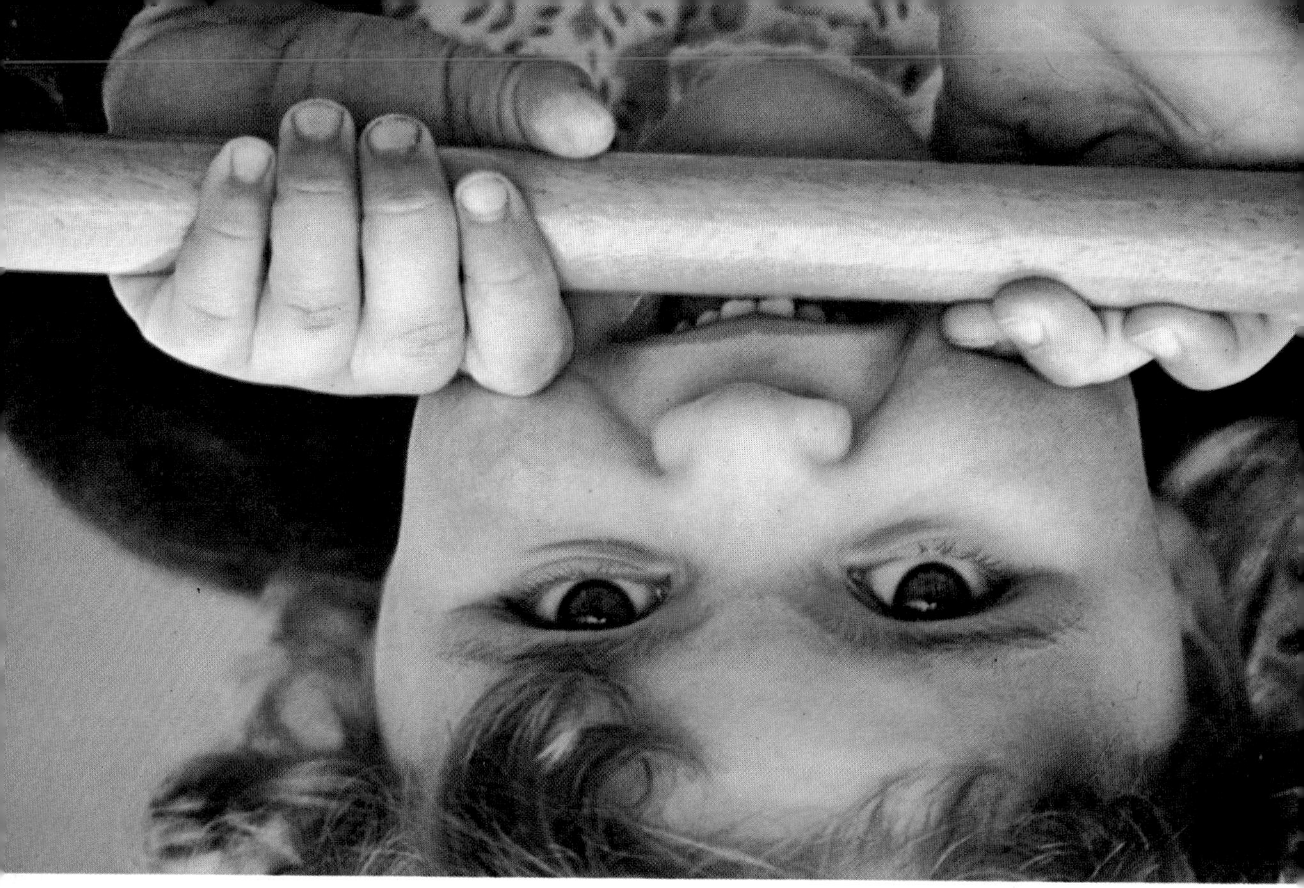

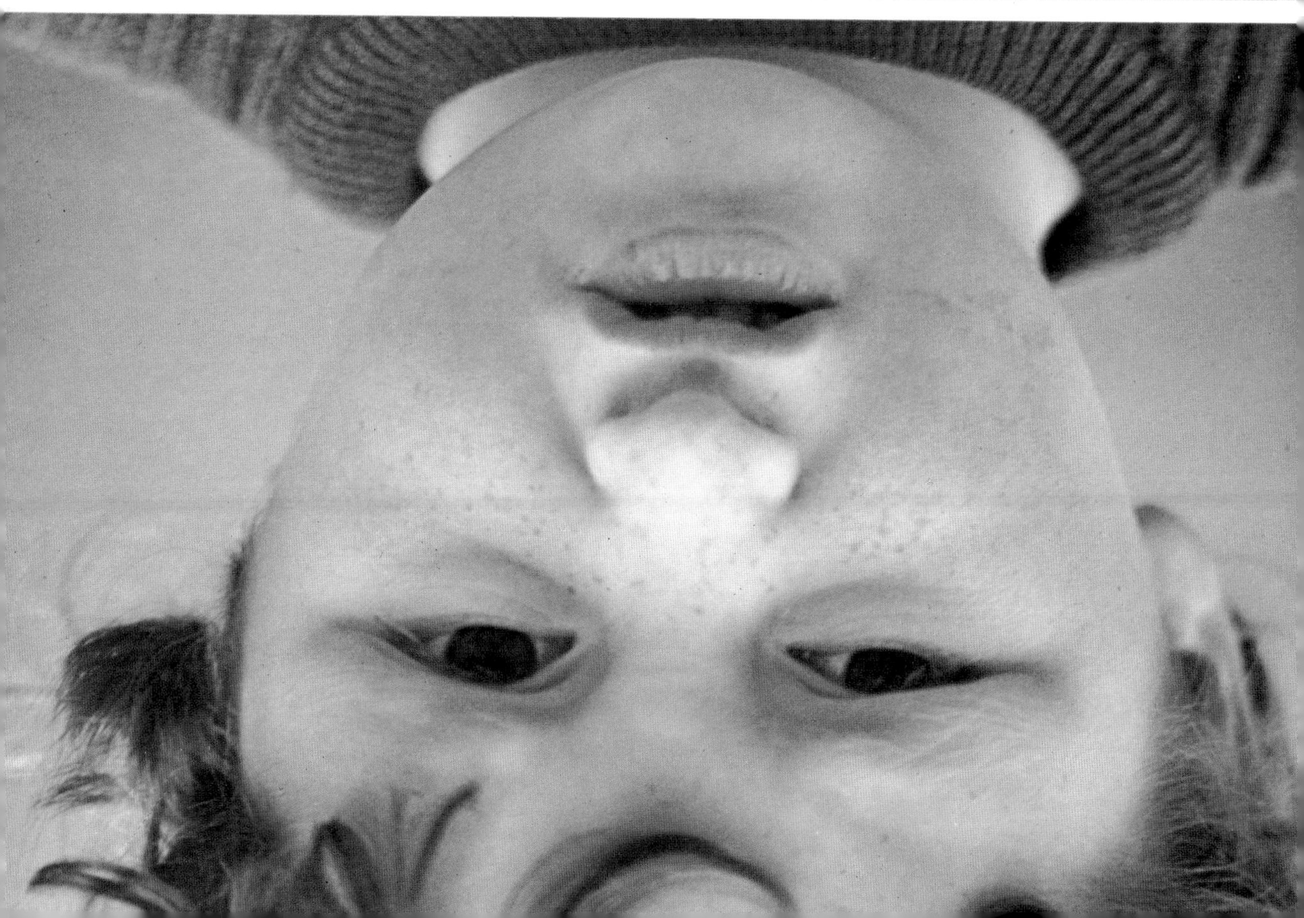

condescending. How more than pretty she is; how fair of face is Monday's child, for no other day would have done for Sarah, destined to break so many hearts in 1992. Andrew, intent upon some act of chivalry, touches Sarah's dark curls and sniffs, Sir Galahad with runny nose again.

'I'd like to marry a girl from Flagg': will Mark or Andrew ever say as much? Will the village contain them, can it offer enough? When you count the blessings they do not seem to add up to much: no riches certainly from these small fields; good air, it is true, except when wind hangs a gauze of limestone dust over the land; for peripatetic villagers there are a couple of buses a week to Bakewell. Sheffield and Manchester are only an hour by car, if you can buy the petrol; more often than not the garage is dry as an abandoned oasis, the pumps wearing slitted canvas hoods like Ku Klux Klan nightriders. It is as though there is a conspiracy to discourage an exodus; anyway, who would want to leave in July, the time of peonies, vulgar and passionate, later than in the south, all over in a day or two.

Sarah, Mark and Andrew are too young to leave; Maud Murray, on a kidney machine in New Building Cottage, cannot leave, and Vera Brough, school care-taker, would not leave for all the crown jewels.

Mrs Brough and Frank, her husband, live in the cottage next door to Vera's mother. Her father, now dead, worked at the quarry; she remembers him setting off in the dawn mist, four-and-a-half miles across fields, to pass each day breaking stones. 'We worried about him in the snows,' she says. 'It was so easy to lose your way, to fall into a mere or down a disused mine shaft. In bad weather he'd tie sacks about him, bind his legs with puttees to keep the wet out – it was a job drying them, but we never let the fire out. Then Friday night was bath night, an old tin bath in the kitchen – the whole village bathed on Friday, ready for the weekend. All the veg was prepared on Saturday for Sunday dinner – no one worked on the Sabbath. At midday Sunday you'd hear knives being sharpened on all doorsteps, ready for the joint.

'There was a lot of wisdom among the old people . . . father had no education but he knew exactly how to cure illness – he'd get rid of chesty colds by rubbing in goose grease. My husband still uses it for his slipped-disc, it's very searching, it'll go through stone.'

Vera Brough attended Flagg school herself fifty years ago: 'The teachers were real school dames, severe they were, put fear up us . . . I remember Mrs Smith, she had a thing about fresh air, she'd make us stand in the icy playground, "Breathe in, breathe out, mind the germs," she'd say. Boys were caned, girls too – I remember being stood in the corner all afternoon, I can't recall why. That wind, it chaffed our knees all winter, we'd try to warm up by chasing barrel hoops and whipping tops and playing "Old Roger is dead and lies in his grave". And we were always being warned not to go near holes because they might be mine shafts. But Flagg children were always tough, they got that on the farms, helping at an early age – the wind hardened them compared to town kids. I can't remember ever catching cold . . . it was bonny, fat children who ate sweets took sick – we had dripping toast for breakfast and tea, nuts and raisins for a treat.'

She is a very upright woman, quiet-spoken and controlled; all her life she has made little notes about the past, she shows you these notes, recipes and cures in a firm, sloping script. 'We were dad's life, us children,' she continues. 'After years and years he bought his first bicycle, £3 10s. it cost, and he thought it was heaven, he'd go riding and come back with icicles on his eyebrows. He'd stroll about the village in the evening, they all used to – the men would sit under the wall and chatter, "frumping" they called it. But in winter we were shut in, winter nights are long in the village – life was so quiet we'd celebrate anything, we were told they were like pagan rituals . . . like when mother made cow pie. She'd take a pint of beastings, the second milking after calving, add salt and sugar, pour it into a dish lined with shortcrust pastry, then grate nutmeg over the top and bake – it was delicious served very cold.

'There were five of us kids, several families had eight or ten – we made our own entertainment, father played the mouth-organ. We'd go looking at the pansy hillocks, all yellow and purple, and bird's foot trefoil – eggs and bacon, we called it. We used to lie on the hills and just sniff, and then come back to Sunday dinner all full of that scent. I think we were very happy . . . there was so much to see and enjoy if you looked for it. There were bad things, like we had to empty the toilet buckets and the newspaper – no toilet rolls in those days for us – we just pitched it into the field opposite. Mother, next door, still has a bucket toilet to this day – no bathroom either. And father and I used to go to the village pump to draw water.

'They were proud people – men like Elijah Middleton . . . Will Allen, a dry-stone waller, old men when I was young. Debt was a dreadful thing, it brought shame, they never owed money. They're straight people here, and careful – we don't throw it about. Mother asked father what she could have so that she could plan her week to the penny.

'I like to think I belong to Flagg, I'm very lucky. I've always hoped that the outside world wouldn't creep in . . . father would hate supermarkets and all that rushing about. We know people have got to live and we've got to make room for them, but it seems all wrong someone buying up three cottages and turning them into one big place . . . I've always wanted to see more trees, not houses.'

Vera Brough's memory is acute: 'Do you remember baking bricks in the oven, mother, and putting them in our beds in the cold? And how we had Sunday School out in the fields, where it should be . . . and how I wondered why there was only one grave in the churchyard?' Her mother is on the sofa in Vera's sitting room; it is polished bright as a moonbeam this room, knick-knacks galore – she treasures her knick-knacks, says Vera. The village street runs by outside, and across the way there is a view you would motor a hundred miles to see. Vera's mother does not say much, she is not at ease with strangers; few visitors penetrate the very special

153

apartheid practised in Flagg. Her hands rest in her lap and she will have her say eventually, when the kettle is on and they are on their own.

One of the games Vera played as a child was 'Ring-a-Ring o' Roses'; legend has it that it came into being at Eyam, the Peakland village not far away, in the autumn of 1665, when migratory birds were preparing to leave their woodland haunts, and death was stalking many provinces of the kingdom. Death came to Eyam concealed in a bolt of cloth sent from London to a tailor, George Vicars, lodging with the widow of a lead miner, Mrs Cooper. Upon opening his consignment the tailor found the material to be damp, placed it by the fire to dry, thus increasing the potency of the Black Death virus. Within days the tailor was dead; within months five-sixths of Eyam's parishioners were in their makeshift graves.

One man defied the Plague: the Rector, the Reverend William Mompesson, who with his wife Catherine did his best to comfort the sick and dying. Such was their faith, or such their bodily resistance, that they both survived until the following August, at which stage the tale relates that they were walking in the Rectory garden when Catherine plucked a rose, commenting, 'Oh! Mompesson, the air – how sweet it smells!' With which the good pastor knew his wife would soon be dead.

A sweet smell was the first sign, followed by a rosy rash; posies of herbs were carried for protection, sneezing was the first symptom, and 'all fall down' was exactly what happened.

> *Ring-a-ring o' roses,*
> *A pocket full of posies,*
> *A-tishoo! A-tishoo!*
> *We all fall down.*

What was that about there being only one grave in the churchyard? Now why should that be: another tale perhaps? Only one way to find out. A few paces from Vera Brough's cottage, and there is the church she attended 'freely' as a girl: no delight to look at, this sombre, sinister building squatting in its allotment of overgrown grass and weed. The door is bolted against intrusion, so although you may kneel to pray on Sunday, for the remaining six days you must apparently take your business elsewhere. Vera's memory serves her right again – there is a single headstone in the entire churchyard, no inscription on the tablet, not even 'Here rests one soul sent to Coventry'.

There is a tablet telling that the church, box-like construction that it is, was built in 1838; there is a board, neglected and peeling, mentioning that the Vicar, the Reverend Thomas Robertson, is to be found at Taddington Vicarage. Nothing else; just the solitary headstone, lank grass, weeds and a gripping sense of desolation. We know where the young men have gone; they are in the fields, every one.

But where have all the old men gone, who should be recumbent, their feet towards the east, waiting for the resurrection?

The Vicar would know, no doubt; but his explanation might be mundane, too reasonable and true to death. Whereas Vera's secret, Flagg's secret of the empty graveyard, may contain the mystery of the Universe. Perhaps village elders, who cannot escape Flagg in life, are unable to find release in death; perhaps they still drift from Town Head to Town End, spectral bubbles refusing to fade away. Maybe they live to such great age that they wither, like leaves pressed between pages of a book, drying, shredding, turning to dust until, at a change of wind, they finally dissolve into nothingness.

Sarah, Mark and Andrew will have no views on this, for they have far to go; how many foot-loose journeys from the morning horizon of Town Head, to the dusk horizon of Town End? What will become of them?

Perhaps they will go to Malawi or New Zealand or Muswell Hill; perhaps Mark will become Prime Minister or a prisoner of conscience, leaving Andrew far behind to marry a girl from Flagg. And should that girl be Sarah, upon whose shoulder a dragonfly once settled, and should they never stir beyond the limits of their village or the limits of their love, they will not have lived in vain.

The Thatcher

CHAPTER XII

THE THATCHER

Hugh Dunmore Walker

In a way Village England is a glorious cosmic accident whose precise origins defy explanation. Historians of a future age will have a sickeningly easy time: it will be there, on micro-film very likely, and all they will be required to do is press the right button to find out who invented the pop-up toaster or laid the foundations of Milton Keynes. Scholarship will be as obsolete as the vermiform appendix.

To discover the first usage of the inclined plane or the wheel, to unearth the first bricks that built the village of Exton in Rutland – this takes more academic muscle . . .

Exton. Well, there is an *ox* thereabouts; and in *ton* there is a *tun*, or settlement. So we can identify the *Exentune*, given to the Countess Judith, who married Waltheof, Earl of Northumberland, at the Norman Conquest. Their daughter Maud married David, the Scottish prince, later King. From him Exton passed to the Bruces, from whom it was seized in the wars between England and Scotland, and granted to one Green, who passed it to the Culpepers and from them to the Harringtons who held it for six centuries, selling to Sir Baptist Hicks, Kt. It then went to his son, created Viscount Campden in 1628.

Now we are getting warm. Dying without issue, his estate and titles passed to Edward Noel, first Baron Noel of Ridlington, whose grandson was created Earl of Gainsborough in 1682. The title became extinct in 1798 until it was reinstated in the name of Charles Noel Noel, created Earl of Gainsborough and Viscount Campden in 1841; whether Noel was duplicated by reason of vanity or speech impediment is not clear. Today Anthony, fifth Earl of Gainsborough, lives at Exton Hall; he will be succeeded by his son, Lord Campden, so the *status quo* is secure for a while yet. Which is immensely reassuring, but contributes little to answering the fearful question to whom Exton belonged *before it was given to Judith*. It happened all over the place; so now is it clear that the entire complex of Village England is nothing more than haphazard cosmic chance?

There are those – and May Wigginton may be among their number – who could wish history had been a fraction less baroque. May helps to clean the church of SS Peter and Paul, and a taxing job it is with such proliferation of effigies cluttering up the place. Not that 'cluttering' would be a word to meet with

Pevsner's approval: 'There is no church in Rutland and few in England in which English sculpture from the sixteenth to the eighteenth century can be studied so profitably and enjoyed so much as at Exton.' Mr Pevsner might have ingratiated himself further upon May Wigginton had he added the rider . . . unless it is incumbent upon you to keep them dusted.'

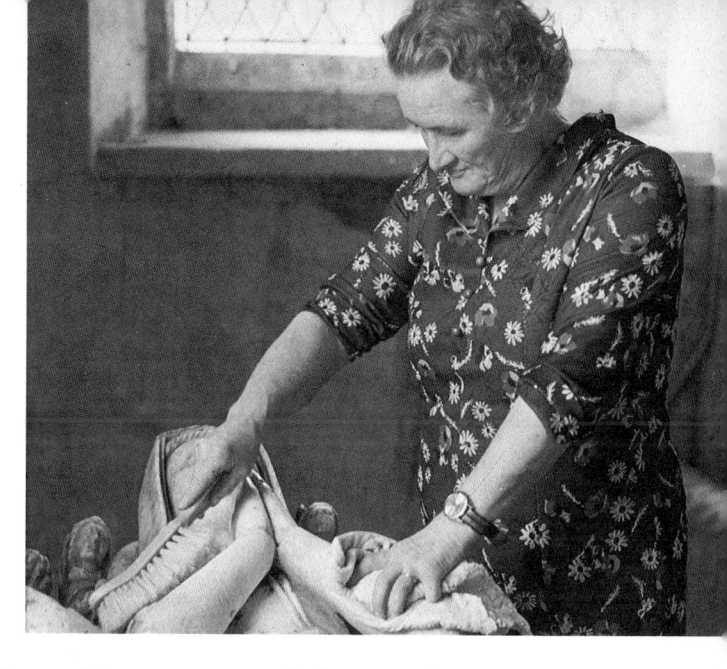

Mrs Wigginton is presently engaged in administering a bed-bath to John Harrington, Esq. and his wife, Alice, who sought refuge on a higher plane at some time during the mid-sixteenth century. They lie, side by side, on an antique table monument, their eyes raised devoutly heavenwards. John is accoutred in armour, sword at rest, gauntlets at his right side; Alice wears a gown the hem of which is tugged between the teeth of two pet dogs, willing their sleeping mistress to take them for a walk, to throw a stick for retrieval among thickets abounding the Elysian fields. About her throat is a delicate necklace from which is suspended a crucifix; and there are rings of betrothal upon her fingers, worn above the knuckle as was the custom. A handsome couple if ever there was, intact apart from a little nasal trouble which cosmetic surgery could fix in a jiffy; they were spared Cromwell's despoilers. There are still traces of colour on Alice's gown, surviving the centuries and the warm soapy water from Mrs Wigginton's bucket.

In the south aisle, dressed in his official robes of lawyer, rests Robert Keylwey, Esq., father of Ann, Lady Harrington; John, Lord Harrington, kneels beside his father-in-law. There are monuments to Sir Jas. Harrington, Kt., and his lady, Lucy; to Baptist Noel, fourth Earl of Gainsborough; to Lieutenant General Noel who died in 1766 and is especially favoured in having an anonymous but stunningly pretty girl weeping in effigy over an urn on which is the bust of the departed General.

In 1846 lightning struck the church tower which crashed on to the body of the church causing such damage that complete rebuilding was necessary, including a light taper tower. The interior is chastely Gothic, and the spandrels of the arches support banners of the Harringtons and Noels, accompanied by their bards, pennons and helmets, waiting it would seem for the next call to arms.

But the *pièce de résistance* undoubtedly is the wordly, florid edifice constructed by Grinling Gibbons to the memory of Baptist Noel, Viscount Campden, who died in 1683. It is a splendid confection of cherubs, medallions, cornucopia, with figures in diaphanous Grecian costume sporting themselves along friezes in the way of a strip cartoon. It is all there, an idealized version of the Archers, a story of simple country folk, headed by a cast of the Viscount, his four wives and their nineteen children. It could entertain one for hours.

'A trifle ostentatious, don't you think?' sniffs Mrs Alison Stewart, leading the way to the graveyard. Mrs Stewart lives at Tudor Cottage and her late husband was Bishop of Jerusalem before coming to Exton. 'But not quite so bad as the Victorians . . . I must show you a headstone.' And there it is. Mrs Stewart stoops to read aloud the inscription: 'Sacred to the memory of Thomas, George and Albert, sons of John and Lucretia Fancourt of Exton Rutland, the first of these Thomas died in infancy on March 20th 1840, the two others George and Albert were cut off by fever aged respectively six and eight years in the month of September of the same year 1840 after giving cheering evidence of their faith in Jesus and their being born again of the spirit.'

'Cheering evidence of their faith in Jesus, at the age of six,' snorts Mrs Stewart. 'Those Victorians!'

Fancourts are legion in this place of rest; and how the Christian name Jasper pleased this pious tribe. The Hibberts are pretty thick on the ground as well, in a manner of speaking. So too the Messings, one of whom, John, 'Departed this Life ye 3rd day of June 1792 Aged 70 years after ferving the prefent Earl and his Father 54 years.'

Behind the church lie the ruins of Exton Hall, built in the Elizabethan style and destroyed by fire in 1810. Nearby is the present Hall, not a great house by any means, but not an eyesore either, set amid verdant parkland. Not far from the house is a swimming pool. There is something slightly shocking about a stately home with a kidney-shaped swimming pool. An orangery is one thing, a croquet lawn even – but kidney-shaped swimming pools are rather frivolous surely?

Exton Hall lies in a hollow. If you could walk, in more or less a straight line, from SS Peter and Paul graveyard, cutting through the gardens of the Hall, emerging into Pudding Bag End, you would be a couple of minutes' walk from the Roman Catholic cemetery, where you will find Dan Colin, retired gamekeeper, tending the pasture of the dead as if they were his very own. A few indeed are his own, of his flesh and of his blood: here lies his son, Eammon, who never made it beyond his fourteenth birthday; here too lies Sarah Colin, the girl Dan took for his lawful wedded wife until she slipped away in 1953. She was a 'dark redhead', Sarah Malarkey was her name, and she came from Londonderry. Dan's grandfather and grandmother are close at hand; the family have not wandered far.

There are six Colins beneath this well-mown, springy turf, and six Sanders, six O'Hallorans; there is Romolo Ricci from Saint Omero, Italy, prisoner of war who stayed on. There is Dom Samuel Gregory Ould, OSB., Monk of Augustus, whose name you will find in the hymn books. There is Alexander McIntosh, landlord of the Fox and Hounds; and there is Janet, daughter of the present Lord Gainsborough, who drew too little breath to carry her through even a single day.

It is late July and there are twin inconveniences of drought and a plague of green-fly. The former is not serious, the wheat is standing well, the harvest will be early; as for the green-fly, well, they're a damned nuisance, the air is thick, you could slice them with a knife and spread them on buttered toast. Dan Colin is in shirt sleeves and a Panama; he is trimming a hedge, sweaty work on a breathless day. His grandfather was a Daniel and his grandson, rat-catcher on the estate, is another Daniel. His family has been in Exton, marrying into the Tyler family, since the Wars of the Roses; they converted to Roman Catholicism in 1870 – at a time when it was expedient so to do.

He pushes the Panama brim up: 'That lady there,' he points to a headstone marked 'Margaret Gruer', 'she came over from Ireland to work at the Hall. She married a village lad – he had to convert . . . there's a row of Gruers.' A few yards on: 'Now that gentleman there, that's old Charlie Williams, coachman up at the Hall, died in 1913 he did, I can't remember him.'

A couple of weeks ago hooligans broke into the cemetery, tearing up headstones, smashing three or four crucifix. The culprits were caught, two boys of eight years old. Dan cannot understand what is going wrong.

'You asked me last night if there's any animosity between Anglican and Catholic here, and I said no. I've been thinking . . . the Catholics were better looked after, it made for bitterness and maybe it got handed down . . . it's a thousand pities it ever happened.'

At Tudor Cottage Mrs Stewart remembers her gardener, Albert Tyler, who died in 1973, once telling her that his father was 'obliged' to embrace the Catholic faith if he wanted to keep his job as woodman on the estate. 'It was quite feudal until recently,' she says. 'You worked for the Gainsboroughs and that was it – nowadays there are the council houses, factory buses taking workers off to Leicester, Peterborough, Stamford – and the Gainsboroughs are benevolent today, although one rarely sees them in the village.

'Do you mean to say you haven't noticed the difference in people here? I'm

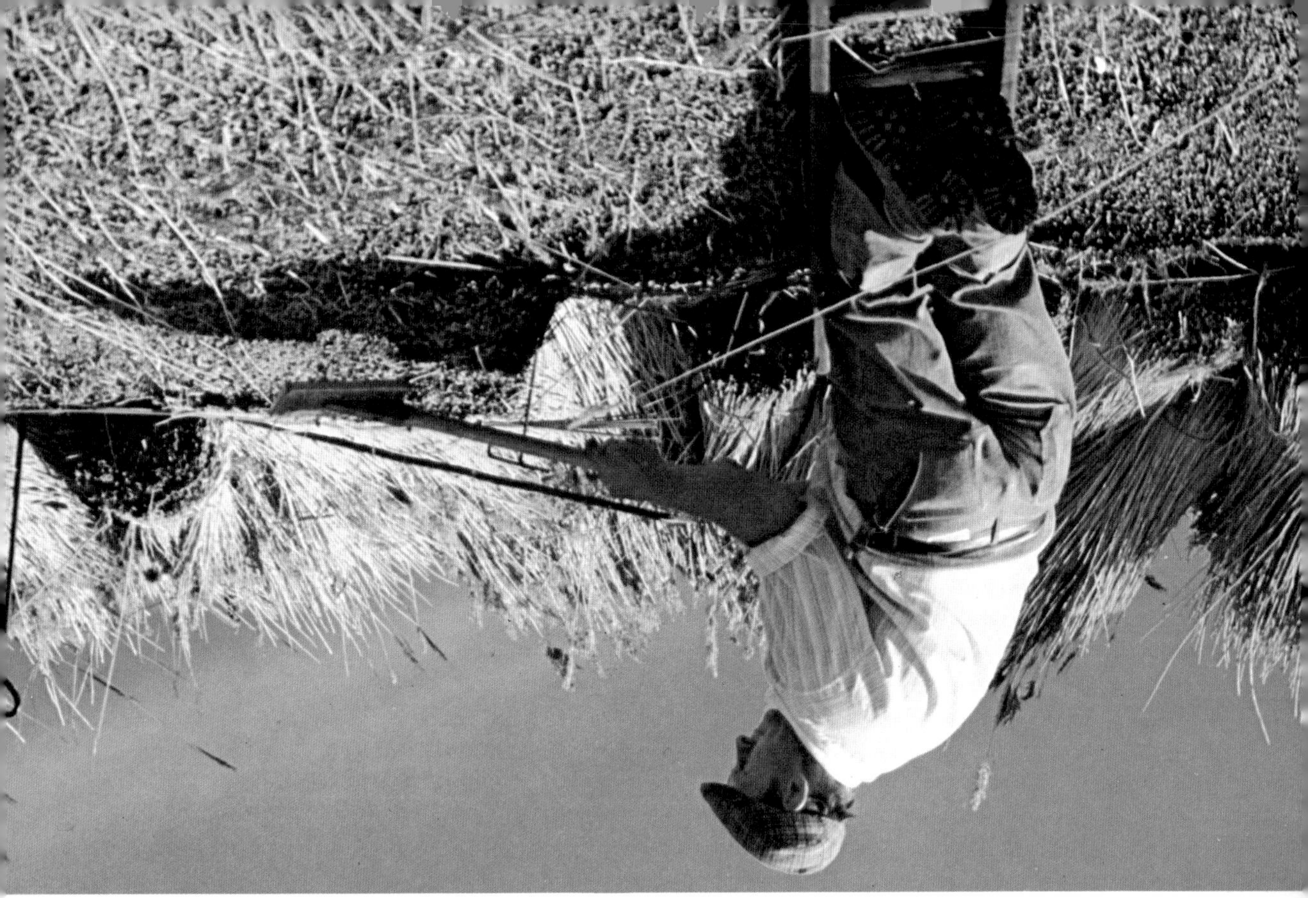

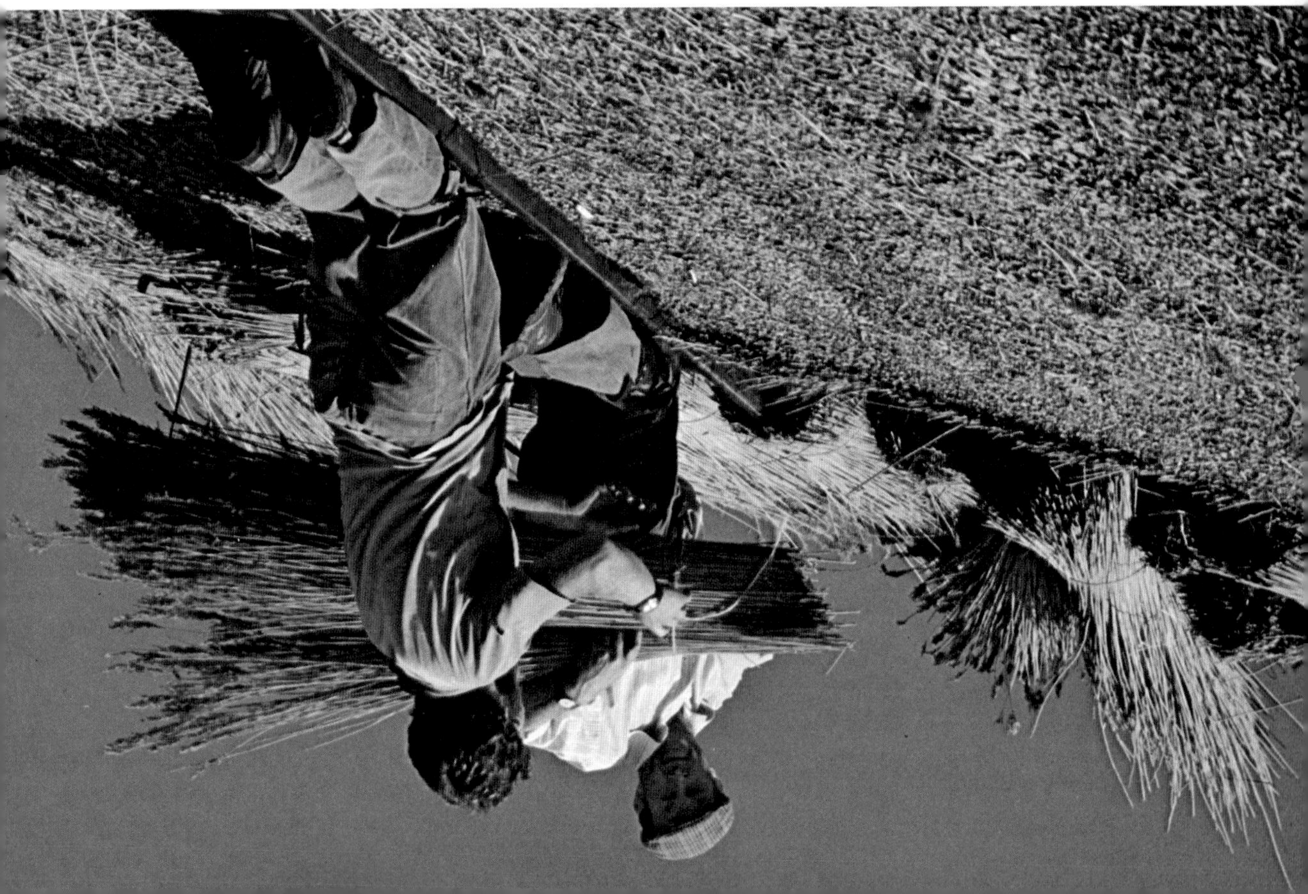

astonished, it seems so obvious to me, they're from different worlds . . . there's what I call the fair, square Anglo Saxons, and the others . . . they're dark, vivacious and Celtic, they've got noticeable eyes put in with a sooty finger. You can see it all over the village . . . the Bells, and as for the Maidens, they all look like colleens.'

'A thousand pities it ever happened,' Dan Colin has declared. 'They're from different worlds,' says the Bishop of Jerusalem's widow. But no one has made a statement; no one has come out with it. And what is the 'it' that generates such evasion, such furtive response to probe? No one actually puts 'Mind your own business' into words; 'Leave us alone' has not been uttered, for Exton is a friendly enough place. They do not stone strangers.

Yet there is a secret, a skeleton in the communal cupboard. There is a reticence, a look that comes from a long way behind the eyes. You will gather such looks in the Caribbean Islands, where the only culture is a slave culture. The West Indian negro's birthright was not as our own; his ancestors were stripped of dignity, and this brands him. His wounds went deep, and whilst perhaps his people have forgiven, they have never quite forgotten the sins of our fathers.

A fanciful equation? Perhaps so – except for certain tenuous evidence which should by right be in custody of the Anglican church, but which is in fact in Mrs Stewart's safe-keeping.

Years ago loose papers were unearthed in a chest belonging to the long deceased schoolmaster of Exton, Herbert Robert Wilton Hall. From 1857-77 Mr Hall kept a meticulous chronicle of parochial goings-on; some of his comments are mildly scandalous, gossipy in vein, others are more searching. His writings were bound, and they open a revealing window on the times.

One such entry reads: 'In 1866 Charles George Noel Noel succeeded his father as eighth Earl of Gainsborough. He had turned his back upon the narrow Protestantism of his immediate forbears, and had become a Papist. Thus the coordination of religious, moral and social forces in Exton which had so long ruled came to an end and thence forward there was a divided village.'

Which lets the cat out of the bag. Although details of the Earl's conversion remain obscure, the most prevalent theory is that he experienced Vatican influence whilst honeymooning in Rome. The only certainty being that he and his Countess engaged in a period of fanaticism which, in 1867, built and consecrated a Roman Catholic chapel at the Hall, imported labour in the form of grooms and parlour maids from Ireland, revived the seigneurial iniquity of imposing religious convictions upon their estate by threats of duress.

Thus, Woodman Tyler, Protestant by persuasion, became Woodman Tyler, RC – or else. Thus village intermarriage guaranteed a progeniture of robust Catholic babies whose eyes had been put in with a sooty finger. It is possible that Woodman

Tyler, with more pressing business on his mind – such as dread of the workhouse – would have merrily turned to Mohammed, Confucius even, if that was his lordship's wish.

And it would be naive to imagine such coercion to be unique: it was the basis of the parliamentary 'Pocket Borough' system. It was only notably more insidious in this case because it reeked of the Star Chamber, the Earl as self-appointed Grand Inquisitor manipulating the minds of the mindless and the helpless. The shame, if shame there was, rested at the gates of the Hall, not on the village green. Historically, the haves triumphed over the have-nots.

A hundred years on and it seems to have settled down well enough. The village green has witnessed no sectarian murders; Exton has not degenerated into an Ulster in miniature. Blinded by faith, Charles George Noel Noel committed an act of tyranny which marks him as a bigot, a man of small stature and misguided vision. Exton lives on, relatively unscathed; whether your name is Fancourt or Bell, Hibbert or Maiden, the follies of an earlier generation will not disturb your sleep beneath eaves of warm thatch.

It is a village of thatch and iron-stone, so there is a golden hue wherever you look. Cottage and grander house blend well together, they are of style, in harmony; and where the occasional bungalow has gate-crashed this gathering, it stands out as an intruder. It is not a relentlessly pretty village, it is too workaday for that; so charabancs do not turn off the Great North Road in search of Exton, and visitors from Nagasaki do not smile and bow at anything that moves, or steal away the colleens' souls on Kodacolor.

Summer is full-blown; the air is torpid, the tortoise undisputed Victor Ludorum. Hollyhocks, delphiniums, sweet-peas, roses and rhubarb and runner beans – all at once and all too much. In the fields the grain is turning, winter wheat is nearly ready for combining . . . more straw then for the thatcher's craft.

And Hugh Dunmore Walker, rolling his own Old Holborn cigarettes tooth-pick thin, hunched by the lifeless summer grate, does not want to know, does not care one single jot. Summer or winter, it is much the same: he has thatched his last roof, put away his hand-fashioned tools, the 'stingers', 'eave knives', 'Rutland bill'. He will never climb another ladder; the years of thatching, of leaning, lifting, twisting have bent him into a human comma.

Hugh lives in Pudding Bag End – except that, by squeamish touch of euphemism, the street was re-named West End to take away the nasty taste. 'Pudding Bag End' was the scraps, implying poverty, the slummy side of life. Then the newcomers, who did up the cottages on the other side of the street, applied to have the old name restored because it sounds – well, sort of rustic, picturesque.

Anyway, Pudding Bag or West End, this is where Hugh lives, on the *uncon*-verted side of the street, two up, two down, thatch trim as a Trumper's haircut. In the sitting room Hugh's chair faces the fireplace, his walking stick beside him; his arthritis is so bad that he relies on the stick for his brief forays about the house. His

165

bed has been brought downstairs, it is against the sitting room wall, discreetly draped in episcopalian purple. It is not a particularly welcoming room; neither does it repel – it is neutral, a place to put your feet up, a bolt-hole. There are no flowers, no feminine touches.

Hugh Walker does not take treatment for his arthritis, he suffers it in the way of a leper, drawing back from offers of help. 'It wouldn't be right somehow', he says, 'if I was cured, with Anne in the state she's in.' Anne is his wife, a chronic arthritic for fourteen years, a wheelchair case for the past ten. She has two artificial hips and has lived in ten different hospitals – Buxton, Mount Vernon, Harefield . . . at present she is in Peterborough Hospital; Hugh visits her as often as he can, the Rotary Club from Oakham drive him over once a week.

'She's in a lot of pain,' he says. 'She's alert, always grappling for news of the village . . . she'll come home. She'll come home again, I know that. I know it in my heart.'

Meanwhile, it is a silent house and Hugh a silent man. He was born in 1915, but looks older: older but handsome, his complexion the ruddy colour of an old penny, his white hair leonine. Bushy eyebrows take an upward sweep, interrogatory, giving him a Mephistophelian look. His fingers are long, tapering; he flicks ash from his cigarettes on to the tiled grate so that it seems like a hibernating ground for dormant grey insects. He is like a man in a station waiting room, rolling cigarettes until the arrival of a train that never comes.

Hugh's childhood was spent at Preston, just a few miles away. His father, Herbert, was master thatcher, as was grandpa Tom Walker and great-uncle, Charles William. Herbert married Sarah Anne, who came from a family of gardeners at Barnack in Lincolnshire; her father developed the Barnack Beauty apple. 'They weren't young when they married, getting on for thirty. I was the only child and not spoilt – although I was never struck in my life. They were outspoken people, didn't take any old buck from anyone . . . I found out right from wrong by their example.

'I'll never forget two so-called village ladies asking mother what right we had putting up socialist posters in the window – no one did that in our village, they said. Well, mother chaired a meeting soon after at the old school, and next day there were socialist posters all over the village.

'Some toffs used to call father – and then me – by surname. That made my blood boil. I was thatching once and a big farmer said, "Morning, Walker." I looked down at him and replied, "Morning, Oakley." He never called me "Walker" again. Some people are like that . . . now Lord Gainsborough here, "Lordy" we called him, talks to us like equals, knows us by Christian name.

'I've always been socialist and always will, nothing would change that, no argument in the world – it's fair shares for all . . . but they say a prophet has no honour in his own country – I'd be better off preaching that twenty miles from home.

166

'Cricket was what we lived for in our village, it was the highlight of the week – no, not on Sunday, no one did anything on Sunday except dress up and go for a walk to look at the allotments. Mother always wore a big picture hat – I liked her in that – and father put on his blue suit. There was Sunday dinner, of course, we had sirloin and Yorkshire pudding – everyone took the dinner out to Jack Scott at the bakehouse to be cooked for a penny, then we'd rush it home under a steaming cloth. Rich living that was – we'd save money making cake, bread, wine – rhubarb, parsnip, mangel wine . . . I fell off the roof at fifteen, drunk on parsnip wine.'

Unpractised at talking so much, he loses thread. He rolls another cigarette, lights it with one of his lighters: he keeps one in his left pocket, another in his right. 'Where was I? Cricket, that's it . . . we fielded a strong team, the wheelwright, wagon-builder, shoe-maker, butcher, baker, thatcher – yes, father was a fine bat. No toffs – the squire played in most villages, ours didn't seem interested. There were big families too – the Naylors could field a side against the Tylers.

'No one had special kit, they'd play in grey trousers, black boots and white shirts – cash was raised by jumble sales and whist drives for bats, pads, stumps and suchlike. They'd travel to away matches by horse and wagon – there'd be a bit of needle, but friendly. Matches started at 2.30 pm, we'd draw stumps at 7 o'clock. The Ladies' Committee had tea ready on trestles on the green or in the black-smith's shop – a rattling good tea for sixpence . . . salad, sandwiches, homemade cake, cups of tea. After the match we'd go to the pub for beer at fourpence a pint, Woodbines at five for twopence – oh yes, I was with them by that time, I'd got into the Ist XI when I was fourteen.

'Father liked his drink. Saturday midday he'd have a session, get a bit slewed – Mother ignored him until he sobered up. He was never unpleasant, he'd just sleep it off.'

It was the village school for Hugh until he was ten, then the town school in Uppingham, best part of a six-mile walk each way: 'I'm not being big-headed but in ten terms there I was top of the class ten times. The headmaster got me the offer of a job at the Midland Bank, then the butler to Major Furlong – who owned the twice-winner of the Grand National – said he could get me a position as footman . . . I said no to both. Couldn't have done jobs like that because I never wanted to take orders or bow and scrape. So I left school at fifteen and joined father as a thatcher.'

Among his skills, the thatcher includes a working knowledge of joinery and masonry. He carves his own hazel rods, and forges his own spikes on an anvil – so he is something of a farrier too. The rods secure each bundle of thatch, the spikes are driven into rafters. When a load of straw is delivered it is shaken into smaller heaps, cross straws are raked out as the straw is tidied and moistened for the yealming process. A 'yealm' is a tight, compact layer of straw, approximately eighteen inches wide and five inches thick, having both ends level. Straw is wetted

167

to make it flexible, less stubborn, and to enable it to be compressed when applied to the roof.

'You'd take one "bottle" at a time up to the roof – a "bottle", that's ten "yealms" – lay it, peg it . . . pegs went into a roof like hairpins. How long's a roof last? – one of father's was done in 1929 and it's got to be coated this year. Average is twenty-five to thirty years, I'd say. It's good insulation, a thatched roof, cool in summer, warm in winter. Disadvantages? Fleas, of course, you'd have to chuck a bucket of water on the bits you worked on to drown the fleas. Wasps' nests too. I've been stung everywhere, mouth and all.

'The war came and I stayed behind – reserved occupation they said it was – people thought, "he's a thatcher, he's different, thatchers don't go to war" . . . and I'd met Anne. I was rather keen on her sister, Poppy . . . we had a date in Oakham to go for a walk and I don't know to this day whether it was a put-up job, but Anne was there instead – said her bike tyres were flat. I had my bicycle pump so I pumped them up and we pedalled back to Wing where she was cook to a country toff, Mr Niell. We arranged that I'd call for her next day off and when I picked her up in the kitchen I had to hide behind the door because Mrs Niell came in to give her menu orders . . . oh, it was frowned upon to visit your young lady at her place of work.

'She moved then, to Major Adkins at Manton, next village to Wing, and I used to go courting her four or five times a week. He was all right, the major, he'd even send me down a drink – and when he opened a new box of cigars he'd send the first layer down to the kitchen . . . "They're rather dry, perhaps you'd like them", he'd say. Well, I didn't know whether they were dry or not.

'We courted for three years and married in 1940. I was twenty-five, Anne nineteen . . . her father didn't think much of a thatcher, he'd been wounded at the Somme. Perhaps I was too like dad and mother, too outspoken – we're meant to be the most cussed of all craftsmen, we'd tell anyone to go to hell, we always had that much work in hand. But we married at Oakham church and had the last wedding cake before the shop stopped making them in the war . . . went to live with mother and father then, and Anne went on munitions work at Luffenham factory.

'Father died on Christmas morning 1944 of cancer of the stomach. He was sixty-three and quite pleased to go, I think – he just quietly went to sleep and we went out to a party that night. Dad knew about the party and said he wanted us to go, so we went. It was difficult getting flowers at Christmas . . . mother took it bravely, she didn't say anything, just carried on as usual until she died herself six years later. I had to carry on too, with the business . . . friends said to me: "Think you'll manage? You'll be playing cricket instead of thatching", but I kept it all going, if I was playing cricket that afternoon I'd be on the roof at four in the morning, I'd get my hours in – then I'd play . . . anything – cricket, badminton, football. I was always a competitor, a pot-hunter, I'd win if I could.'

He looks defiant, daring you to question his competitive spirit, his ability to

win. He glares, his blue eyes hot; he says that people are put off by his glaring. His gamesmanship is something of an obsession, a statement of his virility, his manhood. He has played cricket, badminton, football, all manner of games, except the war-game.

'No, we never really wanted children. Anne had never done much sport . . . I'd got into fishing by then, coarse fishing, and she came with me, the only woman among 400 men. We kept pigs, poultry, there were flower shows . . . we never discussed children. We discussed anything and everything, but not children.' He turns the key in the padlock of this particular conversation: it is at an end.

'After Preston, we bought our own house at Ridlington, twelve miles from here – but Anne was getting worse and Lord Gainsborough offered me a job doing the estate thatching at Exton. I said I'd come if I could fish his three lakes – bream, roach, tench, pike, eel, using maggot or worm . . . so we moved to this cottage in 1969. Lordy thought I should have an apprentice, so young Michael Franklin came in and I was made redundant eventually . . . it suits me very well. I still fish as much as I can – and there's television, if only there'd been television when I was young. I'd have learned so much more about sport from watching professionals.'

You have to coax Hugh from the house; he is not anxious to leave the sterile room, the still fireplace. He eases himself into the car; he has never had a car himself, only motor bikes, cars are 'boxes on wheels, you can't get at the air'. He turns his glare on to the newcomers' cottages across the way and tells you that there are twelve motors to the cluster of five or six cottages. Driving through the village, he stares directly ahead, showing no interest; again you must coax him to acknowledge the buildings bearing his mark as thatcher. In the bar of the Fox and Hounds he drinks whisky and peppermint, and talks of sport, of fishing, of Rutland Water: 'I was never against the flooding, it's beautiful, although I've never fished with the fly. Fly fishing's for toffs, £120 a season to be a member . . . maybe I don't understand it.'

Persuading him to talk about his craft is like getting a child to swallow castor oil. When his father was thatching, a cottage might take four or five weeks, all long straw thatching, wheat straw; it was a thin straw, farmers being only too pleased to sell. He would make £18 to £20 for those weeks. When Hugh started, the fee had gone up to £40 or £50; today it has risen to £6,000 or so. How many houses has he thatched? 'I don't know – hundreds it must be, from Rugby to Skegness . . . there was one place, at Medbourne, where I replaced blue slates and zinc with 1,400 square feet of thatch. Took eight months – then I fell off the roof and broke my arm.' For a moment there is a spark; connected perhaps with the sport of falling off roofs, and arm-breaking.

'This pub,' he says, 'you used to know where you were sitting, you had your own bench. They said they did food, so you asked for bread and cheese and pickle – no, they said, they didn't have that and gave you a bag of crisps and nuts if you were lucky. I hear they've put in a special restaurant, with a chef.' He places the kind of emphasis on 'chef' that he might on 'ballet dancer'. He glances through the menu: Chef's *hors d'oeuvres*; house *terrine*; kidneys in red wine; trout grilled with herb butter, lemon and prawns. 'I might come down one day with some friends for a meal,' he says. But you know he never will. He doesn't say so, but you know he disapproves – of the tasteful wallpaper, modern bar stools, framed engravings, the *Pouilly Blanc Fumé*.

'When I was young,' he reminisces, 'every Friday a horse and cart came round collecting lavatory buckets to take over to the allotments . . . there was one driver who'd gallop his horse to lighten the load.' Whereas today we're all sitting around eating *hors d'oeuvres*, lapping up *Pouilly Blanc Fumé*. He does not say so, of course. He is inscrutable. He rolls a cigarette, orders another whisky and peppermint, and glares at the barmaid, who is young and pretty, who wears a suggestive invitation stretched across the tight front of her T-shirt.

Outside the Fox and Hounds potato crisp wrappers litter the village green, and pools of yellow light spill from the public bar where Exton bucks and their colleens feed the juke-box . . . 'If I said you have a beautiful body, would you hold it against me . . . ', goes the song. Over and over again. And the twilight is

170

crepuscular, the high mackerel-sky smeared with graphite streaks; and there are sulphurous murmurs, sulphurous looks and sulphurous thoughts put in with sooty fingers.

In Pudding Bag End, on the better side of the street, net curtains are drawn and Kellogg's Corn Flakes are on the breakfast formica surface and twelve cars line the verge, sleek metallic slugs. The light in Hugh Walker's room still burns.

'There was always a perk with thatching,' he says. 'Cups of tea, cake, lemonade . . . one lady made us suet puddings, just plain suet, weighed a ton each. Dad and I couldn't eat them, so when she wasn't looking we buried them in the garden. One day the local hunt went by and a pair of hounds got in and dug up those puddings right under her nose.'

He does not smile; his smiles are rare. He seems like a man drained of enthusiasm, a master craftsman without pride – but it is late and he brings out a book: 'EIIR Coronation Scrap Book 1953'. It is full of photographs and newspaper cuttings of houses he has thatched; there are no dates, no locations, no comments. There is no photograph of Anne, his wife, of the Manx cat they once cared for, of cricket on the village green – just page after page of thatched houses.

Sometime he must go to bed, he cannot sit up all night rolling cigarettes in this silent room. But his wife is in Peterborough Hospital – the girl whose bicycle tyres he pumped that Oakham Sunday long ago. He courted her instead of sister Poppy. What endearments did they exchange; what were the love potions of the day?

The Publican

CHAPTER XIII

THE PUBLICAN

Reg Honeybun

The year 1888 saw a rare event in the London borough of Bermondsey; for there, in Balaclava Terrace, was born George Metcalfe. George was destined to lead no revolt against an established order of inequity; neither was he fashioned to swim the Channel, or score a century at Lords. Instead, he became apprenticed in the printing trade.

His revelation, if you could call it such, came vicariously – through his sister, who had shown the good sense to marry a boy from Dorset. Shortly after the wedding it was suggested by his brother-in-law that George, who had never strayed far beyond the East End, should accompany them on holiday . . . to Thomas Hardy country, to the Dorset village of Hazelbury Bryan. That was in 1907, when George was nineteen.

And what, you may enquire, has this to do with the price of beer and a publican called Reginald Honeybun? Directly, it has little to do with either; indirectly, now that is a very different matter.

On that first occasion, in 1907, George Metcalfe found his way into the bar parlour of the Antelope. In fairness, one should add that it was a question of chance, for in those days when Hazelbury Bryan had four blacksmiths, three harness-makers, its own brewery, it also had five pubs. In the Antelope George found something unobtainable in Bermondsey; he couldn't quite put it into words, just that it was worthwhile, worth coming back for. Which is precisely what he did.

Every year since 1908 George Metcalfe has returned to Hazelbury Bryan for his summer holiday; and that makes seventy-two holidays. Mind you, he has given Brighton and Bournemouth a try, Clacton too, and Poole, Portsmouth and Ramsgate, but: 'Well, I don't feel I've had a real holiday unless I come here.'

George lodges with Mrs Vaile nowadays; that's at the far end of the village, the Droop side, a mile from the Antelope; a nice quiet walk on a summer day, the hazel hedgerows murmurous with insects, deadly nightshade, alluring harlot offering bright berries. A mile to the pub and a mile back; George takes it slowly, firmly, barely needing his stick, smoking St Bruno, still seeing something to delight him on every round voyage.

'Morning, George,' says Reginald Honeybun, as George approaches the bar, resting his *Daily Express* on the counter so that he can reach into his pocket for change enough to buy a glass of Guinness. 'Used to be 3d. a quart,' he grumbles. 'St Bruno was 5d. an ounce . . . you could have a real pub evening for a bob. We played cribbage and we talked. Oh, I knew them all . . . and they've all gone, every man jack.'

He moves over to his regular spot, a bench beneath the window, laying his stick, his tobacco pouch, the *Express* on a table. He takes a slow sip, froth settling on his upper lip like a furry moth. He loads up his pipe, methodically, he is not a man to be hurried, not the sort to be ruffled; he may not have made a century at Lords, but he will make it at Hazelbury Bryan.

'What do I do here for a month?' He puts a match to his pipe, which gurgles, like defective plumbing. 'Well, I don't rightly know . . . the time passes. I read . . . no, not the *Express*, nor any newspaper, they all contradict each other, can't get the truth from them. I used to come here from Waterloo, changed at Templecombe for Sturminster Newton, eleven bob return.

'I'll tell you something,' he pauses, weighing up the implications of divulging information that may come under the Official Secrets Act. 'The country'd go bonkers without telly.' He nods. 'Bonkers,' he says again. 'There are no real characters left, the world's all bloody pop music, it's degrading, going back to barbarism. Worst hour for this country was when they introduced betting shops . . . bloody scroungers. Another thing,' he jabs his pipe stem in the direction of the multi-coloured android against the bar wall. 'Bloody fruit machines.'

It is nearly midday in the Antelope; so far George is the only customer. He stares balefully at the fruit machine, although in truth he has little to complain about . . . there is not much wrong with the Antelope. There are no frills here, not a horse brass or post-horn in sight, no twee little fairy lights dangle from the bar. The floor is part polished board, part stone flag. There is a dart-board, table skittles, a rings board; a notice reads 'Love thine enemy' and an adjacent one, 'Drink is the enemy'. There is a pair of antelope horns and an upright piano which one of the customers, Len, plays on Thursday evenings when he's a mind to; then there is a sing-song.

When the pub was built is anyone's guess, although there is a beam in the kitchen marked 1567. Occasionally the Blackmoor Vale Hunt meet in the forecourt, and a colourful spectacle it must be judging by the snapshots in the Honeybun album. Thickly wooded copses and gently rolling hills make this ideal hunting country . . . whereas the chivalrous offices of the brewing house of Hall and Woodhouse, from Blandford Forum, make it ideal beer-drinking country. 'Badger' bitter is the brew men of Hazelbury Bryan appreciate, with Taunton cider taking second place; the ladies prefer a drop of refinement that comes in little bottles labelled 'Cherry B', 'Babycham', and 'Pony'. There is no demand for cocktails with fancy sounding names; Reg Honeybun says he heard of a drink called Harvey Wallbanger, but thinks perhaps someone was having him on. There is an unopened bottle of Martini on the premises, but you would get a funny look if you asked for a glass.

'Gentleman from London lost his way a while back,' Reg recalls. 'Parked his Rolls Royce outside and came in to ask directions. "While I'm here," he said, "I'll have a gin and tonic, landlord, with ice." I told him we couldn't help with the ice because there was no frost last night.

'There was this lady got lost as well . . . it's the only reason we get casuals . . . she asked if I had any sherry, and I said we had this dark stuff and a lighter one. She said could she taste it and I told her we didn't allow tricks like that. So she asked which one I'd recommend . . . I told her, I said, well, I'd given a dose of the darker one to a heifer with scour and that didn't do her no harm.'

Honeybun is a Dorset name and Reginald of the clan was born at nearby Lychett Minster in 1897. His father was groom to Sir Eliott Lees at the Manor, while his mother's side of the family ran a dairy; Reg remembers his grandmother selling milk in the town, wearing a wooden yoke about her shoulders. There were six children, four boys and two girls, who were tutored in the three R's at Dorchester until their fourteenth year. War came soon after; Reg reported to the Dorset Regimental depot where he kicked his heels for three days before being sent back home to milk the cows. Brothers Philip and Bill were shipped to the Dardanelles and were lost to Dorset for ever.

'I think Mr Churchill made a mess of that,' is Reg's verdict. 'We'd have been better to have bought the Turks instead of fought them . . . it cost us the cream of the country.

'Well, I came home to milk cows and that's what I did for twenty years . . . and the best part of my life was being single! Ena and me met at a village dance, as I remember . . . she was from the same parish, farming people. We spent two years courting, then I married her at twenty-seven.

'I'll tell 'ee what happened – 'tis like this . . . I wasn't a big drinker, but I got in with a fisherman who put the idea in my head that a pub would be a good thing. I applied to the brewers and they offered me the Antelope. I came over, had a beer

176

and that was it. Hitler's war was just ending and I was forty-eight. I took over a case of dry ginger, a few glasses and that was the lot. One bottle of whisky a week was our ration – tell 'ee what I done . . . I let them have as much beer as they liked till it was finished, then I shut the door. You'll excuse my language, but the publican at Shillingstone put up a notice: "Sold out of beer. I've buggered off and suggest you do the same."

"Tis a job to say what a good pub is – some do cooked meals. These people don't like that. Lunches and dinner, that's all wrong. Country people want a pint and a chat, not all that cooking smell . . . puts a man off the taste of his beer. Home's the place to eat. I know what these smart restaurants be – scrapings from one plate to another . . . you can't do that to bread and cheese. Ploughman's lunch was what the horsemen ate, not with all those silly bits of lettuce and cucumber – 'tisn't to our palate here.'

At eighty-three, Reg Honeybun must be one of the oldest working publicans in England. There is not much of him in height; he never grew that tall and he never really grew up. He is a leg-puller, out to shock if he can; his nose and thumb are inseparable. He is rubicund, with the corncrake voice of Walter Gabriel.

'Being a landlord is being a personality, nosey like, you've got to enjoy a conversation . . . strangers lose themselves and come asking the way. Only two charabancs have lost their way since 1945 . . . damned good thing too, they steal glasses, that sort. A pint and a chat is what a pub's about – not machines . . . our postman was feeding that damned fruit machine and he said, "This machine doesn't pay out, landlord," and I said, it ain't meant to, it takes all and gives nothing.'

'Oh, father,' reproaches Peg, 'you ought to know better than say things like that.'

Peggy Honeybun is the sweet voice of reason at the Antelope. In her way she is beautiful, shy at forty as she was at sixteen; it is said that she and Fred have been courting for twenty-three years, but Fred had parents who relied on him and Peg would never leave home as long as her parents needed her. The older sisters could make the break: Doreen married Stuart who works for British Rail, they live at Streatham in London; Rita married Bill, a Hazelbury timberman; and Margaret married Philip, the village plumber. That leaves Keith; but we'll come to him later.

So Peg stayed on. It is her duty, but no sacrifice; or if it is, it does not show in her face. The world turns on its axis and even Hazelbury Bryan is exposed to centrifugal forces; but not Peg – Peg has remained untouched. When the sun rises, Peg gets up; if needs be, she milks the cows at 5.30 am. There is Buttercup and Pansy, Bambi, Claire, and Mary . . . Mad Mary, they call her, because she has a temper and shows it from time to time. Peg sweeps the yard, feeds the geese and chickens, and by opening time she has put on a summer frock ready to serve in the bar.

When village work is done the football team practises on Alec's Field, across

177

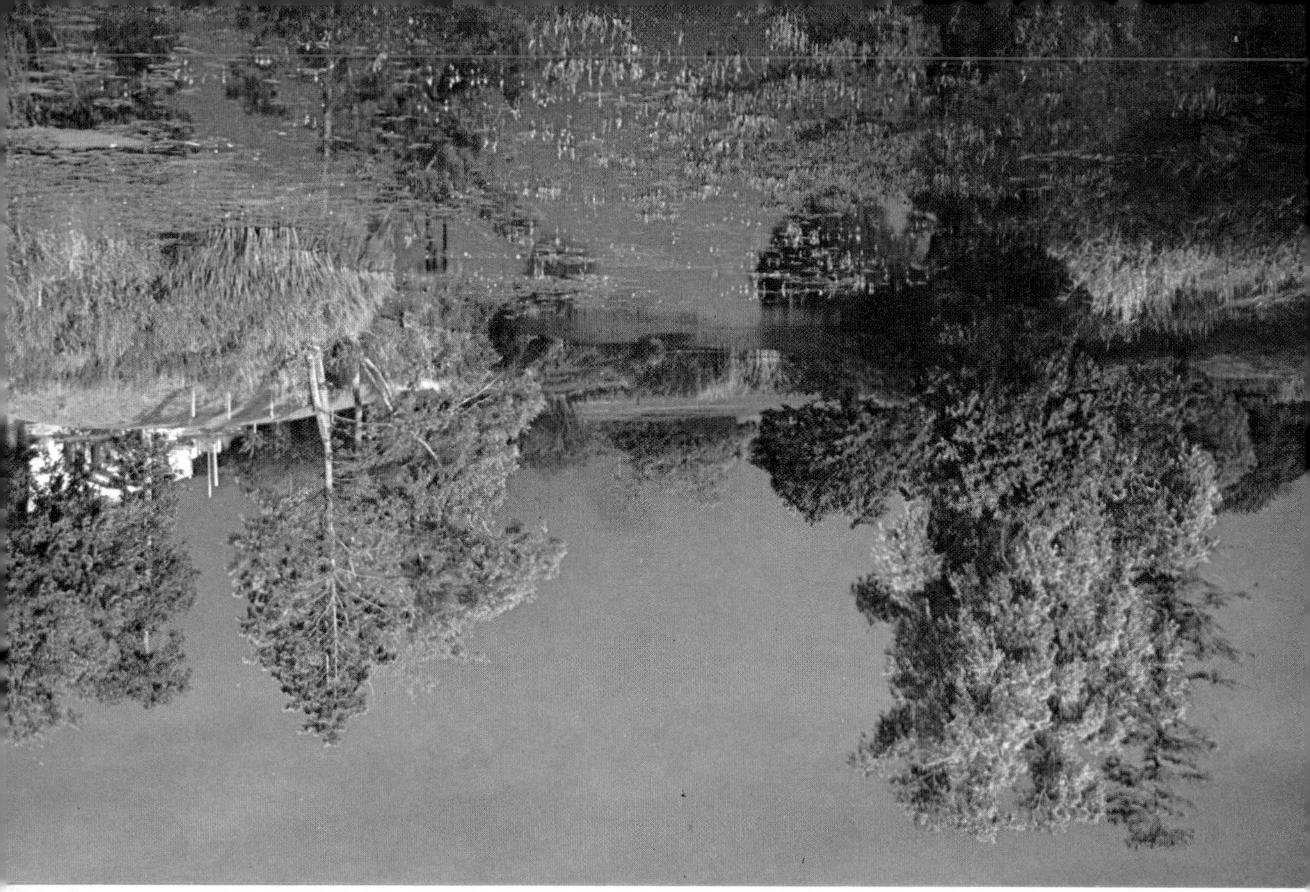

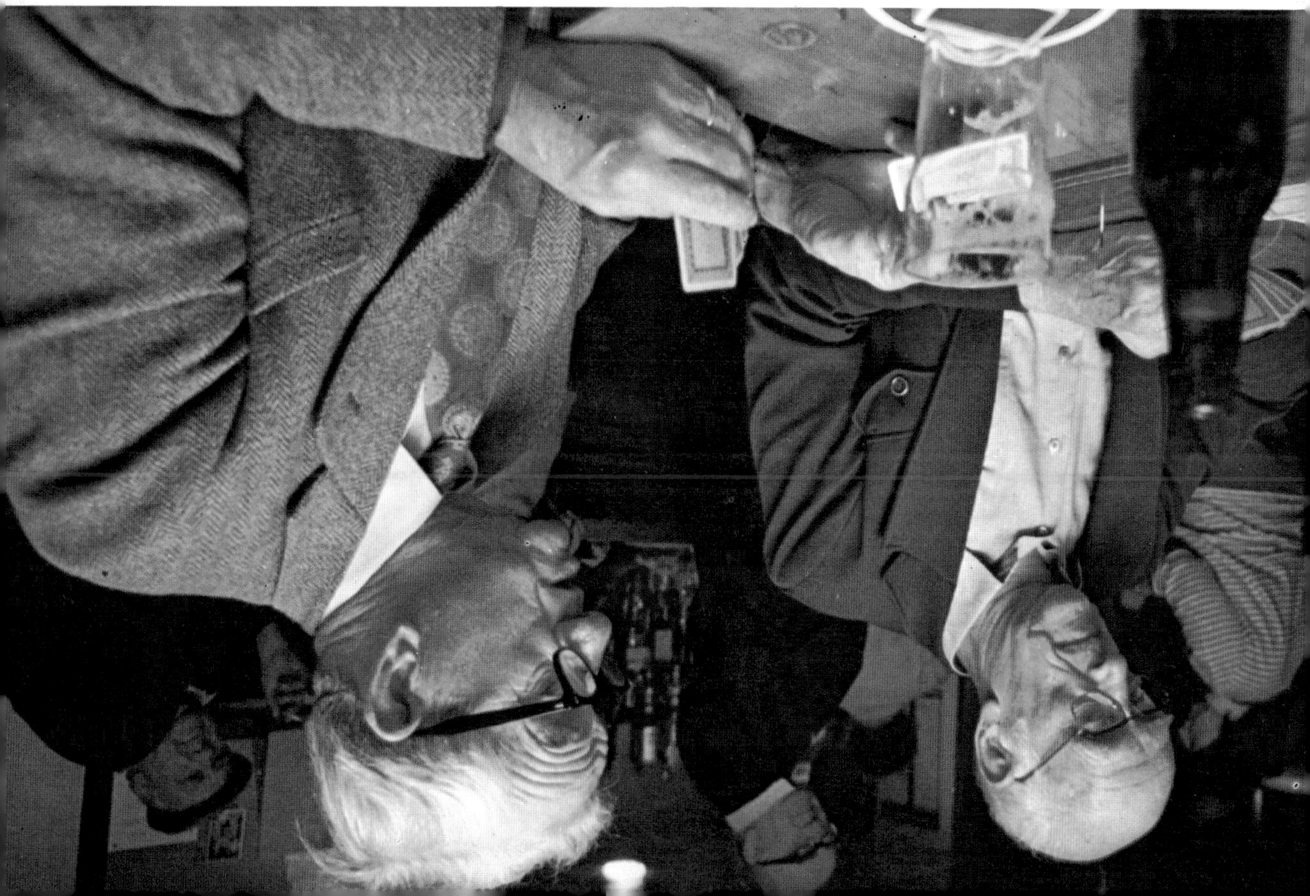

the road; others play skittles in the alley converted from a World War I barrack hut Reg bought on Salisbury Plain. And when shadows are full stretched on the rack of sundown, there is a sly movement towards the bar, where Peg helps her father at the taps. Most evenings Fred comes in, nurses a tall glass of Badger's, talks to his neighbours, and looks at Peg; and she in turn draws him a pint and looks at Fred, and never in a thousand years could you tell what she is thinking. When Reg calls, 'Time, gentlemen, please,' she rinses the glasses, empties the ashtrays, and soon goes to bed. It is a pattern, orderly, uneventful, and probably filled with secret happiness. For these are the days and the seasons of Peg's life.

'The future?' She looks startled, then amused, as if the question is of such fatuity that it seems almost improper. Why, there's milking, straw to bale, the future is the morrow: this is not what she says. What she says is: 'You can't tell with the future . . . mother has a chest in damp weather. I don't know . . . this is as much as I want. I'd never move . . . I'm satisfied.'

Hazelbury Bryan is a maze; small wonder that gentlemen in Rolls Royces lose their sense of direction. If you turn right outside the Antelope, there is a group of bungalows with names like Madrian, Greenleas, Vale View; further on is Badger's Cottage where Big John with the beard lives; next comes the Primitive Methodist Chapel. Three Ways is a house before which is a signpost pointing to Mappowder, Piddletrenthide and Bulbarrow.

There are ancient thatched cottages, neo-Georgian villas; Trenwyn has a Hollywood touch, and Chycoll must surely be an anagram. Then it is a long haul to the church and the school; past the war memorial, and you are back where you started, outside the Antelope, with an unquenchable thirst in August heat.

Why, one wonders, is the church of SS Mary and James such a step from the village centre, a wholly long march to shine the pews. Truth of the matter is that years ago, in the fourteenth century to date it accurately, the village got itself moved. It was at the time of the Black Death, and Hazelbury suffered the scourge worse than most, so it was thought that the only course to salvation was in burning down the entire village clustering about the church, rebuilding on higher ground to the west, now known as Wonston.

And why Hazelbury Bryan; how did such a name derive? Hazelbury is easy enough, considering the hazel hedgerows enclosing smallholdings: no big farms or big fields here, a fifty acre farm is thought pretty vast, a hundred must be the size of Texas. The land is heavy, solid blue clay much of it, with nine inches top soil, and wet with it, too wet for sheep; but it is some of the best dairy grazing in the country. The stock is mostly Friesian with a sprinkling of Sussex for beef. Even so, the herds are brought in for winter to have their bellies filled: 'If it doesn't pay to feed, it doesn't pay to starve,' is the local maxim.

'Bryan'; now that takes some poking and prying: old parish records have it as Brienne, Brian, Bryan, leading us, by way of the valiant Lord Chandos, to Sir Guy de Bryan, Lord Bryan, Knight of the Garter. There is no documentary evidence, but it could be that his ancestors were connected to John de Brienne, last King of Jerusalem, from whom the Lords Beaumont descended. Lord Bryan himself was a distinguished soldier under Edward III, discharging himself honourably at the battle of Sluys and at the siege of Calais; he was prominent in the Black Prince's wars in France. His daughter by his first wife married the heir to the Fitzpaynes, which may have influenced his acquisition of the Manor of Hazelbury, close to the Fitzpaynes' favourite Manor of Okeford. Just below the church a signpost indicates Okeford Fitzpayne . . . England is, after all, a very family affair.

As a family the Honeybuns may be less bellicose than the Bryans and the Fitzpaynes, yet their colonizing instincts seem as sharp. With the Antelope came a field behind the pub, belonging to the brewery; today their conquistadorial advances have brought them four fields, twenty acres in hand, farmed by Keith. The land is scattered, in four or five acre parcels, too wet to plough, fine as permanent pasture.

Over towards Buckland Newton, in the 'corn belt' eight miles away, drizzle is holding up the harvest. Keith follows in the combiner's wake, baling straw for winter feed . . . so he is at a loose end, waiting for showers to pass, the sun to dry to readiness. He is waiting for word from Farmer Needham, whose land is being worked. The best part of an afternoon is at waste.

He drives the pickup to Pleck's Field, one of his pastures; it is steep, rising high, the wind is cool, damp-laden after noonday's heat. This is Keith's favourite spot; he stretches out on the grass, not caring about the wet. He chews a blade of grass, cradling his head in his hands, the peak of his orange baseball cap shielding his eyes, keeping specks of rain off his tinted spectacles. Directly below is Deadmore Common, rough ground; Keith points suddenly, eyesight keen enough, as a deer quivers, freezing into its background. Here and there smoke signals drift to the horizon, telegraphing the word that in places the harvest is in; the time for burning has come, flame sears the stubble, incinerating all life. Some say it is a crime, this annual holocaust.

Keith Honeybun is thirty-four, a bachelor still, with bachelor ways. Until recently, that is; he will need to toe the line more now. The tender trap has finally closed and Keith is engaged to Gillian, a hairdresser from Stalbridge, the other side

of Sturminster Newton. They have even got as far as buying a secondhand mobile home, towing it to one of Keith's fields while they apply for planning permission.

'I was always keen on the girls,' he says. 'Friends thought no one would tie me down . . . reckon this has shaken them. How did we meet? Well, I'd fallen out with the village football team and felt I might give Stalbridge a try, but I thought I'd better get to know the place first . . . and there's no better way than by courting a local girl. I told Gillian that beer, skittles and football came first but, well . . .' he puts on a face, rueful but unrepentant.

He is darkly good-looking, debonair; you can see that he may have a way with girls, be hard to tie down. It is difficult to think of him sitting down to meals at a regular time, to putting on his Sunday best and pushing a pram.

'If I'm like dad at his age, I'd be pleased with myself – but I'd never take the pub on. I don't like being nice to people to order . . . it's bloody hard work agreeing with people. But I'm a village person, in towns people walk past you – the pavements are too hard for me. Went abroad once, with the skittles team to Cherbourg for the day . . . didn't think a lot of it, we couldn't get any decent beer, and they didn't speak English. I was disappointed really . . . thought they'd all look like little frogs.' He squints up from under his baseball cap to see if you are taken in.

'I've got this thing about boats though – after milking on Sunday, Gill and I drive to Poole to look at the yachts, and I think that's what I'd like to do . . . then you look down into the cabins and see them sitting there watching *Coronation Street* or something, and I think I'll stick to the land.

'I wouldn't mind being an in-work actor – I'm a show-off really. I've read a lot of stories by Stanley Morgan, about a character called Russ Tobin, a sort of adventurer. It'd make a great film series with me as star . . . I'm a dreamer, that's what I am. When I'm in the straw, I'm dreaming all the time – day dreaming.'

Someone else with a dream, a dream that shattered, is Miss Cross, who lives at the Manor House, whose father was inducted to the church living at Sturminster Marshall 106 years ago. She lives alone and points out that she can see three churches from where she sits, looking towards the hazy distance. Quite vividly she remembers as a little girl being clothed in raven black for Queen Victoria's memorial service at her village church. She remembers too the hedge in their garden being decorated with hundreds of small Union Jacks in celebration of the Relief of Mafeking.

'1914 broke,' she recalls, 'and I found myself in France in response to an urgent appeal for nurses to care for the terrible casualties of Verdun and Flanders. The world emerged from the wreckage . . . we raised monuments to our dead and forgot the living. We went our several ways and closed our eyes.'

Then came 1939 and Violet Cross returned to France at the same time as the British Expeditionary Force: 'The Germans took over . . . it was concentration camp or run, so I removed everything English except my face, hid in a convent in Paris, finally made my way home via Lisbon.'

The Manor is a big house for one person, however indomitable; there is a notice by the door instructing you to go in and loudly call her name – she is a little deaf, and sadly disillusioned by what her world, her England, has come to. She was a fighter always; she is a fighter still; once there were comrades in arms who would ride with St George to slay the dragon. Now the troops have deserted.

'We were worth fighting for. Today I'm ashamed of my country.'

She says: 'In the old days you could cash a cheque anywhere in the world – they won't trust us nowadays.'

She says: 'They've sold the old Rectory for £100,000 at auction, I believe. I'm so glad they haven't turned it into a night club. People with a foreign-sounding name have bought it – bankers, I believe.'

She says: 'Dr Beeching ruined England.'

She says: 'Certain things remain constant. I've had the same gardener forty-two years. Someone asked if he used a spirit-level to do the hedges, and I said, no, he used his eyes.'

Keith Honeybun, alias Russ Tobin, resting after his latest MI5 assignment, has said: 'Things are different – but I don't know how much it's the village that's changed or me that's changed growing up.'

183

Different generations are talking; different perspectives. One thing is certain: no cause is so lost that it is irretrievable. Battles will still be fought, and who knows that Hazelbury will not be called upon again to show that same cunning, that same contempt for the forces of evil that it did in the hour of peril in 1940. In the church porch a framed notice proclaims: 'During the imminent threat of invasion in 1940, the name Hazelbury Bryan was obliterated from this board in order to help foil the enemy should he succeed in landing. It has never been replaced in order to serve as a memorial of his defeat and the deliverance of our country.' It was spirit such as this that toppled the Third Reich.

It is the 30th August, summer draws out, much of the corn still stands; it is bright brittle gold no more. The colour is fading, pricked black in parts, beginning to wilt. An air of fecundity is in the countryside, a swollenness which must be eased.

'SW England,' reads the area forecast. 'Dry and sunny after early fog. Wind E to SE, light. Max. temp. 23°C (73°F).'

At milking time the mist is thick, clammy as Mad Mary's breath. By eight the sun, a great fog-lamp, scorches through, burnished like an inverted brass bowl. But the night was chill, dew heavy, the sun must work harder – so it is nearly midday before Farmer Needham is satisfied.

Seen from afar, there is something primeval about a combine-harvester at work: it shows a dinosaurian clumsiness, a too-small brain directing too-massive a body. There is a stupidity, a blindness in its groping gait, in the lowering of its jaws in search of food. Its armour heaves and shudders, hewing a path of hot destruction. Periodically it stops, snorting in bewilderment; then it lowers its head again, myopically swallowing its vitamin deficiency. Its blundering raises clouds of dust, a myriad insects; its bellows drive farm dogs into yapping frenzy as they snap and snarl at the monster's feet.

From a distance Keith, intrepid white hunter, stalks his prey; from his safari Jeep he assesses the killing ground, adjusts the sights of his high-velocity rifle. A slight tic of apprehension licks his lean jaw; his eyes narrow to a slit lest the beast, down wind of him, should catch his scent and charge . . . a bale of straw falls to the flint-strewn field, jerking him back to Buckland Newton, to his tractor cabin.

It is a muck-sweaty job, harvesting; it is a struggle against the clock, against the din, the filth, the lung-clogging dust. You can wear mask, helmet and headset – but how can you tell how the combiner is running if you're kitted like a spaceman? The old ways are best; let's get it done, get the harvest in. That's what counts. When you come down to it, there is no pleasure in harvesting, only in the harvest home.

Shadows lengthen again; dusk comes early. There is a ring round the moon, yet the light is pellucid; the effect is somehow contrived, theatrical, the harvest scene becomes a tableau. Then, one by one, engine sounds die; Keith turns his tractor towards Hazelbury.

The journey is through a weird inferno; stubble is ablaze, sparks crackle and jump. The good earth is being cauterized; and in the morning it will be scorched wasteland. The breeze will lift black corn dust, and what yesterday was yellow gold will tomorrow be base.

Trade is brisk in the Antelope this evening, you can barely get to the bar. Reg has slicked down his hair with water, he has a scrubbed look, cherubic as a choir boy. Peg is anxious because there has been a run on pork pies. Big John-the-beard is at the bar, so is George of the red woolly hat with the pom-pom, so too Vick and Pam Cornick who have parked their tractor outside. Fred is there, dependable as the Rock of Gibraltar. Gillian has come over from Stalbridge; she is talking to Vic and Pam, waiting for Keith.

A game of cribbage is going on; Chris is trying for a double-one on the dart-board, avoiding Dossy's Hole as it is known. And why? Because long ago Dossy the baker, who dipped his darts in beer to make their flight more true, missed double-one so frequently he dug a cavity in the wall. In the alley Nick, Tony, Andrew and Vaughan are bowling down the pins, waiting also for Keith . . . Gillian or beer and skittles with the lads? It's a terrible dilemma for a man who's been in the straw all day.

185

It is half-past nine when he turns up. No time to shave or change, straw catches in his jersey, his face is grimy; when he removes his spectacles he looks like a panda. Peg pours him a lemonade shandy as he makes his peace with Gillian before heading towards the skittles . . . Gillian catches Peg's eye for moral support, but Peg knows better than that.

Reg winks; he knows the form. Mum's the word. His face shines as he leans over the bar: ''Tis like this,' he says. 'All my life I've been up at five in the morning to breathe fresh air, and I've got a contented mind. I never dwell on anything. Peg worries, the wife worries, but worry never helped anyone. Someone said to me, how could I sleep if I owed money and I said that's where you're wrong, it's the ones I owe it to can't sleep.

'Those people in the town worry. They sit up looking at each other, then one says what's the time? And they look at the clock and say is that all, we can't go to bed yet then.

'I've never known about time, never worried and never been ill in my life. I may not know much, but I know one thing . . . I know I'll reach eighty because I've passed it.'

The
Coal Miner

CHAPTER XIV
THE COAL-MINER

Wilf Simcock

The following is taken from *Coal Mines Inspection* by R. Nelson Boyd, FRGS, FGS, published in 1879:

> It is only within recent years that we have acquired any accurate knowledge of the habits, customs and inner life of the labouring class. Few authors have devoted their pen to this subject, and those few have been hampered by lack of data.
>
> Sir Frederick Eden, writing in 1789 on the history of the poor, says: "I was persuaded that the scanty materials which were to be found in our old chroniclers and annualists would necessarily confine that part of my subject to a very narrow compass."
>
> The same may be said of any writer compiling the early history of the labouring part of the community. As Hallam says: "We can trace the pedigree of princes, fill up the catalogue of towns beseiged and provinces desolated, describe even the whole pageantry of coronations and festivals, but we cannot recover the genuine history of mankind."

It is a point well made, a reasonable conclusion. The tapestry of working life, both in town and country, was indeed threadbare, remaining so until Dickens, followed by Hardy, thought to weave in the neglected threads. It could be argued that those merry wives of Windsor speak of Pistol and Mistress Quickly; but they speak volumes more of Falstaff. Pistol lives on to fight at Agincourt; but it is good Hal, his dukes and earls who carry the day more than the rank and file. As for the 1381 Peasants' Revolt, how little we know of feudal conditions leading to rebellion. The Great Unwashed were only great numerically; that much is known.

Wilf Simcock quotes Nelson Boyd; it is something he read long ago, something he cannot forget. In simple translation Mr Boyd's statement is chilling: the working class was a commodity, an article of convenience, expendable and insignificant.

Into this generic order Wilfred Simcock was born seventy years ago in the Staffordshire mining village of Ball Green.

'I'm the fourth generation to go down pit – there were probably more,' he says. Of those four generations, two perished underground. Wilf is lucky; he was

never in a bad fall, the dust has not rotted his lungs. He is a fit man still, compact, sturdy, five feet two inches tall. He has lost his hair, but none of his pride in having spent his life below ground: 'It's not really fit work for human beings, but I was always as happy as a lark . . . except that I really believe a man is meant to work in the light, not in the dark.' He is retired, but not retired; he is an ex-miner who cannot keep away from the colliery.

'People don't seem able to talk about miners without getting political,' he says. 'The sort of coal-mining you see on television and films and how-green-was-my-valley is a load of codswallop . . . blood, sweat and tears, that's all they see – but there's a lot of laughter down a pit. Hard swearing too . . . that's because there's no women down there to offend. Miners stick together like few others, for good or evil . . . like in the strikes of 1921 and 1926. There was bad feeling then, we knew something was wrong with the system, we recognized that much . . . but we never saw the mine owners, they were another breed of people. The manager and his wife were the ones we looked up to, they were somebody in society, like the parson.

'In the strikes we lived off hope and extended credit – and that was shaming, working people had a fear of debt. But you took credit or you starved. We used to say, "The Lord will provide", but He didn't always make a good job of it. Today they say, "The government will provide" – and it does. We knew real poverty, but we were still taught manners . . . aye, if someone came to the house and I was reading, I had to stand up and stop reading. Father said, if you go into a house, knock first, take off your cap and once inside, live pleasant.'

Wilf's great-grandfather was down the pits from the age of ten; he supplemented his earnings from Chatterley Whitfield colliery by a bit of poaching at Westwood Hall. One night he was involved in an affray with the gamekeeper, during which the keeper's dog was killed. For this the miner was convicted and transported to Australia to serve out his sentence, leaving behind a wife and four children.

'Great-grandma walked from Brown Edge to Leek to buy butter from the hill-women who came down to market – she'd buy as much as she could afford, then she'd walk all the way to Burslem to re-sell the butter at market there. She kept herself and the kids alive by that, and had something put by for when he came home from the penal colony. He went back down the mine and was killed by a fall.

'I was thirteen when my grand-dad died . . . I remember him, he was a rough man, a miner and a pugilist, a bare-knuckle fighter before it was outlawed. He'd have a gutful of booze, strip to the waist and see who the best man was . . . bets were placed. He worked the boats too, moving coal from the Potteries to the mills at Leek along the Cauldon Canal. Aye, he was an ugly looking man who'd had a few good hidings and it showed.

'My father was called Daniel after him, but they were a different sort . . . he'd been taken in by Old John Sherratt, landlord of the Rose and Crown, he and his wife virtually adopted father – a marvellous man, I called him grandfather Sherratt. Mother, she was called Edith Rosa, was reared on a smallholding at Whitfield Farm, near the colliery . . . they met somehow, I don't know how, and married in 1908. They had four sons and four daughters, and they were always happy – I don't know how they kept happy, they just did.

'We lived at Number 49 South Street then, at Brown Edge, a two up and two down . . . a bog down the yard next to the coal place, one cold tap, oil lamps, two or three to a bed . . . segregated. Father had gone down the pit at twelve – he walked home, forty-five minutes it took, and when he got to the fields he took his clogs off to walk on grass. Aye, you could say it eased his feet.

'In those days you brought your dirt home, no pithead baths – he'd wash under the tap as far as he could and he'd sleep in long pants so's to keep decent. Friday night the whole family'd bath in the kitchen . . . an old doctor said the wives worked harder than the miners, keeping clean. It was a terrible job keeping clean.'

Wilf's own house is immaculate, scrubbed and polished with an almost forensic passion. It is a red-brick, detached 1959 house, with a garden front and back, a driveway, fine views overlooking the valley. Although it is September, with

an Indian summer heat-wave, a coal fire burns in the grate. A bowl of fat tomatoes ripens in the window, brass sparkles like church plate, there is a 'forget me not' milk jug, a Coronation mug and a tea-cosy. Chairs and sofas have antimacassars, there is a tasselled pouffe and an embroidered fire-screen portraying a country lane leading to a chapel in the woods.

Mary Simcock is at war with dust and dirt, they are the foe against which she is constantly vigilant. She finds the house too big these days, too much to manage for the two of them. But Mary hasn't been very well, she's had a nervous breakdown, she tells you brightly; she smooths her hands on her pinafore, dabs at a cushion. 'No,' says Wilf, 'Mary's not been too good lately.'

At five Wilf went to the village Church School; it was demolished years ago, there is just a gaping space where it stood. 'It was a good school for those days, one big room with curtains separating classes – there was bible study every morning and the Friday hymn was *There is a Green Hill Far Away* . . . there was a harmonium the headmaster, Mr Rhodes, played. He'd make us do physical jerks and deep breathing before prayers . . . they even taught algebra at that school, and gardening on Tuesdays and Thursdays – if you took gardening you needn't do history, so I chose to be outside.

'There was a rough field for playing marbles, flicking cigarette cards . . . in the summer dinner hour we'd go down to the sheep-wash, it was a wide place in the brook, for swimming – oh naked, no swim suits then. We played street cricket and football, there was no traffic – we'd go mushrooming and blackberrying to help mother. I'll never know how she managed, there was always good wholesome food – dumplings, pies, oat cakes, stew, we never went hungry. Washday was Monday, with a dolly peg, washboard, tub and mangle . . . sometimes the wash would take two or three days. We'd sometimes get a penny a week pocket money – it went on gob-stoppers, bull's eyes, pear drops . . . I can still smell those pear drops to this day. As I said, we were all happy in that house.

'But I had aspirations to do anything but go down pit – to get a scholarship, go to secondary school – but that would have put too much on the parents . . . there was no choice, pit or Potteries, and the Potteries were too far away.'

By his fourteenth birthday Wilf had joined his father underground. There is a snapshot of him taken with another lad: they look small and daunted, hollows round their eyes, children dressed up in men's clothing, as for some charade. They wear huge cloth caps, miner's lamps hang from their broad leather belts. No smiles for the camera; perhaps there wasn't much to smile about at two shillings and fourpence for eight hours at the seam, with an hour's 'winding-time' – the journey to the surface. That's fourteen shillings for a six-day week in old money – more than a farm labourer's wage.

'Aye, but only if there was work – some mornings you'd hear the "buzzer", one long half-minute wail – no orders coming in that'd mean, no orders, no work. "No trucks," they'd say . . . no trucks to fill.

'No training – you were just put with another lad. I went as fireman's lad . . . a fireman examined for safety and when workmen wanted shots firing, he'd do the blasting. Men carried powder, but firemen were the only ones to have detonators. It was all hand work then, coal was hand-won . . . after eighteen months I went on to haulage, pony driving . . . worked with horses for years. They stayed underground all the time except for holidays. When it was mechanized we said, "They've taken the horses out and left the asses behind." '

At the same time as he was below ground, Wilf had 'aspirations' (a word he uses frequently) to study pharmacy; he even worked part-time at a chemist shop in Norton. Eventually the proprietor persuaded him to go full-time, so he left the colliery for two years: 'But I couldn't raise the money you needed to qualify . . . so I took to bricklaying, then to the silk mill at Upperhulme . . . trade went bad and I found myself back in pit for the rest of my life.'

Wilf is a man without rancour and without regret; life has treated him kindly, he is owed nothing. 'I'd not like you to make much of that,' he says, as he describes hardship, deprivation. There is a lot of laughter down a pit, he has said. He is a modest man, a good man, patient and gentle; he would have made a teacher. 'You

192

think so?' he asks, pleased but not flattered. 'Not with my writing . . . my writing's like bagpipe music. We'd have liked our own kids, but they never came along . . . we thought of adopting, but you know what it's like. We're not great socialites – Mary's always a bit under the weather . . . I wish she could be well.'

Mary was the girl next door, more or less. So they met, they just met; they met in 1939, the month Germany invaded Poland and Wilf's father was killed by an underground fall. Mary had generations of coal-miners behind her; so they had much in common, breathing the same air, listening for the fateful buzzer, watching slag heaps take over the landscape, sharing friends and superstitions. Down the pit men feared the 'Bloo Mon', the legendary bogy, the mine ghost defaced by the blue flash of firedamp; men on early shift would turn about in their tracks, staying at home all day if they met a woman on their way to the pit. To this day Mary will buy nothing new on Friday.

They married at Brown Edge church in 1942, moving in with Mary's parents for seventeen years until they saved enough to put down the deposit on their present home in Park Lane, Knypersley. By then Mary's people were getting on, so they joined their daughter and son-in-law in the move, remaining there until their death. They all got on, there was mutal respect; mining families hold together in this way. Mary worked at a draper's shop in Tunstall and when he was not down the pit Wilf grew runner beans, cauliflower and cabbage; he planted potatoes, pruned roses and put in snap-dragons – nothing tall because the wind is mean, sweeping up the valley. He built a greenhouse and kept clear of the working men's club: 'I've never been a club man, it's habit forming – you lose your freedom if you have to go to same place at same time.'

And when his mother died – she'd held on seventeen years after her husband was brought back dead from the mine – Wilf buried her next to his father. They share the same gravestone in Norton churchyard. The children, as many as they could, got together; Dan and Harry from the pit – except that Harry turned to coalman, delivering coal, 'fuel distributor' as it is now called – Jack who became a medical representative, Edith, Kathleen and Mary from Leek mills, and Irene who had gone to Canada. They thought what to put on the headstone, coming up with 'Parents Indeed'.

'I still miss dad,' Wilf says, 'like most miners, he'd sit around and talk about pit. It wasn't pride, it was his trade . . . we worked in the same pit. As for me, all I wanted was work, to be doing something . . . I've known them that's packed up, gone to America, Australia. It's never occurred to me to leave here – it's how people's hormones are. I just stuck at it . . . from hand-drilling to when coal was cut by machines, fed on to conveyors, wages went up to seven and sixpence a day. War came and went . . . we got Displaced Persons down the mine. We had one of Rommel's men working alongside a Desert Rat – they'd been fighting each other, now they were chaffing each other.

193

THE PROTECTOR LAMP & LIGHTING CO LTD
TYPE
SL
M & O
SAFETY LAMPS
ECCLES
S
624

'I took a correspondence course in mining, went to Stoke Technical School. In 1945 I got my under-manager's ticket, my manager's ticket in '46 . . . no, I've never managed a colliery, I've not the ambition for it. All I've wanted was to find out things, that's been my aspiration. Nationalization came, that was a big upheaval, everyone said, "What are we going to get out of it?" Nobody said, "What are we going to put into it?" There aren't many Tolpuddle Martyrs left.'

One day the clock hands stood at 1975; Wilf had been underground fifty-one years, so they retired him. A reporter came over from the *Hanley Sentinel* to interview him: had he had a happy life, was the question. 'I've had a good home, good health, good friends – and there's no Value Added Tax on those,' said Wilf. And that was that. He is entitled to 3¾ tons of free coal a year and all the hours of the day to do as he pleases.

Except that he is not entirely pleased with his surfeit of freedom, the twenty-four thin hours that make up each day: 'I've seen a lot of retired miners doing nowt and all it does is make them old.' He says this on the way to Norton Church; it is a Ford Fiesta spin to youth revisited, easier on the feet than the shanks's pony he used to ride. There is the Rose and Crown where grandfather Sherratt lived, there the church where Wilf wed the girl next door. 'Look for stone houses, not bricks and mortar, to see how it used to be,' he makes the distinction, looking down the decades to fewer streets, more fields. Here and there rise outcrops of millstone grit from which cottages were built, 'miners' farewell' as it is known because where such outcrops occur there is no coal beneath.

He waves to a figure walking slowly, alone, a spindly figure, curiously isolated from his environment, like a Lowry matchstick man: 'That's old George Frost,' says Wilf, 'he could make a mouth-organ speak in his time.'

He parks the car beside a farmyard, locking the doors carefully, climbing the steps to Norton Church. It is a gloomy edifice, house of a stern saviour; a saviour, if appearances are anything to go by, with little interest in gardening, for the graveyard has returned to nature. Weeds choke paths, brambles suffocate headstones, blackberries are ready for the picking in this garden of the dead. Too many weeds, too many dead by far: St Peter must be busy with applicants from Norton. There are stunted trees, burnt black in burnt Norton; away to the west smoke trails from a thousand chimneys, slag heaps sprawl. It is not a sight to make hearts rejoice.

Wilf tut-tuts his way through overgrown thickets, making erratic leaps like

a wildebeest dodging predators; he has not visited his parents' grave for a while and is disorientated by the profusion. He finds the plot and is dismayed: 'I hadn't realized . . .' he begins, then lowers himself to his knees, attacking the weeds with his hands, pulling, tearing; and there is the inscription, 'Parents Indeed'.

And there, at 49 South Street, Brown Edge, is the two up and two down with the bog down the yard, where Wilf and his seven brothers and sisters spent their early years; and all one can think is how they all fitted in and how Rosa kept them clean, fed, and so happy. She must have been a woman of great strength; she must have been a wonderful mother.

You can see Chatterley Whitfield Colliery from South Street, the mine to which – so we read in Shaw's *History of the Potteries* – Ralph Leigh of Burslem travelled twice a day for coal in 1750. Each of his six horses carried two to three hundredweight of coal along lanes impassable to wagons; for this he earned one shilling a day. By 1838 the proprietors were listed as the representatives of William Harrison, and coal and buildings were collectively assessed at a value of £154.7s.6d. By 1853 Hugh Henshall Williamson was the owner, by 1880 143,283 tons of coal were produced in the year, and 1900 saw the colliery reach the one million tons mark, the first pit in Britain to achieve this output. In 1935 the Cockshead workings, scene of the 1881 underground explosion which killed more than twenty men, were reopened, in the process of which old tools, jackets and caps were discovered, as well as the skeleton of a pit pony still attached to a tub of coal.

In 1976 extraction of coal ceased at Whitfield and the dust was allowed to settle; but not for long: in 1978 the Chatterley Whitfield Mining Museum Trust was formed to convert surface buildings and underground workings into the country's first living mining museum.

Meanwhile, Wilf had retired to concentrate on his cauliflowers and snapdragons – which, when he came to consider, were in pretty good shape anyway. Then you must take into account the feeling, the actual *feeling* Wilf has for coal. It is not just black-solid-opaque-carbonaceous substance of vegetable origin to him; coal to Wilf is a plant which lived and breathed hundreds of millions of years ago. This is what he tells you, this is what he explains to children, his eyes alight with quiet passion. When Wilf went to London he didn't go to Twickenham or the Talk of the Town; he went to the City where, in EC4 not far from Ludgate Circus, he had heard of Seacoal Street. He took a bus there and walked its pavements, enquiring about the derivation.

When Whitfield became a museum Wilf volunteered to act as trustee, which gives him a chance to go underground again. Quite regularly he conducts visitors, safely helmeted, with lamps and self-rescuers, to the old workings. Authentic conditions are simulated: rubber soles (no nails) are worn, two metal tallies are collected, one to be clipped to the belt, the other handed to the banksman at the shaft-head. At the pithead the cage rises to the surface, held in the grip of a giant chain claw. The gate clangs to, the cage drops – into total dark. Lamps are switched on, dazzling the cage's twelve occupants on the 500-foot journey to the bottom, where the onsetter releases the gate. For the best part of two hours Wilf leads his visitors from one seam to the next, showing by exhibits how coal has been won over the years, from hand-drilling to mechanized excavation. It is an orderly, civilized business – in no way like the real thing.

In most mines you slither down sharp inclines, clutching at a guide rope; there is sludge and water which closes over your boots. Arches have snapped in places, rock has rolled off the sides of the tunnel; some of the rocks are massive, they could break a man's back. Wind from the ventilator shaft howls like a banshee, drying sweat, chilling bones. In gullies sit men with blackened faces, eating their snaps, waiting relief.

The seam could be an hour's walk from the cage; then it is a crawl, hands and knees, then frequently on your belly, head down, bottom down, through sludge to the shearer at the coal face. Men squat, in semi-foetal position, eye whites luminous, jaws moving on the chewing gum, or tobacco, which helps them salivate. Some wear masks to keep dust out, but masks are an encumbrance, so the majority take risks: 'If the dust's going to get you . . . ' The cutter attacks the face like a bacon slicer, spewing coal, spitting chippings like bullets, so that you duck, turning away, waiting for the shift to end, longing to stand, to stretch, see daylight, breathe pure air.

It is a man's world down a pit, exclusive as a St James's club, alert as a front-line trench. There is leg-pulling, humour, profanity; but no fooling. Each man's life is in the other's hands. There is always a chance of firedamp, explosion, a fall: there could be a fatal accident today. Many face workers have, at one time, been buried by a fall, have been dug out by their mates . . . but, 'I'd not like you to make much of that,' Wilf has said.

Given the choice, many men might accept a long term in Wormwood Scrubs as an alternative to life underground. Wilfred Simcock's sentence in the pit was fifty-one years (one of the Oxford Dictionary's definitions of 'pit' being 'hell'), but he does not recognize it in this context. He is now seventy; he is 'on overtime', as he calls it; he is a retired miner who cannot retire, who cannot bring himself to break with the job. Cauliflowers, snap-dragons and Ford Fiestas are all very well; but coal dust and comradeship are Wilf's very creed.

At the pithead he rummages in the pocket of his overalls: 'Take this,' he says, pressing something into your hand. 'Have it as a bit of a souvenir like.' It is a lump of coal.

The Shopkeeper

CHAPTER XV

THE SHOPKEEPER

George Kyle

It could warp a man's mind, the wind on Holy Island. It bears no name – though it should, and a bad one at that – yet it is full of malice. Coming from the northwest, it cripples trees, prostrates headstones in St Mary's cemetery, tugs at human reason. In these farewell days of autumn it offers no respite, savaging slate roofs, snatching at chimney smoke. It is an ill-wind, bastard progeny of tempest and fury; it lacks all grace, being disfigured by malevolence.

At such times Islanders turn in upon themselves, burrowing from the elements like hibernating creatures. Visitors have retreated to the mainland, all but the most stoic ornithologists come to spot the greylag goose, to listen for the bittern's boom. Market Place is deserted. Sanctuary Close, Straight Lonnin, St Cuthbert's Square, Popple Well are all deserted. In the harbour five fishing boats strain and jerk at moorings, five survivors from times when herring boats brought a whiff of prosperity to the Island. In Tripping Chare is a figure, bent at work. The work of chasing swirling leaves scurrying along gutters. The figure is Arthur Shell, street cleaner by trade, solitary by nature.

In summer, when tides are favourable, the tourist throng is like a football crowd. That's what the Islanders say – a football crowd. The Northumberland

Arms, Crown and Anchor, Castle serve beer non-stop; beer, crisps, sandwiches, egg, sausage and beans. Sally's souvenirs do well: Holy Island ashtrays, tea towels, spoons. Lindisfarne Mead sells well too, brewed to a recipe guarded jealously for over a thousand years . . . the water is important, that much we know, clear water and pure honey. Which is how the word 'honeymoon' came into being, deriving from the ancient custom of having newly-weds drink mead for a whole 'moon' in order to increase their chances of happy marriage. In an age of spray-on-flavour, the taste of Lindisfarne Mead is reassuring.

'Twice isle and twice continent in one day, being encompassed with water at every flow and dry at every ebb . . . a semi-isle,' was how the Venerable Bede described Lindisfarne, the Holy Island off Northumbria's coast. To Alcuin, eighth-century monk, it was 'the very cradle of Northumbrian Christianity'. It is a place of pilgrimage still. It is a place not quite of this earth, a place for spiritual re-examination and prayer. The power of prayer, the quality of devotion left an imprint on the Island long after the monks fled the Priory at the Dissolution. Yet there is an unease, an indefinable mood of conflict; the feud between God and mammon continues, leaving you wondering where it will end.

Lindisfarne. An early writer says that the name came from a stream called the Lindis appearing at low tide; 'farne', found also in the Farne Islands, is from the Celtic, meaning 'land'. It was to this remote spot, eight miles south of the border with Scotland, that Aidan arrived with his mission in AD 634 Oswald had just made himself King of Northumberland by his victory over the Welsh prince Cadwallader. Being a Christian he wished his subjects to forsake their pagan customs. To effect this change he sent to Iona for teachers, but these first missionaries failed, to be replaced by Aiden with a body of Irish monks who established an ascetic monastic community in the way of the Celtic Church. From Lindisfarne Aiden evangelized Northumbria, becoming first of the sixteen bishops, of whom the best revered is Cuthbert, shepherd boy from the Lammermuir Hills.

The fortunes of the sacred order rose and fell: in AD 875 the Danes reduced Lindisfarne to rubble and ash, the miracle being that the monks escaped, taking the Lindisfarne illustrated gospels and St Cuthbert's remains with them. By edict of Henry VIII the monastery, now ruled by the mild Benedictines, was dissolved; the Priory was demolished in 1541, leaving remains to the climate. The Priory Church stands today, roofless but awesome, the distinguished 'rainbow' arch showing delicately against the sky.

Adjoining the Priory is the parish church of St Mary the Virgin, built about 1140. Early records are incomplete, but it is possible to count the Reverend Denis Bill as thirty-fourth incumbent to the living since 1544. He was once a monk himself, so when he came to Holy Island in 1964 he was, in a way, coming home.

'I think they like me, I feel accepted – but I'm not an Islander and never will be. It's a place of vision, of spiritual vision. I'd like the Islanders to be more aware of what they're sitting on spiritually, they don't appreciate it. I'm glad I wasn't here before the causeway, it would have been too isolated . . . isolation of this kind breeds fears that are exacerbated by the confines of small communities.

'Heaven knows how, I just do my job. I'm here as shepherd of my people – I must be careful what I say . . . I'm cagey in talking, but I have to be. There's no concept for the word "ought" here . . . I ought to go to church, I ought to do this or

that. They're independent to a degree – men will come to village hall meetings late, not because they're unpunctual, just to prove they won't be disciplined.

'Whatever else they may be, they're not suburban – their natural defence against that is a kind of surliness. Personally, I think it's shyness, they're very shy at expressing themselves. What they understand is the sea, nature – I'm told that's what they talk about among themselves. I've heard that whenever they're persuaded to go away on holiday they head for other fishing areas and go looking at the water and the boats. The men are spoilt by their womenfolk, that's obvious – and if you care about them there's an underlying loyalty . . . there are patterns to their lives that nothing can alter. They're tough too. See through that window, where the tide's out? In January you'll see them gathering mussels – they'll be there hours when it's almost too cold for me inside the house.

'The main thing is this: whatever happens, rejoicing or bereavement, it affects the whole community. If you're an Islander, you're an Islander, and there's no escape, no trying to be something different – they feel and think as one. They're far narrower than even they know. I'll tell you about my daughter's wedding. I'll get the photos.'

Before the Causeway: it is less an expression, more an incantation; in the years BC life was better, life was worse. Well, in the years BC life was certainly different: the most direct route to Holy Island from the mainland was over the low tide sands, across a way marked by 270 wooden poles, many still surviving along this, the Pilgrims' Way. A further 100 poles indicated the South Low, now taken by the metalled road. Two refuge boxes built on stilts offered safety to those who misjudged the 3½ mile crossing. Even so, the sands claimed life, as parish records show:

> 'Jan. 8th 1584, old John Stapleton drowned.
> Jan. 13th 1723, Thomas Wardle and James Wilson lost in the tide.
> Jan. 24th 1796, Martha, wife of Robert Mort, a soldier, perished in the sands.'

There were more, drowned in passing the sands, in the years BC. Then pony and trap made the crossing, to be followed by model-T Fords which made a lucrative taxi service ferrying visitors from the mainland railway station at Beal to the Island . . . thus was Lindisfarne modernized when, in 1966, the final two mile stretch between Snook and Chare Ends was completed. But you must watch the tide; forget the time and you will be marooned on Holy Island the night through. There might be room at the inn, but chances are there will not – and you cannot buy a cooked meal on the Island.

The vicar's wedding album makes a pretty picture. The vicar and his wife, Minnie, who is the Island nurse, have a daughter. Mary is her name, a girl with a shapely turn of ankle. At University Mary met Bruce and they fell in love. The wedding, on a Saturday in July, was an Island affair; that is how it has to be, you cannot ask just a few friends and leave it at that. The whole Island must be invited to see that tradition is upheld: after the blessing the bride must jump the 'petting stone' supported by two fishermen – giving us a chance to glimpse a shapely ankle. The stone, situated between the chancel of the church and the Priory, is thought to be the base of a pre-Norman free-standing cross. A clear jump signifies good fortune and fertility. Next the couple is greeted by a fusilade of shots fired skywards by Island men. The lych-gates are tied by ribbon and a 'fine' must be paid before bride and groom are allowed through to their reception, when a slice of cake is passed over the bride's head, the plate being shattered on the floor.

After which there is kissing and dancing, eating and drinking, joy being shared among the Island 'family' 150 strong. The Islanders come together, close-knit in revelry at a time of giving, of laughter and happy tears. The Holy Islanders came together in celebration, all on a Saturday.

Three days later one among their number, a twenty-three-year-old male with the world to live for, climbed the stairs to the bedroom next to where his parents slept. There he placed the barrel of a shotgun against his temple and squeezed the trigger.

So it was that the Islanders came together twice in a week, both times in church. Tears were shed again – and they are a hard, tough breed who loved this young man who destroyed himself. They put him in the ground and then went home, and a pall, dark as of the devil's making, settled over Lindisfarne. This is their tragedy, this their sorrow and their secret; to discuss it is taboo.

Opinions.

'The Interlopers': Ian McGregor, sub-postmaster, came in 1964 from Ford, fourteen miles west on the mainland. 'It's a different community, nothing is planned, they live from day to day – nothing will change them. I'm "local" but that doesn't matter. I'm still an interloper . . . they're all related, if I fell out with one they'd close ranks against me . . . three times I tried to get on the parish council, three times they squeezed me out.

'The families are Luke, Kyle, Brigham, Patterson, Allison, Douglas, Lilburn, Wilson, Cromarty . . . an Islander married an Islander . . . then the causeway came and men went across to meet mainland girls at dances. The older ones resent this, as they resent tourists. If you see an Islander shopping in Berwick, you'll see twenty – they're clannish . . . mainlanders think Islanders are backward. They live to a good age, they're heavy smokers. I sell cigarettes although it's against my

principles, but they won't see it's harmful. There's a lot of beer drinking too, it's the only sociable thing to do. They're ultra-conservative – they think something different, like vegetarianism or sea-bathing, is almost sinful.

'They sit on their backsides and let the world go by – if it wasn't for the interlopers the community would fall apart. No, they haven't changed me, but if I see something I dislike I keep quiet about it – I'd never stand up to them . . . there's a vindictive streak.'

Michael Hackett is Managing Director of the Lindisfarne Liqueur Company, which he founded in 1961. Coming from County Durham, he settled on the Island for fifteen years; now he comes and goes with the tide: 'They're avaricious, you'll get on well with Islanders so long as you're giving – stop the one-way flow and hostility sets in. They think they're splendid, they're used to being told so by pub visitors . . . whom they laugh at behind their backs . . . those navigational hazard obelisks? They were telling visitors before the First World War that they were moon launching pads.

'I've nothing against them, but it's hard to find a single good quality – they've made a lifelong study of idleness and fiddling. To them I'm just "Hackett", without the "Mr" . . . "Hackett", they use it like a title. I employ thirty-two here, only one of them an Islander, they can't keep time . . . although it's *their* mead, not mine . . . they've got pride all right, so long as no effort is needed.

'There's always an undertone of battle here, a fight in the air . . . they hunt in packs, they won't stand up for a one to one situation, kindness is taken for weakness – they're cowards. The wind has something to do with it – they're in a good mood, then the wind gets up and day by day their mood grows uglier.'

Peter and Margaret Nelson retired from Leeds in 1975. He was a billiard table maker. Their house looks across the water to the mainland; it is a view you would never tire of. 'We came for a weekend and it had a massive impact on us – we knew we wanted to stay here and felt it would be possible to live with these people.

'First thing we did was to give the village hall a billiard table, then they made me treasurer of the hall. I call out the numbers at bingo. Winter is when the Island comes into its own, when the tourists go . . . there's a bit of late drinking . . . no policemen, so the pubs may stay open a few minutes longer.

'We've made friends. Ask anyone where Peter and Margaret – not Mr and Mrs Nelson – live, they'll tell you. There's Melville – he's mongol – he calls every Thursday evening for his 20p for doing the dustbins for us. He likes sweets and show jumping on TV and if he dislikes someone he'll not come near. He's forty now, the Island looks after him.

'We love their company . . . we joined them, accepted their ways, didn't expect them to accept ours. They're very jealous of being Islanders. We're interlopers, not presuming to be Islanders. If they hadn't accepted us, they'd have forced us back to Leeds.

'When that boy shot himself the whole community cried – it was like a shock wave hitting the Island. Apparently he felt no one wanted him, a persecution complex if you like . . . he was a quiet chap, thoughtful, everyone loved him.

Opinions.

From the past: 'It was in January 1907, that I commenced to pen the initial pages of the little book on Holy Island, which the general public took up so responsively,' wrote W. Halliday, schoolmaster of the day. 'The inhabitants are robust and self-reliant in character, with a fund of energy which comes well to their aid in the struggle for existence, as it did their ancestors, under different conditions

. . . they are kindhearted and hospitable. If they are brusque in manner, they are also patriotic and interested in things national. The people of the Island are kind to a degree, and it is a pleasure to see their frank but tanned and weather-beaten faces. Their physique is very fine, capable of almost boundless endurance and fatigue – a race eminently fitted for this bleak and isolated region.'

In conclusion Mr Halliday entreats visitors ' . . . as they wander o'er the sandhills and inhale the life-giving breezes of rich ozone, or quietly sit and watch the ebb and flow of the tide, to think kindly of this little Island and its inhabitants, and to send up to the Heavenly Shrine a silent prayer that this little speck of land may be blessed with peace and prosperity.'

It would seem, delving further into the past, that prosperity, if not exactly peace, also featured in the Islanders' prayers. With the Dissolution a new chapter opened on Island history: the Priory became used as 'the Queen's Majestie's storehouse', and a castle was built on Beblowe Rock – thus making Lindisfarne an important naval base . . . little of which rubbed off in improving the Islanders' lot. Isolated still and poverty-stricken, lawlessness prevailed for 300 years.

Nefarious activities were confirmed by the Governor, Robin Rugg, in 1643: 'The common people do pray for shippes which they sie in danger. They al sit downe upon their knees and hold up their handes and say very devoutedly, Lord, send her to us, God send her to us. You, seeing them upon their knees, and their handes joyned, do think that they are praying for your sauvetie; but their myndes are far from that. They pray, not God to sauve you, or send you to port, but to send you to them by shipwrack, that they may gette the spoile of her. And, to show that this is their meaning, if the shippe come wel to porte, or aschew naufrage, they get up in anger, crying, "the Devil stick her, she is away from us." '

The castle on Beblowe Rock was destined to become one of the few permanent garrisons in England, the establishment consisting of a captain, two master gunners, a master's mate and twenty soldiers. But the garrison dwindled, being withdrawn in 1819. From time to time it came into its own again – as a coastguard station, headquarters of the Northumberland Volunteers – but by 1882 the castle was abandoned and fell into ruinous condition.

In 1903 Edward Hudson and Peter Anderson Graham, founder and editor of *Country Life*, saw the possibilities. Hudson purchased the castle from the Crown, persuading his friend, architect of New Delhi and the Cenotaph, Sir Edwin Lutyens, to convert his acquisition into a private residence.

So Lindisfarne Castle came to life again, becoming the scene of house-parties still remembered by some Islanders. Among the best celebrated visitors was Madame Suggia, the cellist whose portrait by Augustus John, playing the Stradivarius given her by Hudson, hangs in the Tate Gallery. It is said that when she practised in the Castle, Islanders gathered on the rocks below to listen. It makes an appealing, if wistfully romanticized picture, to imagine the motley gathering, their frank but tanned and weather-beaten faces aglow with rapture, straining to catch Madame Suggia's notes as they were swept away by force eight gales.

Other guests included William Heinemann, Lytton Strachey, Lord Baden-Powell, Lord Asquith, Lady Violet Bonham-Carter, Madam Markova, Sir Malcolm Sargent, the Prince and Princess of Wales . . . then Hudson, surprisingly, sold the Castle in 1921 to a London banker, O. T. Falk. After a short time Falk sold to Sir Edward de Stein who, with his sister Gladys, used it as a family home until giving it to the National Trust in 1944.

Today the Castle is in care of National Trust administrators, Martin Parr and his wife Ann, who in the season escort perhaps a thousand guests a day along the galleries, through dining room, Ship Room, on to the Upper Battery . . . but somehow the fun has gone out of it, the maintenance has become a duty, a chore. The party is over, the laughter dead, Madame Suggia has played her coda. Participation is reduced to expressions of *ooh's* and *ah's*, the purchase of colour transparencies, bookmarkers, postcards. Martin and Ann Parr live in semi-isolation in a Castle flat buffeted by wind, as emotionally remote from organic Holy Island as they would be in Kensington.

Ann Parr recalls: 'We first saw the Castle in a mist, it was damp and clinging – but the Island had something, a mystery. It's out on a limb, the mystery of the tide, being imprisoned . . . it attracted us. We moved in, April 1978 it was, in a storm, a howling gale, torrential rain.

'It's still mysterious – you've got to come on the Island's terms. There's something, you can't put your finger on it, that separates these people from others. They think it's *their* Castle, they resented Sir Edward handing it over – the National Trust warned us of friction . . . ' She seems distracted, melancholic for a young woman of twenty-five. The wind howls, lashing against the windows, maniacal almost. 'We walk along the beach, collect shells, watch fulmars nesting – it's a kind of petrel . . . it makes a strange cry.'

And you can't help thinking: the Parrs are in transit, they won't stay, they're interlopers and they are not welcome. You cannot join the Islanders if they don't want you; and you can't fight them. What is the alternative? No, there must be other islands, if such is your need. Better go while the going is good. Unkind thoughts, cruel too in a way; but the evidence is accumulating.

The Islanders.

Linda Lilburn and her sister-in-law Jean share a cottage, St Oswalds, as it is named. It is the last house of the village before the harbour, looking directly towards the Castle. The sea, sky, and Castle fill their sitting room window. The Castle has filled their lives.

'When Mr Hudson bought the Castle,' says Linda, 'he saw my father, Jack

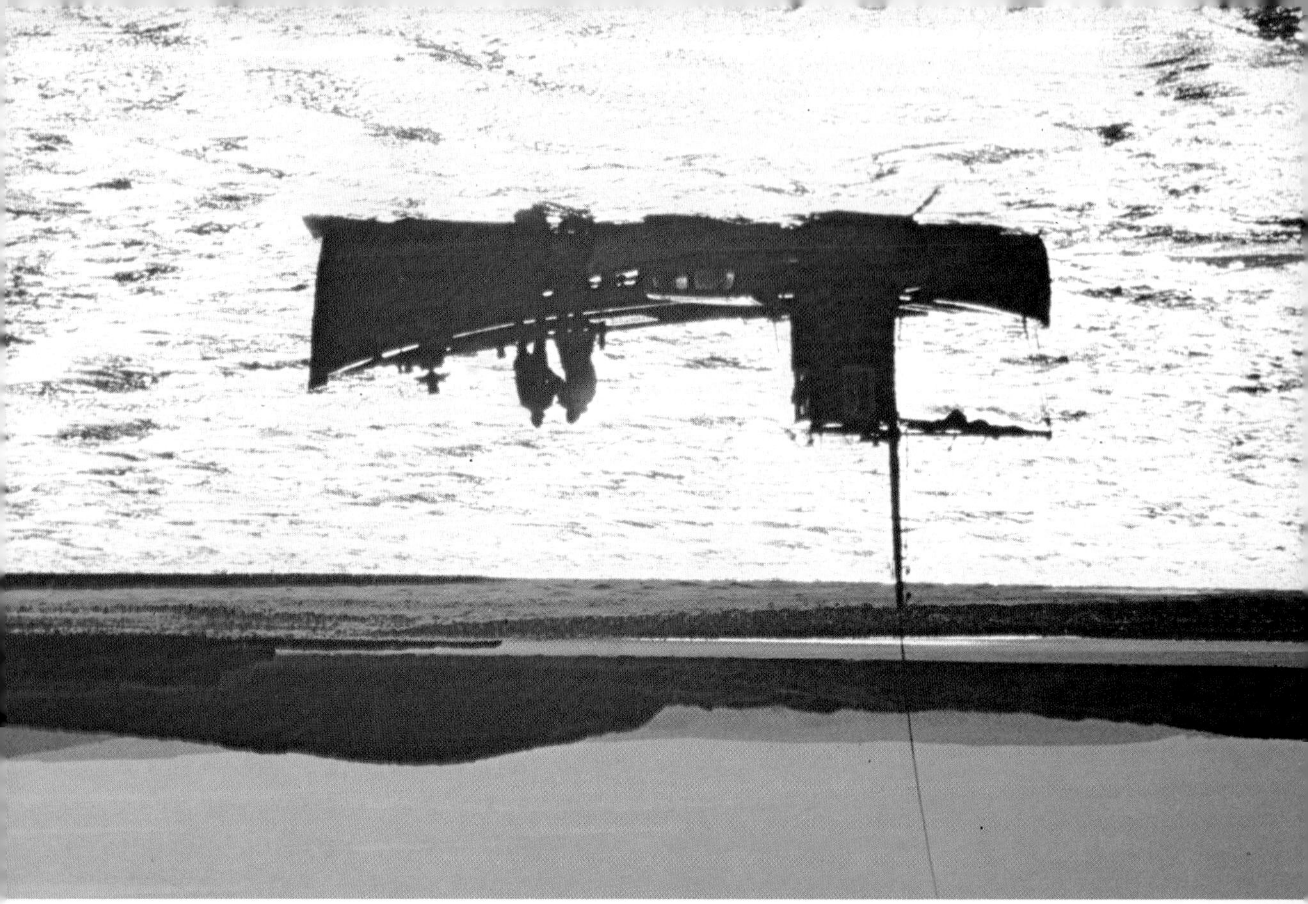

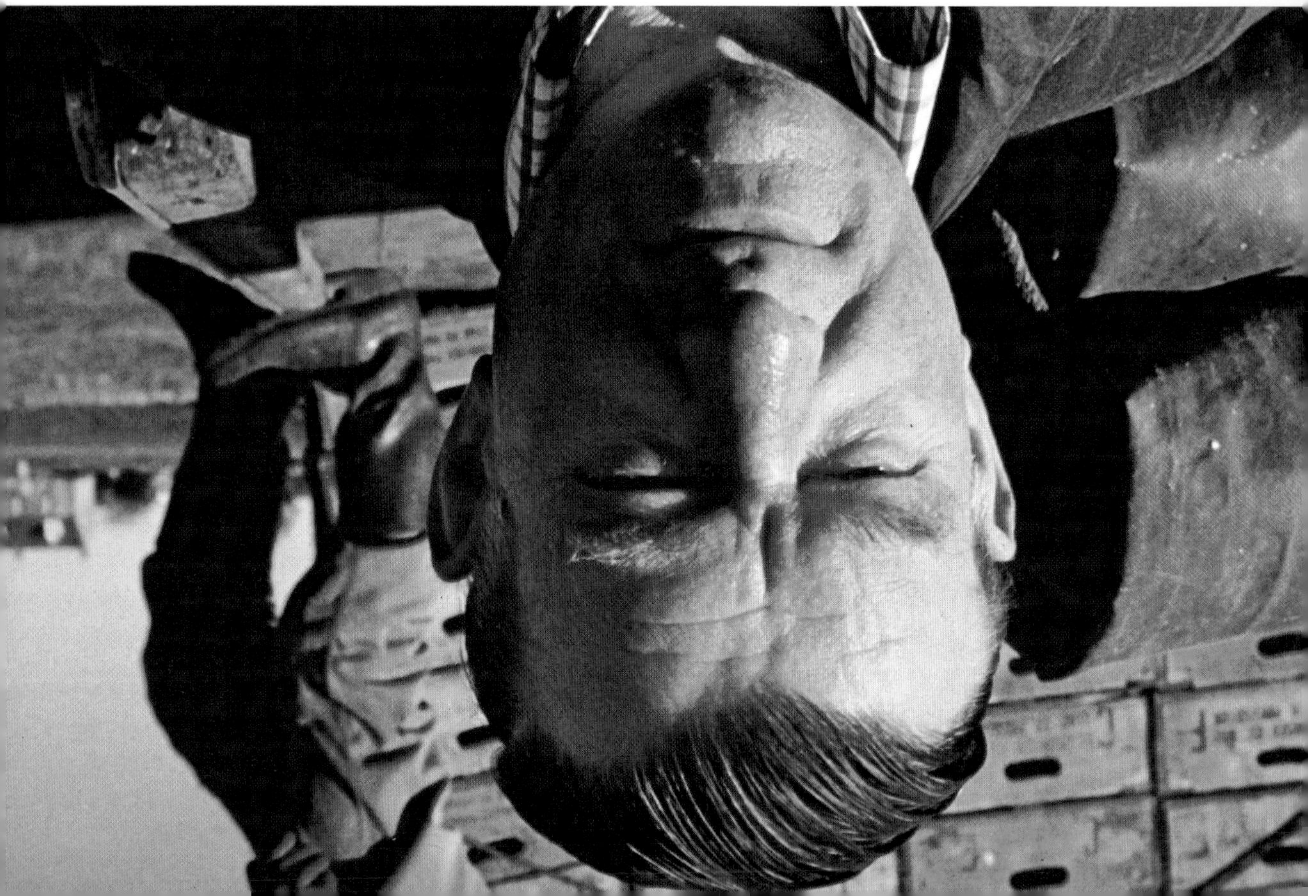

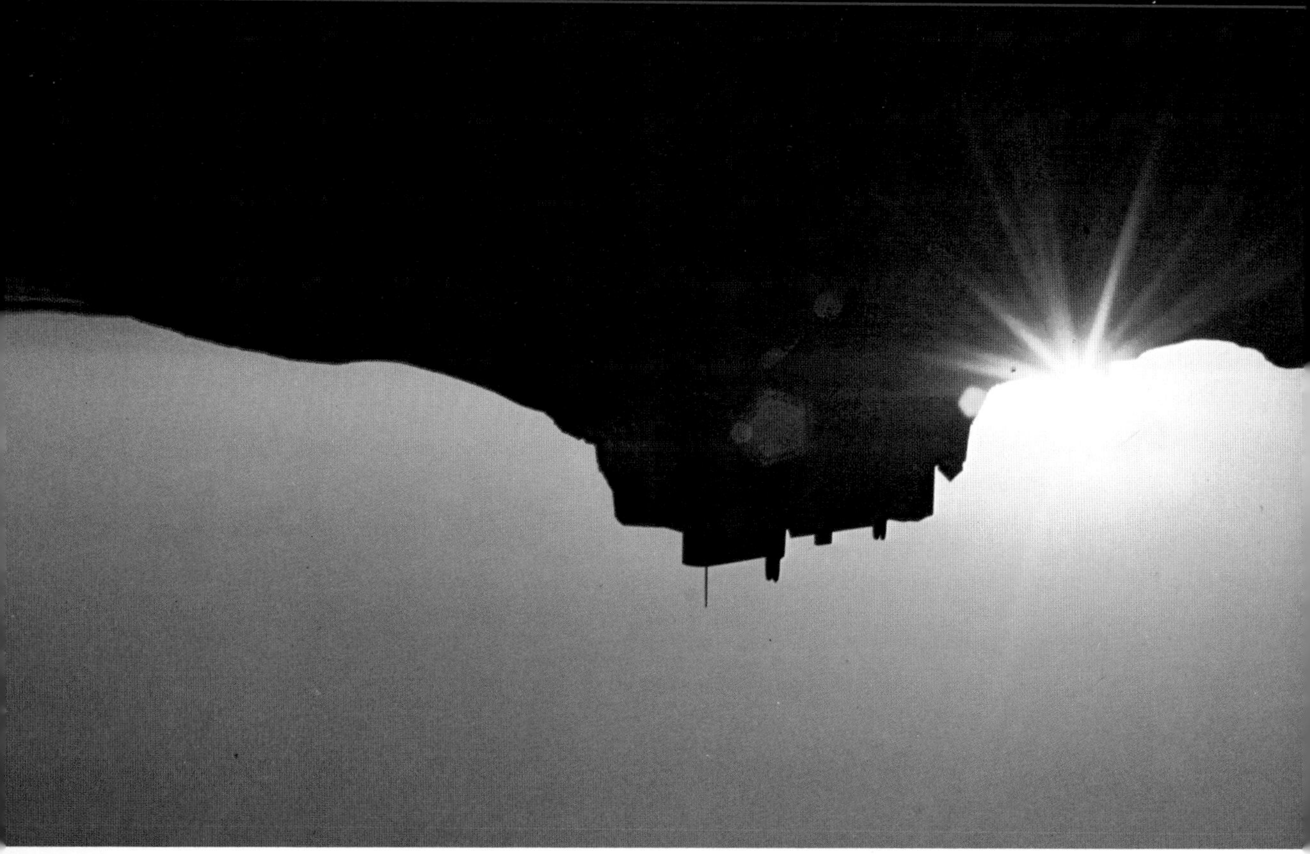

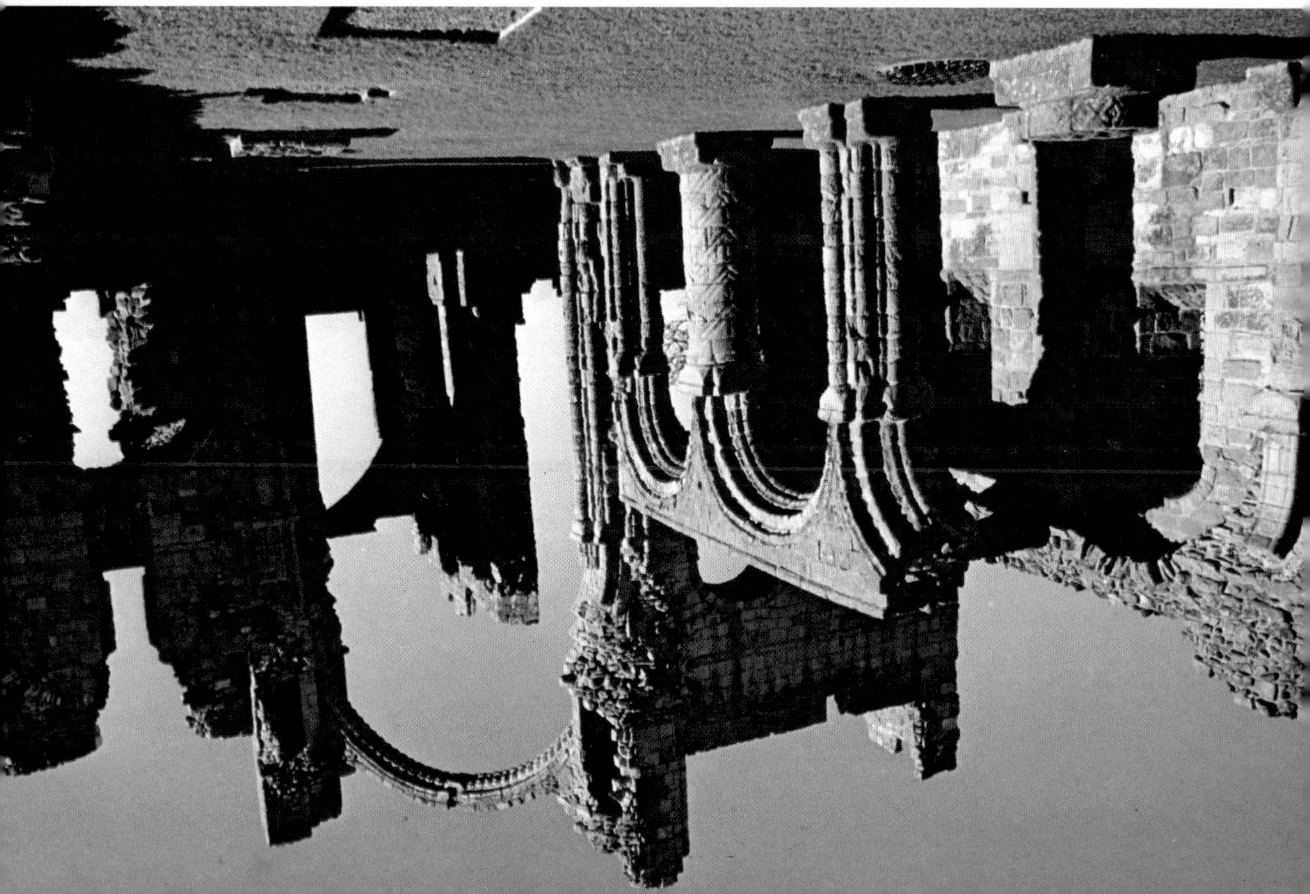

Lilburn he was, working at the boats. Father was a fisherman then. He took a fancy to father, said he had an open, honest face and that he wanted him as caretaker . . . he'd brought the rest of the staff, cook and so on, from London. Well, father went . . . he died there, so did mother, and I spent sixty years there.'

'Sixty years there,' repeats Jean. They echo one another in the way of people who have grown close.

'It was a real old castle – seventy brass candlesticks to polish . . . they're all lacquered up there today! Log fires, wood to carry, we were battened in by wind and storm – oh, it was hard . . . but it was a happy house, father liked things just so when guests were arriving . . . "the first sight's the best," he'd say. And they were such nice people, the guests, they spoke to you as equals.'

'Spoke to you as equals,' interjects Jean.

'All that fetching and carrying,' continues Linda. 'We had old Robert Kyle to help – he was simple-minded, but strong as a horse and willing . . . he'd carry groceries, coal, logs all the way to the top of the Castle. Islanders are one big family – we used to depend on the sea, women used to bait the lines. Today . . .' she starts the sentence.

' . . . we live off the tourists,' Jean completes the sentence. It is rather uncanny.

212

In 1936 Jean leaped the petting stone to marry Linda's brother George, after which she went to work at the Castle too. 'We went back last year,' she says, glancing out of the window towards the Mount, five hundred yards away, 'but it's all changed . . . it's nice, but it's just run to make money.'

'To make money,' nods Linda.

They have a lovely book on Lindisfarne and its Castle, written by P. Anderson Graham, who came to see the possibilities with Edward Hudson. It is inscribed by hand: 'To Jack Lilburn from his friend Edward Hudson, June 15th 1920.' Man to man, equal to equal.

They have been welcoming, Linda and Jean, friendly and helpful. But they haven't given much away, no secrets, no skeleton-in-the-cupboard.

In Marygate, behind a yellow door next to the Northumberland Arms lives Olive Luke. 'Northumberland Arms – N. Kyle Luke', reads the sign. 'N' for Norman, Olive's son, who runs the pub since his parents retired. Norman is taciturn, withdrawn, charging as much as he should, if not more, for his drinks . . . you could say it's a short season and a lean winter.

Olive was born in 1906, leaving school at fourteen to help her parents in the Castle pub – they took on the Northumberland in 1930, and Olive leapt the petting stone in 1936, same year as Jean.

'Father was one of eleven children,' she says. 'Grandfather, father, two brothers were all in the lifeboat crew when she overturned – no one was lost. We played in the street then, drew water from the pump twice on Saturday to preserve the Sabbath . . . electricity came in 1957 . . . always an Islander married an Islander . . . it's a proud business being an Islander . . . I've about eleven cousins on the Island, I forget how many. If we get ill? Why, Dr Byers comes over from Belford every Tuesday and leaves all the pills we need.'

She is a warm person, she'd like to help. She is expansive and reticent, both at the same time. She is very watchful. Her husband remains speechless, drawing on a cigarette, wrested no doubt from the sub-postmaster's principles. He joins in the conversation briefly, when it becomes neutral, discussing tides, how life is governed by the tides. There are no revelations, no scent to follow.

In the open once more, in the wind, down among the upturned herring boats, hulls tar-blackened, converted into stores. There are piles of fishing boxes stencilled 'Aberdeen Inshore Fishselling Co. Ltd.' But no fishermen. People do not seem to congregate as in most places, you do not see clusters gossiping on doorstep or street corner. At eight-thirty at night you hear no footsteps, no murmurs from lovers on the loose, just the wind picking and nagging with a sharper tongue than scandal. Near the harbour children have built a bonfire upon which to burn the effigy of Guy Fawkes, the fifth of November a fortnight away.

Children? There are children, ten on the Island, thirty older ones as weekly boarders in Berwick. There are old men too; they are halt, some of them, afflicted by what is known as Brigham Hip, hereditary arthritis passed down among men of the Brigham family.

Selby Allison and his brother George have Brigham Hip, Selby's is more acute . . . he has been operated on five times, is confined to a wheel-chair. He wears a tam-o'-shanter and is chirpy as a linnet, ready to sing, content to sing. 'I'm a cousin of Brigham, a cousin of Patterson too – mother was a Brigham, born and died at the Crown and Anchor . . . grandfather was a fisherman. Sixty-five boats then, now it's the odd five. I ran the pub there for forty-eight years . . . one blow struck in anger in all that time. We ran a pony and trap service to the mainland – England, as I call it – then motor taxis, aye.

'Used to shoot a punt gun – widgeon, brent geese – out on Fenham Flats. Marry? No, neither me nor George married, too busy both of us. My sister and aunty cooked for us – they've died, so I'm learning.'

He propels himself towards the front door as if warming up for a Brands Hatch circuit. 'I still get out for a drink twice a day. Going to see George Kyle are you then . . . oh, aye.'

His attitude does not change; his expression does not alter. 'Oh, aye,' he says.

Exploring Holy Island is like being in a psychological maze; it is punctuated with false starts, dead ends, clues that lead nowhere. It is different, different and complex. Like the dialect, heavily Scottish, yet as you listen it is laden with undertones, a gutturalism from across the water, from the Norse or the Low Countries. It is quite inimitable.

You cannot probe, ask too many questions or too pointed. There is a code, ritualistic, cabbalistic. It must be observed, respected; or there will be penalties.

The Shopkeeper.

Kyle's Souvenirs. Fancy Goods & Toys, Postcards, Confectionery, Pop, Fruit & Groceries. There is a board on the wall of a long, low dwelling in Fenkle Street, facing Market Place. There is a penny weighing-machine outside, souvenir mugs in the window. 'To my wife and sweetheart, may they never meet,' it reads on one; 'I'm boss in this house and I have my wife's permission to say so,' on another. Kyle's sells Lindisfarne Fudge, Holy Island Rock, Milk of Magnesia, Aspirin, beach balls and baked beans, Sellotape and Scott's Porage Oats, apples and pears, Treets and Munchies, funny hats and tennis bats, over-heated love stories in paperback and frozen cod in breadcrumbs.

There are no wire-framed perambulators for humping your purchases; neither is there a line of check-out girls in nylon overalls – just Mrs Kyle, Lina, at the till. Both George and Lina serve in the shop, keeping overheads down. It is the only grocery shop on the island. During the season there are well over a quarter of a million visitors . . . Kyle's must be a gold mine.

214

George has been in a Newcastle hospital for tests; he returned on the evening tide. He gets abdominal pains, but tests reveal no cause, doctors can find nothing wrong. He is a thick-set man with high colour in his cheeks, hair showing no grey, black still, well cut and combed. He has green eyes, closely set, wary – Islanders' eyes.

Despite an appointment made a week ago, he does not think he can spare much time; his wife says she really can't get involved and returns to the counter. George settles into a sofa. There is little sympathy in his look, scant encouragement in his manner. He is flushed, his eyes hot.

Born in 1919, his forbears had all been Island fishermen, until his father, Ben: 'He never went fishing, he started the shop in 1920. Mother came to the Island from Scotland, I was their only child. We were poor, you realized your parents couldn't afford to keep you so you went out to work as soon as you could . . . we never went hungry, there was always plenty of fish.

'I came into the shop because I wouldn't like knowing that every Friday my pay packet would be fifty quid come what may . . . I like private enterprise – although when you're in business you've got to keep your mouth shut. But I'll tell you, the fishermen aren't partial to weekenders, that's pub talk . . . some of them, the fishermen, remember hard times with women baiting sixty score of hooks – they'd shell mussels, then hook them, all for three bob from five in the morning.

'Two sons we had. George runs the Manor guest-house – no, he doesn't own it . . . it's owned by the Lord of the Manor, Colonel Crossman, he's got a place on the mainland. The other son, Ben, worked in the shop here . . . he died.'

Recently George Kyle put the business on the market: when it's doing so well too. 'We've had enough,' George says. 'We need a rest. Only good thing about it is we still take the customers' cash however nasty they are. It'll be better to have the money before we've one foot in the grave. Tell you the truth, I'm sick and tired of holiday makers.'

There is silence, not an easeful silence as between friends or those who understand one another; more listless. George answers questions with apathy, a huge weariness, resenting intrusion.

He again mentions his visit to Newcastle: 'I feel sorry for those people, they're pushed around. No, the hospital couldn't find anything wrong with me – perhaps you just get more aches and pains at sixty than you do at sixteen.'

He talks about Lindisfarne's New Year custom: Islanders, armed with bottles of whisky, call on every household, pour out a tot for each host, moving on down the street. There are, apparently, those who fall by the wayside. A couple of years ago there was a bit of a scene when an interloper, insisting on being one of the boys, became insultingly drunk.

Suddenly there is nothing to discuss; the atmosphere is arid, it is pointless to continue.

*

George Kyle could have said so much more. There is one thing he could have said that would explain everything, that could only be received with humility and compassion. The boy who killed himself three days after Mary's wedding was his son, Ben. This is the truth, this was how it happened.

The
Country
Journalist

CHAPTER XVI

THE COUNTRY JOURNALIST

Robert Gregson Shepherd

His parents were Bob Shepherd's sun and moon, adored in life, venerated in death. He could talk about them till the cows come home – not that cows do come home along the Fylde coast of Lancashire. The land is not notable for grazing pasture. There is dark loam, wonderful soil; and there are outskirts of mosslands or ancient peat bogs in the area between Stalmine, Garstang and Cockerham; but it is not the stuff for cattle.

In the Ice Age glaciers slithered down from what is now Cumbria, gathering volcanic stone from the mountains, mostly boulders of slate or granite. They ground them into powder, compressed them into clay. When the glaciers melted, the clay remained in heaps; and one of those heaps is Preesall, where in springtime Arthur Shepherd courted Mary Jane Anderson.

'The countryside was full of "characters",' laments Arthur's son, Bob. 'That is – individuals. We look back nostalgically to them now, when everyone dreads being unlike anyone else. We're sheep, running wherever the dogs of bureaucracy and the media direct us – probably over a cliff before we're finished.

'Among the characters I knew father held a high place . . . he began to be an individual as soon as possible, with his christening. He was first of the Shepherds to be named Arthur. His father was Richard, grandfather Obadiah, great-grand-father, who married in 1799, another Richard. He went to the village school when schooling was part-time, mostly in winter after the potatoes were lifted. Children wrote on slates and little boys wore petticoats until they were four or five. On Mondays they gave the teacher twopence; if the family couldn't afford it they'd give peat turf to put on the fire . . . there's a local saying about turf: "Torf warms ya five times – when ya delve it, when ya winrow it, when ya robin it, when ya stack it, and when ya burn it."

'The child production of the last generation was extraordinary – it allowed for wastage, death in infancy. They needed a labour reserve, strong healthy workers at ten years old . . . and winters were long, there was no Dr Marie Stopes. You'd hear: "Aye, I've had twelve an' reared eight of 'em."

'When father grew up he became a farm labourer – with a bit of pig-sticking on

the side. I remember helping him, I'd catch the blood coming from the animal's throat and keep stirring it in a bucket so it wouldn't coagulate for when it was used in black pudding. He graduated later to driving the travelling steam thresher . . . finally he got a job at the Preesall salt mine pumping station, in charge of the horizontal steam engines.

'He was a stocky man, with a square face and a ragged moustache. He had a settled speed of work – slow to middling – that he shared with all the Shepherds. Used to tell me he excelled at pole-vaulting at village sports, but I can't imagine it – it's far too energetic. He was famous for his unflappability, which he developed long before Harold Macmillan was heard of.

'He had a fine tenor voice, and a passion for music which he developed in the choir. He couldn't read music in what he called "th'owd notation", so he had a treasured hymn-book and psalter in tonic sol-fa . . . he was making his way home one night after he'd been blowing the organ for me to practise, pushing his bicycle because he didn't have a lamp, of course – and the dear old vicar saw him:

"What makes you walk, Arthur? Have you got a puncture?" said he.

"No," said my father. "You'll know the story of the unwise virgins who had no oil in their lamps when the bridegroom came?"

"Certainly, Arthur, certainly," said the vicar.

"Well, I'm worse than them. I've getten no lamp!" '

Like father, like son. Bob Shepherd says of his father: 'He was a delightful fellow, not exactly happy-go-lucky or lethargic, more that he didn't go looking for work, he was quiet, philosophical – "Come-day, go-day, God send Sunday," was his attitude.' By his own admission, Bob has inherited the strain. He is not a man to be rushed. He tells his story in his own good time, puffing imperturbably at his pipe; he will not take any short-cuts – if you want to hear about his life, you must listen as it happened, month by month, from the cradle to this very mid-November day.

He fills his pipe from a pouch. The pipe has a metallic alloy joint that shines like an artificial limb. His lighter is made of gun metal, a contraption of wicks, flints and petrol – when it doesn't quite ignite, it gives off muffled crumps like distant gunfire. Once the pipe is going he sits bandaged in smoke, his eyes a little watery.

'There was a stubborn insularity in Preesall, everyone was related, it was one huge family. We said that if you trod on someone's foot on Monday, the whole village would be limping by Tuesday. Newcomers were suspect. "He's getten nuboddy in t'churchyard yet," we'd say of a newcomer. There were words of wisdom: "Never marry ower t'midden," was one . . . never marry a girl from outside the village because you don't know all about her family.'

So it must have created quite a stir when Arthur did just that – married a girl not really of the village. Mary Jane's father came from Wincham in Cheshire; he was a mining surveyor who had come to Preesall to bore holes for the salt mines. Salt miners from Cheshire came in scores at the time – the 'Northwich invasion' – and they were none too welcome. For one thing, their dialects were so different they could barely make themselves understood. The newsagent, used to being asked for the 'Dayally Mayal', had new customers wanting the 'Deely Meel'. A Preesall man, asking a friend if he were going to Fleetwood Market next Friday, would say, 'Arta bahn t'Fleetwood Market o' Frida?' But a Northwicher would ask 'Arya gewin Fleightwood Markit Froydee?'

Neither was the divide between Arthur and Mary Jane simply one of language: 'My maternal grandfather', Bob relates, 'was a respected, fairly prosperous, leading Congregationalist. He was straight-laced, wore a Churchill hat, not bowler, nor topper . . . father was just a labourer, odd-job man. Mother too was intensely religious, with strong sense of duty and an overflowing desire for Victorian virtues. Then there was a big difference between Church of England and Chapel . . . there were two farming families, the Kays and the Threlfalls – they were great friends during the week, but on Sundays the Kays walked to the village fifty yards ahead of the Threlfalls, never uttering a word. Anglicans took precedence, you see.'

Nevertheless, the couple married, parental consent was granted, the main priorities being that a woman could bake a loaf and sew. It seems also that Mary Jane made more concessions than her labouring husband: 'Mother, devout Congregationalist that she was, wished to continue her own form of worship, to which father raised no objection – but when she realized that he went to church, she gave up chapel to attend church with her husband. She was never baptized or confirmed, she just felt it was her duty to worship with her husband. She was a dear person, handsome, her hair in a bun, immensely house-proud and thrifty.' Like most Preesall people, they paid their way, they were self-supporting, living off the land and the sea. An occasional rabbit or hare came their way; they collected cockles and mussels on the Pilling sands. Then, in 1896, their first son Arthur was born.

A bright lad he turned out to be: winning a scholarship from the village school to Lancaster Royal Grammar, from where he would pedal home on Friday evening, returning on Sunday with clean clothes, to lodge with Mrs Woods in Wingate Saul Road.

'It was a meagre scholarship, how they maintained him I'll never know. Father gave mother his wages on Friday and when she'd paid the bills she had sixpence to last the week. One Monday she knelt to pray about the money lasting and next morning my brother's travelling allowance came in the post . . . such was her simple faith.'

Arthur, the academic star of Preesall, won an Exhibition to London University. It was unheard of in the village. He was due to begin in October 1914; but in August Kaiser Bill's war broke out and Arthur volunteered, naturally: 'He had to in a way – he was swept along on a wave of patriotism, another victim of propaganda . . . people actually believed that Germans ate little children.

'There was the idea of "striking at the soft underbelly of Turkey", so an expeditionary force was sent up the Euphrates under the command of General Townshend, a member of that great Cheshire family who owned estates in the district where mother was born. It was a bungled affair – at Kut-el-Amara the wily Turk did a pincer movement, which wasn't considered quite sporting, cutting them off. It was Mafeking all over again . . . a relief expedition was sent, with brother Arthur among their number.'

Mary Jane in Preesall, Lancashire, wrote frequently to her son Arthur in Mesopotamia. This is one of her letters, written in April 1916:

My dear son,

It was with great pleasure that we received two field cards from you yesterday morning. One was dated March 18 and the other March 22. We are so glad to know that you are well; it lifts a great load from our minds.

But we are very disappointed that you are not getting our letters. It is very hard for you to be such an awful long way from home and not to hear from us.

We keep writing every week, and we have registered a lot of letters to see if you would get them any better . . . one contained my photograph . . . I sent two pairs of socks in the last parcel, and in the one before I sent cocoa ready mixed.

We are all keeping in good health. Your Aunt Sarah is a good deal better than she has been for a long time, as she has been poorly all winter. All your pals are going on all right. We are having fine spring weather now; everything is looking nice and fresh after the long spell of winter. Your dad will write next time. Be a good lad.

The Squire and family are coming to Parrox Hall soon; the servants have been there for some weeks. We had a nice service at church last Sunday. It was Easter Sunday. There were 83 at Holy Communion at 8 a.m., and a service on Good Friday morning and a lantern lecture in the evening.

The Scouts gave a very nice concert last night in the school in which most of them took part; also the Misses Gooding, Worsley, Hall, Hayhurst and several others. There was a very good attendance. The vicar and curate spoke very nicely . . .

I must close now with fond love in which dad, Aunt Sarah, Uncle Arthur, Aunt Lizzie and all friends join me.

My dear, dear lad – I keep praying for you and hope that God will bless you.

Your loving mother.

221

CRABTREE
SALE
Students at risk —Poly chief
Flats blaze man dies after escape
POOL BANK ON ANOTHER JOHNSTON
SPORTS COUNCIL BLAST 'LAME DUCKS'
McEwan joins injury parade
Blackpool Schools call for backing
She's beautiful

Arthur never received the letter. Mary Jane's dear, dear lad had been dead for a week before it was even written. It was returned to her with the small belongings he had left at base before he went into the line. So the Exhibition at London University went to someone else, and Arthur's name went on to Preesall's war memorial.

Bob Shepherd, surviving brother and country journalist, has written: 'Mother lived to be an old woman; but on her gravestone are the words she carried in her heart for all those years – "Until the day breaks". And so November comes round once more, with its cold and mist and fallen leaves – and the countryside full of interest for those that have eyes to see. Wild geese cross the sky, talking incessantly to each other in their strange gabble. You may hear them at night although you cannot see them.'

Of his father he wrote: 'Poor old dad! When he was in his early seventies he contracted gangrene from diabetes. They didn't know about antibiotics then, and he had to have his leg amputated at the thigh. He sat in his chair patiently and watched the world go by until, when the other leg was showing signs of infection, a seizure mercifully and instantly carried him off.

'Yes – a "character". And for another reason, too. For the whole of his life, so far as I know, he never got into bed without first kneeling down in his old-fashioned nightshirt and saying the Lord's Prayer.'

Bob, born in 1905, followed his brother to the village school; but at nine polio paralyzed his right leg and no one knew how to treat it. Because of this he lost a lot of time at school and was disqualified from taking the scholarship exam: 'But somehow mother got me into Blackpool Grammar School as a fee-payer at three guineas a term . . . sounds nothing, but it was a lot to us. I biked to Knott End ferry, over to Fleetwood to catch the 8.06 am train to Blackpool.

'One of my friends at school was Alistair Cooke – the BBC lad, you know. His father was an insurance broker at North Shore. Alistair succeeded me as editor of the school magazine . . . oh, he was bright, he had all his buttons on – he's kept the same size in hats too.'

There is a photograph of the cricket team, young men in striped blazers, with a walrus-moustached master; second from the left in the back row stands R. G. Shepherd, who made the first XI despite polio, next to him, sartorial, not a hair out of place, is A. A. Cooke. Another photograph, in the school magazine, shows A. A. Cooke again, bewigged this time, for his role in *She Stoops to Conquer*.

'The headmaster was a snob of the first order,' reflects Bob, 'but by God he turned out gentlemen who could hold their own with the world.' Alistair Cooke seems to share his old friend's regard for their late head; writing of his days at Blackpool Grammar he has said: 'The Secondary School as it was then called, was known to the townspeople as a fount of learning and also as rather a toney place where some boys grew too big for their breeches. To its Headmaster, the inimitable Mr Joseph Turral, it was an oasis of gentility in the desert of the North Country, a fortified town holding the seige against the surrounding Philistines . . . he dominated the school and everyone in it. He is the one great Dickensian character that Dickens forgot to invent.'

In the same recollection Alistair Cooke recalls: ' . . . Phyllis Dunkerley teaching the valeta in the Memorial Hall just before Christmas, and the brunette who hung over the piano as you played "Blue Skies". The picnics to the Pennines. Sports Day and R. G. Shepherd lugging his game leg over the bar to win the high jump.'

But the inimitable, and doubtless inestimable, Mr Joseph Turral, cannot be allowed to take all credit for turning R. G. Shepherd loose upon the world a fit chap for society. Older brother Arthur took a hand in things too, for he had left behind his books for Bob to read: 'He only had about half a dozen, but they meant a lot to me . . . *Pilgrim's Progress, Kidnapped* – but it was *Tom Brown's Schooldays* that made the biggest impression. It was in vogue at the time for Oxford and Cambridge undergraduates to take themselves off on Alpine holidays, clutching their Virgil . . . the modern equivalent of the Great Tour.

'Well, Thomas Hughes said in *Tom Brown's Schooldays* that there was enough of interest within three miles of any English village to last a reasonable man all his life . . . I lived in the village of my birth over seventy years and he was right. Day after day, season after season, year after year, there is something new to be noted. And in a village one is conscious of being part of a long history, one of a long procession of people who have passed this way and who have left their marks and their memories.'

R. G. Shepherd's parents could not afford to keep him at Blackpool Grammar beyond his sixteenth birthday; but the headmaster had other views. There were, he explained, certain funds at his disposal . . . the question of fees in this case could be forgotten. So Bob stayed on until he was eighteen, when he applied for a job on the *Blackpool Gazette & Herald.* There was no vacancy, but he was taken on by the *Fleetwood Chronicle* as a junior reporter at ten shillings a week.

Newspaper reporters did not use typewriters in 1923, but Bob Shepherd, who had already studied shorthand, developed fast and legible 'penmanship'. His area of coverage was home ground: the Over Wyre villages of Preesall, Stalmine, Hambleton and Pilling; his subjects, anything that made the wheels of village life revolve – births, deaths, whist drives, weddings, two-headed chickens, quadruplet lambs, giant mushrooms, potatoes shaped in the image of leading politicians.

'Bazaars and garden parties,' he recollects. 'Local council meetings and football matches, peat moss blazes and subsidences, concerts and suicides . . . I wonder if anyone was as close to the life of the countryside as I was then? And the people . . . farmers and their wives, blacksmiths, carpenters, cobblers, labourers, parsons, all moving in the still unspoiled country scene through all the seasons . . . happy days and lucky me!'

In 1929 the *Evening Gazette* invited Bob to join the reporting staff. Daily he took the ferry from Knott End to Fleetwood, again catching the train to Blackpool as he had done in schooldays; but eventually he found digs near the office, immersing himself in what he then referred to as the 'glamour of journalism'.

'I confess I liked the aura. If I had to look into my heart I'd have to say that the main attraction was egoism – you think you've got something to say to interest people. Vanity it was . . . and vanity feeds on vanity.

'And the people one met . . . the controversial rector of Stiffkey who claimed his vocation was to save London's fallen women – one never fully understood whether his interest in fallen women was entirely altruistic. Anyway, he ended up being mauled to death by a lion . . . they made a musical play about him. It was not a success, I believe. Then I interviewed Edgar Wallace who stayed at the Metropole Hotel when he was campaigning for the liberals in Blackpool . . . a most flamboyant figure in that famous silk dressing gown and cigarette holder a yard long – what a man, an honest man. Then there was the editor himself, he was god was Harold Grime, now Sir Harold. He still goes in, just like his father in his old age – " . . . to make myself a nuisance and to annoy these whizz-kids who run things now."

'Journalism has changed, it's slicker, more flashy than in my time. What people wanted then was a good read, today they want headlines, something they can skim. We journalists were becoming respectable . . . I was envied in Preesall, which was opening up too, the horizons were widening. It was a sophisticated world, it brought me out – I was pretty well equipped with spelling, grammar, and so on. Today I writhe when someone writes "imply" when he means "infer", or "disinterested" when he means "uninterested" . . . solecisms like "meet up with", "meaningful discussion", "at this moment in time". We were always told: "Write it as Mrs Smith can understand" – Mrs Smith being the admirable woman who does the washing. So the standard of English had to be exact.

'No, I never hankered after Fleet Street or Manchester. Maybe I could see what was coming . . . maybe I was cowardly, I was safe where I was in the country, a big fish in a small pond. I also liked what newspapers were about – a paper sold chiefly by getting more news, better news, on the street before its competitor. News today, quoth he sounding like a disgruntled Methuselah, has to do with the shape of a footballer's eyebrows, the endless saga of Rod and Bianca, tittle-tattle about Prince Charles, endless trivia that doesn't matter.

'It will get worse, the appetite is shaped by what it's fed on. I don't expect everyone to read *The Times*, but the so-called popular press should have more integrity, intelligence, humour – look at them, so much flap-doodle.'

On 20 April 1931 Bob married Jennet Wilkinson, who came from a long line of Preesall builders. Bob took the day off, meeting Jennet at the bus stop as she came in from Preesall. They 'picked up' a couple of witnesses and took their vows at Blackpool's Marton parish church. That evening they went to the pictures to see *The White Hell of Pitz-Palu* showing at the Grand. After the show Bob took Jennet back to the bus station to see her off back to Preesall. She went home to tell her parents, to show them the ring. Bob wrote to let his parents know. They didn't meet again until the following weekend.

'Oh, it may have been the Shepherd way of doing things – it saved a lot of effort. It was a "village" marriage . . . I inherited the Faircloughs, Thorntons, Warbricks and Bramwells – she inherited the Jenkinsons, Cooksons, Gardners and Dobsons. The village was one big family, as I said.'

Eventually they rented a Blackpool house for ten shillings a week. At twenty-eight Bob was appointed editor of the *Fleetwood Chronicle* where he remained until 1946; then he was made deputy editor and leader writer of the *Evening Gazette* until his retirement in 1970. The years went by; Jennet had Arthur, Celia and Peter; Bob applied himself to his quiet passion, his *'In the Country'* weekly articles appearing, as they still do, each Saturday.

'My writing is journalism, written for instant effect. I hate sentimentality,

investing birds and dogs with human emotions – that's rubbish. My recipe is that if I see something that interests me and arouses an emotion . . . if it does that to me, it'll do the same to others. It's a trade, like being an electrician. I couldn't handle a novel, because I couldn't invent . . . I've no need to manufacture situations about the countryside because it's all there – in memories, in memories of the dead, the seasons, the village. People come to the country for peace, more and more come, and their numbers destroy what they were looking for. But the surrounding country remains intact, snow on hills doesn't change, hoar frost doesn't change.

'For forty-seven years I've written fifty-two articles a year on the countryside . . . that's 2,382 articles, and it's only scratching the surface . . . it's very frustrating.'

Finding the garden of their Preesall bungalow too much for them, Bob and Jennet moved a few miles to Glasson Dock in 1975. Six months later Jennet died of cancer. Bob is alone; but it is not too bad because his son Peter and his wife Jane run the Victoria Hotel down by the docks. Most days Bob drives his Toyota down to the bar, where Jane serves him steak and kidney pie and a pot of tea. 'Jane is a Shepherd too,' Bob informs. 'She didn't need to change her name because she's a cousin of Peter's.'

Jane, approaching forty, is a woman who attracts lame ducks; they come to her, knowing she will help. Invariably, she does. She is formal in her attitude to Bob, addressing him as 'Mr Shepherd'. She tells you excitedly, on the side, that she and Peter are going abroad for the first time, a week in Tenerife: 'When I told Mr Shepherd – he's never been out of England – we were going, he sniffed and said we'd be better off in Blackpool.'

Opposite the Victoria is a caravan dispensing hamburgers, hot dogs and milkshakes; yards away is the Ba-Ba-Gee floating restaurant. There is a yacht basin offering mooring to spruce seaworthy vessels and a few paunchy gin-palaces. Cargo ships still trade in scrap iron, fertilizer, timber; but the traffic is not vast. It is an appealing place, tangy with salt, not tarted up; but Bob is anxious to be away. You can tell when he is restive; his bad leg fidgets all the time.

He is not a mechanical man; he has a job to make his lighter work and it is much the same with the Toyota – it stalls so that you wonder if he has filled the petrol tank recently. He does not always engage the correct gear for the occasion; to tell the truth, he rarely uses gears at all, being inclined to select one more or less

228

at random, ignoring it for the rest of the journey. Motorists in furious Fords overtake, hooting and glaring; Bob appears not to notice.

'There's Preesall Village School,' he takes both hands off the wheel to point out a Victorian building atop a hill. 'That slope's where Jennet slid as a lass, dirtying her knickers . . . that's 39 Elletson Terrace where I was born . . . there's our bungalow, Milroyd . . . and now we descend into hell.'

You can see what he means: Preesall has been 'developed', that blessed word. The village has been submerged, suburbanized, subverted if you care. No more the fields, the ponds, barns, bakery and blacksmith; Preesall shows a face which has undergone cosmetic surgery. A signboard reads: 'For Sale – 2, 3, 4 bed detached and semi-detached. Built by S. Kelly & Brothers Ltd.' Villas are named Orion, Nimrod, The Tudors, Mandalay; there is a Laundromat, Wyre Salad Bowl.

Bob Shepherd clenches his teeth, his bad leg twitches: 'I may preach the virtues of lost values, but I can be scathing at times . . . the Morecambe Peninsula – the Heysham Power Station will spread all over that lovely land. I preach the gospel that it's all very fine, but when we've developed all the fields, what will we eat? What will happen when the energy is exhausted, when there are *real* shortages – people will fight for them . . . yes, I mean civil war.

'I see a future of unremitting bleakness . . . we're wondering, half of us, how we'll keep warm in winter. I think the country has become damned and I don't know the remedy. Even in Lancaster it's not safe for old people to live alone – the basic moralities my generation was taught do not exist. You do as you like and to hell with anyone else – there's violence, instability all around. The good old days were quite often bad old days, primitive, poor; but we took it as a way of life and we were happy. It makes me chuckle when I hear men complaining that they can't make do on £150 a week.'

He has parked the car on the hard above the ferry terminal. A strip of grey, turbulent water separates Knott End from Fleetwood. The ferry is a ramshackle affair, open deck, thudding through the waves every half hour. On the shore a handful of old people are scavenging, filling carrier bags, sacks, with driftwood, feverishly, as if they have heard Bob's warning about winter warmth. For once Bob is silent, his chin lowered.

Back in his Glasson sitting room, he struggles with his pipe again while tea stews in a pot. At four-thirty it is almost dark, rain drumming at the window with impatient fingers. It would be good to see a live fire instead of fake logs that glow, tonsil pink, at the flick of a switch. He is getting on, he is beginning to talk like an old man, ranting against progress as do all old men; he is becoming querulous. Any moment he will say: In my young days.

'In my young days,' he says, 'we believed in Beecham's Powder and instinct – it's gone because we've lost the basic, cardinal virtues, through exploitation, brainwashing, the creation of false values by the powers of persuasion, adver-

229

tising,, the glibness of non-entities on TV . . . the young who think they're so original and individual are real conformists in the uniform of dirty jeans . . . "blah-blah, OUT, blah-blah-OUT", they chant.

'I know – I'm falling into the perennial trap of all old men . . . like the story of the old fellow of ninety-six being interviewed. "You must have seen a lot of changes in ninety-six years?" he was asked. "Aye," he replied, "and I've opposed every one."

'All the same, I wish I could see a solution except the impossible one of returning to the old virtues. How can one hope for an intelligent outlook when you listen to little children singing the inane jingles they hear on television? Politicians have instant remedies, but there's no such thing . . . there's more sense in my old mother-in-law, still going at ninety-eight. She was remembering a while ago the biggest treat of the year when she was a girl. It was the Sunday School outing to Blackpool . . . she said everyone spent six months before looking forward to it, the following six months recalling what a wonderful day it had been.'

R. G. Shepherd never became a famous journalist, his is not a household name like that of his pal in the first XI, A. A. Cooke. He did not really want it that way, his interests were never on an international scale; he was fettered by the village, a willing captive. He wrote about The Rocking Chair, Girls on Horses, Pilling Lads, Cormorants, Tons of Daffodils, Old Bella, Postman Peter . . . these are the headings of some of his pieces. They are lovely pieces.

This is how he begins 'A Good Winter': 'Most people say that it has been a bad winter. But not we who live close to the soil. There has been rain, gales, frost and some snow. Those – except the gales – are just what we need in winter to make the land ready to grow the food that we all need. A soft winter is little use to anyone. So let us count our blessings.'

This is his ending: 'There is no generation gap in a farming family. The young understand the wisdom of the old, and the old understand the eagerness of the young; and each in turn takes its place in the patterns of the land and the seasons that go on for ever and ever.'

The future? 'Oh, I shall sit here getting poorer and poorer, more and more feeble – and then I shall join Jennet in Preesall cemetery. I get a certain happiness in surveying my gradual deterioration – it doesn't bother me . . . I'm interested in people and I'm a person, it's like being one's own guinea pig. It's curious to think this same body played cricket for twenty years, scored the only century ever made by Preesall Cricket Club . . . today I can't walk fifty yards without getting cramp.'

So Bob sits, not unlike his father, patiently, watching the world go by. The only sadness is that his is a doom-watch. Yet even in his summing up he uses the poetry of country lore: 'We're like gnats dancing in the sunshine, oblivious of the storm clouds building up.'

The
Gardener

CHAPTER XVII
THE GARDENER

Oliver John Morris

'If you want the truth instead of pretty talk . . . well, I'm a stranger in my own village. I can walk the length of the High Street and not see a face I grew up with.

'In my time the place was alive, you heard the sound of children playing on the green, laughing. There's no kids today, not on the green – they're untidy in a beauty spot, so they're hidden away on the council estates. Not that their mums would let them come with all this traffic. The families I knew have gone. Where? Factories, of course, factories in Coventry, Oxford, Tewkesbury. There's not a score of men tied to agriculture in Broadway today.

'The winds of change blow pretty often down this street – people come and go like flies. It's not a Cotswold village any more, it's an international village: Americans, Dutch, Arabs I shouldn't wonder . . . whizz-kids from Brum. Some of the newcomers walk straight through you – they must live in a very small world. Funny, we've become a Mecca for successful Brummies . . . until they discover they can't join what we call the Magic Circle. No, not the gentry, there's precious few of them left . . . just the social circle. So they clear off, carting their money with them. I *hate* money, always hated it. They don't take their culture with them because they don't have any. No bloody culture and no bloody taste either.

'Some of them are interesting, I suppose, but I keep at arm's length. Some you never see, they hibernate behind drawn curtains. There's just three local families in the High Street – and only two of those are *really* local. Go to the council estates and you'll find forty or fifty local families. It's a tragedy, this change. Summer you can't move, chock-a-block with all colours and nationalities doing the trail – Blenheim, Stratford, Warwick Castle . . . we're a whistle stop where they come to buy cashmere sweaters on the way back to London Airport. Some tourists pick our flowers, even take cuttings. The Brummies are worst – some of them lasses have a bouquet by the end of the village. My wistaria suffers, I can tell you.'

Oliver John Morris lives on the green at Broadway, fifth generation of his family to do so. The wistaria, wedded to the cottage, is as thick as your wrist. It must be a treat in bloom. But now it is late November, so it is pruned, scrawny as a witch's claw. Winter arrived suddenly a few days ago, flurries of snow which came and went, playing silly beggars, keeping us guessing. Then it cleared and the sun

232

came out so that from Fish Hill you could see a handful of counties spread below; not the thirteen it is claimed may be counted on a clear day, but not a bad total for all that. Cotswold stone glowed, honey coloured, with rose pink hues towards evening; and there was frost next morning, a chilblain-torturing, good-for-nothing frost. Christmas is coming, the geese are getting fat . . .

At the village grocery, Franklin & Cook – whose sign proclaims them *'Epicureans'* – there is Christmas fare to eat: Elsenham Mincemeat with Courvoisier Cognac, Crêpes Dentelles, Royal Game Soup, Italian glacé fruits, Charbonnet et Walker chocolates. 'Damned Fortnum and Mason,' snorts Oliver John Morris, 'bit of cheese is all we can afford from there. We have to go to Evesham Supermarket, which hurts a bit . . . father was village grocer once, you see. Man of all trades in a way, but the grocer's shop was his mainstay – so we were never short of food. Father's head was too much in the clouds to make money, but the larder was never empty. He had respect too, and that meant something; he was looked up to as last Overseer of the Poor, Steward for the Lord of the Manor, life deacon of the Chapel . . . yes, we were Chapel. There've been dissenters here since the seventeenth century. He was a strait-laced man, sardonic, a good reader. He did us well enough . . . kept a pig right up until we could buy bacon cheaper in the shops. Every family had a pig them days.'

Oliver John Morris was born in 1914, one of three: there were sisters Molly and Joyce, children of the Overseer of the Poor and his wife, an Oxfordshire girl from a family of bakers. 'She had a retiring disposition – not shy, she was well met, but kept away from parish affairs . . . a good mother, that's all you need say.'

Educated at the council school and at Prince Henry Grammar School six miles along the road, Mr Morris was on his way at sixteen, first to the grocer's, then as trainee mechanic at the garage. Herr Hitler caught up with him then, hounding him over Africa and Italy until his tank stopped a shell and he was badly burned. He was demobbed, fitted and kitted with a civvy suit whose trousers and sleeves were too long, whose back was too tight.

For Oliver John Morris is only 5' 4½'' ('Shrinking some these days'),

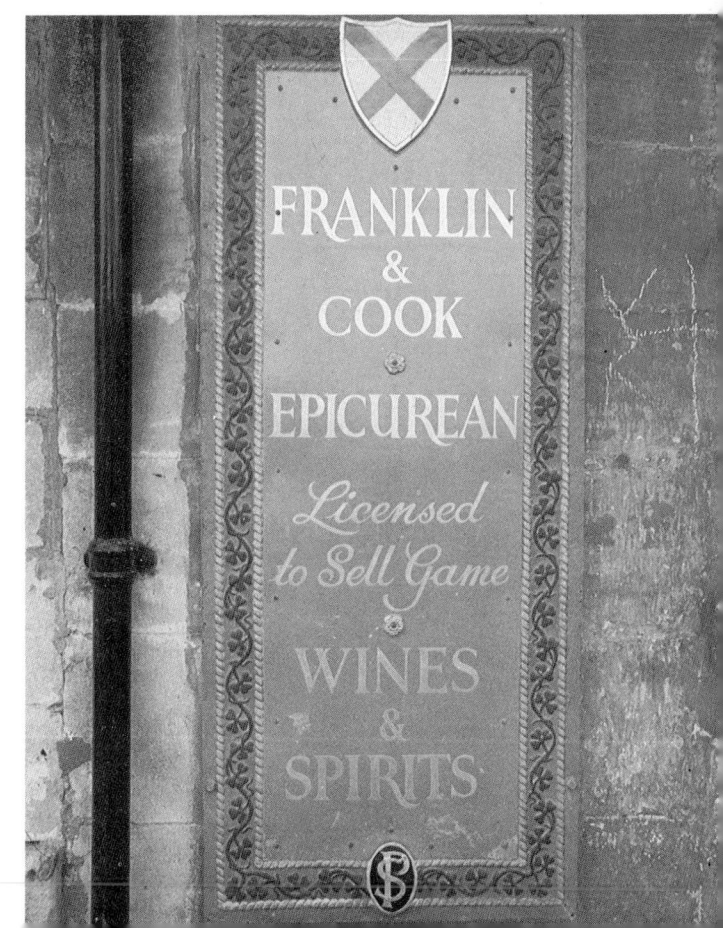

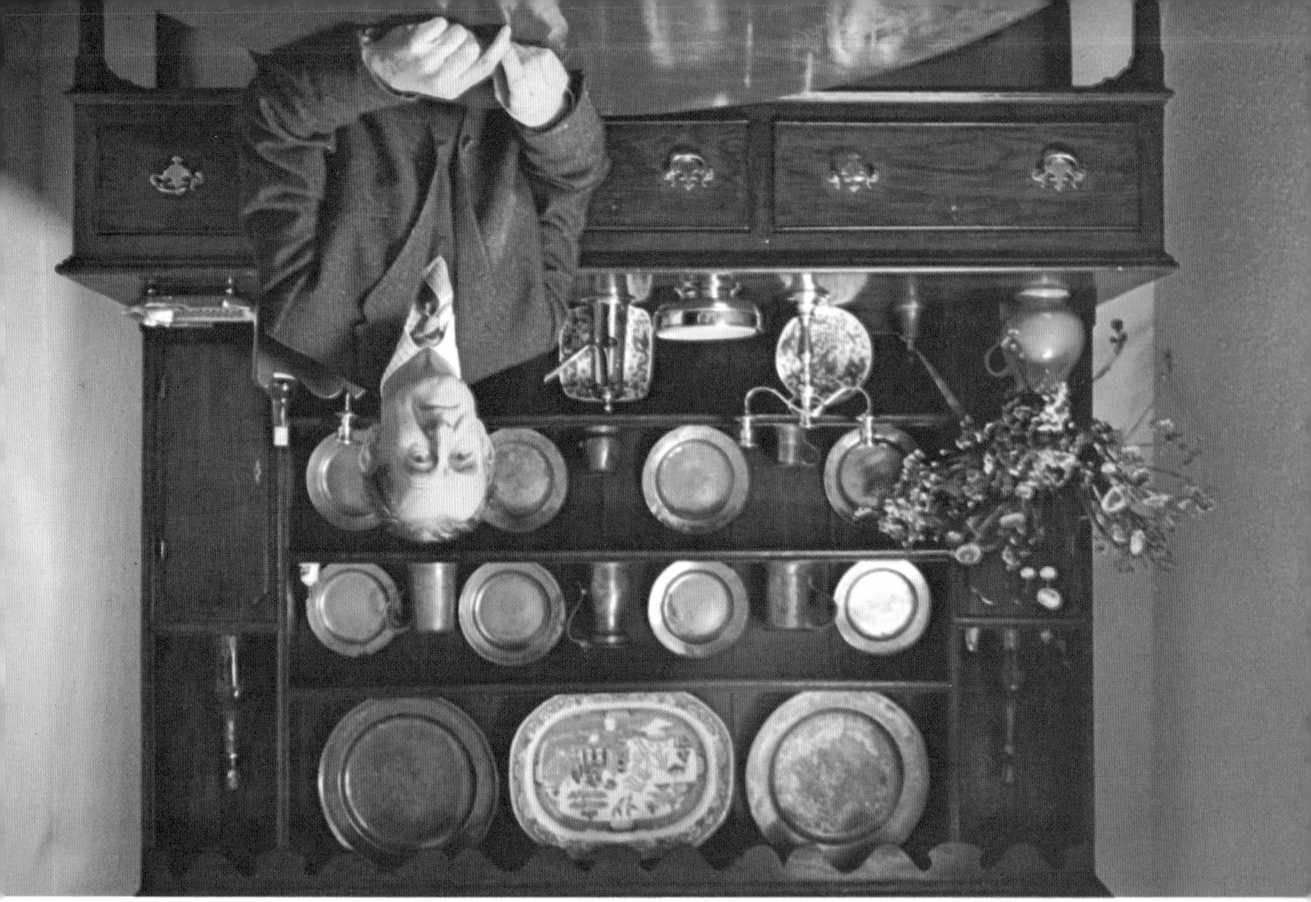

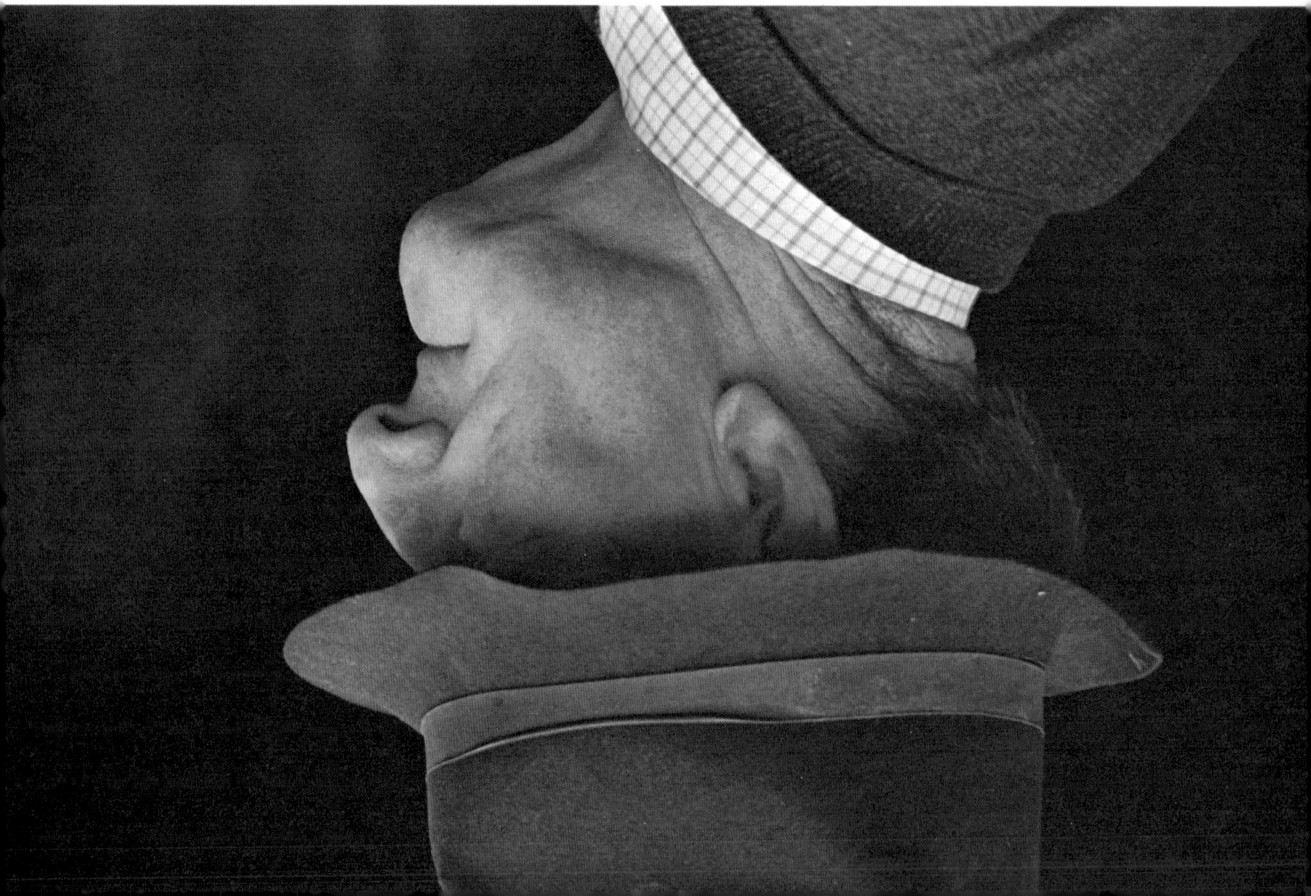

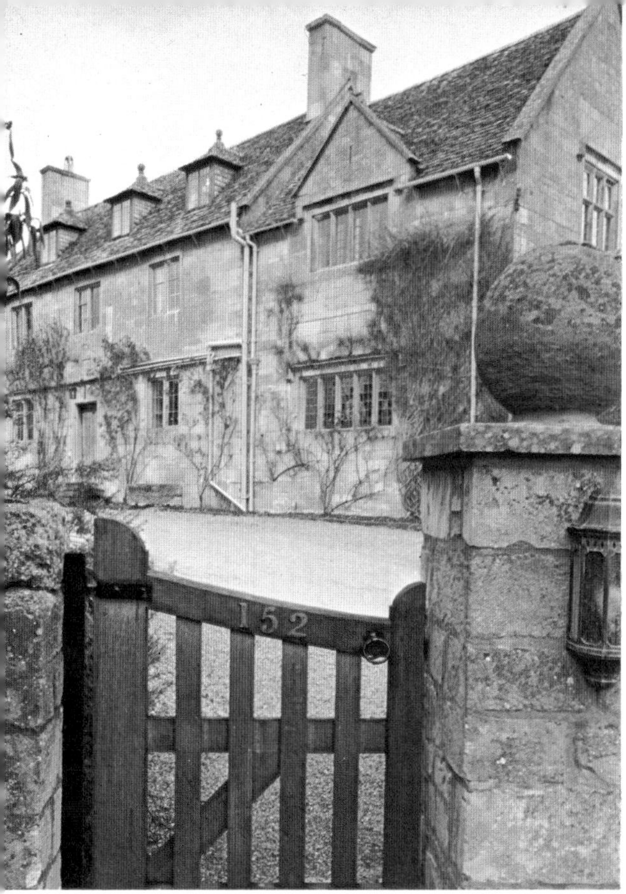
152

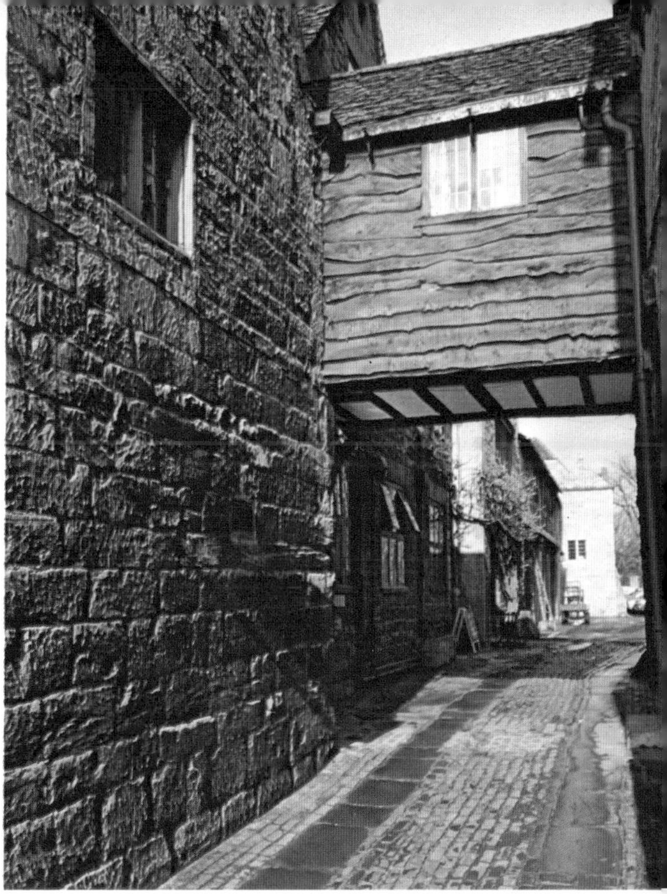

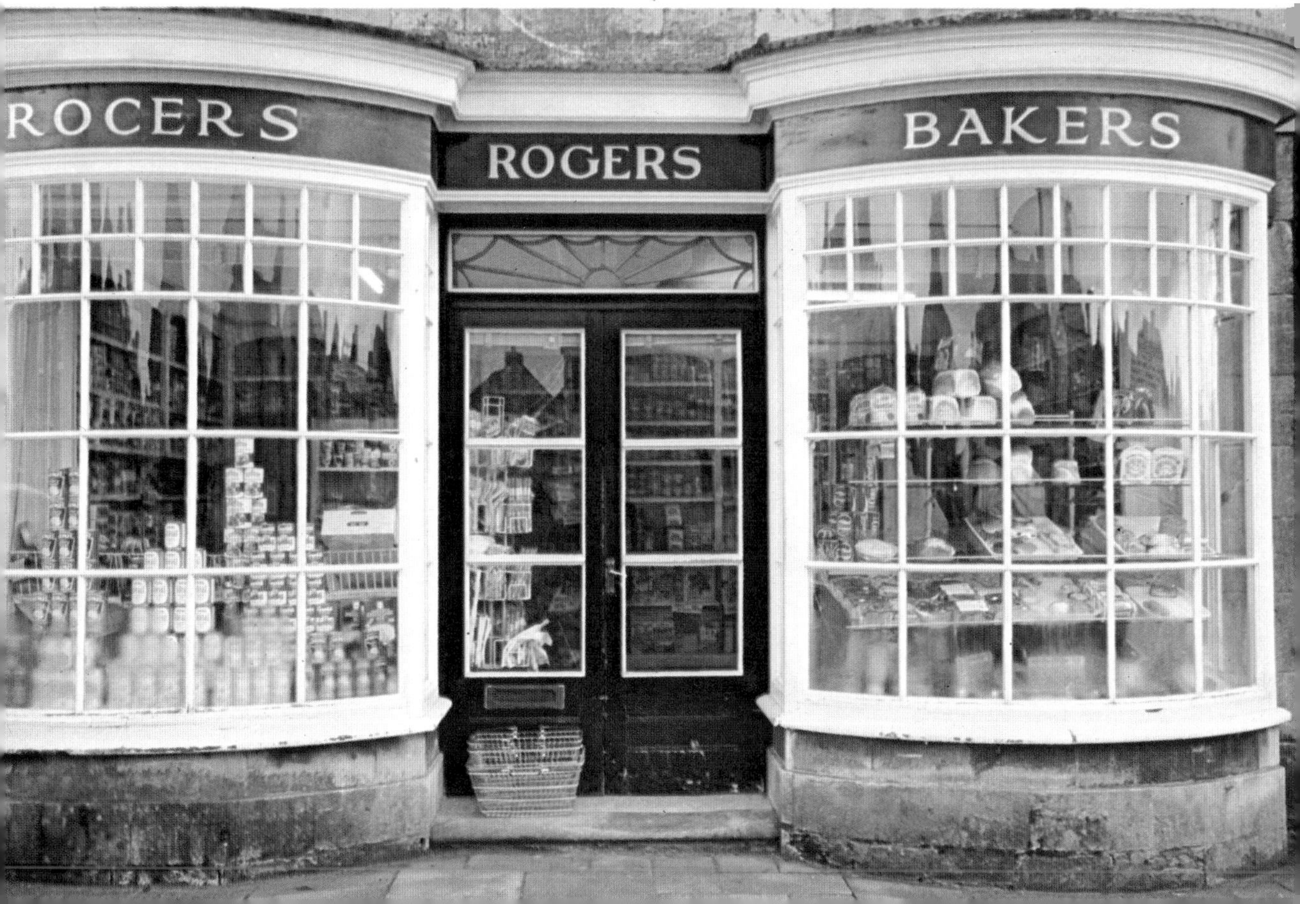
ROCERS
ROGERS
BAKERS

with a pugilist's chest and a grasp that could crack walnuts. There is something of a schoolboy about him, a Just William look, so that it would be unsurprising to find conkers, a catapult, in his pockets. Grey woolly socks are corrugated over stout shoes, a short back-and-sides haircut leaves springy tufts that won't lie down, a trilby is worn at a rakish, devil-may-care angle. Spatulate finger nails are caked with an acre or so of good Worcestershire soil, dark as Bovril. He smokes Players No. I Extra Mild cigarettes, cupping the butt inwards to his fist. His blue eyes are unclouded, bewildered perhaps by the tragedy of change; his humour dry as the dry-stone walls enclosing the fields of Broadway.

'No, I couldn't go back to the grocer's shop. It never went down with me that the customer was always right. Service didn't suit me, I'm not a counter-hopper – I never danced to no man's tune. So in 1946 I joined Colonel Victor Jones on his smallholding. He'd been left in the lurch and I helped with the poultry, only it went wrong – which is how I ended up in the garden. A famous garden in a way, designed by Alfred Parsons RA. Edwardian style it was, pleached hedges, formal gardens, walled fruits, you name them, we grew them. There were three gardeners, I was second man.

'It was hardly a calling, but you've got to love it. It was bred in me almost . . .

I've still got this letter from Sir Thomas Phillips to my great-grandfather in 1840 thanking him for the apricots we grew on the flax-house wall – the apricots are still there.' He gestures towards a building at the end of his own garden where, until 1750, when the industry failed, flax was a working proposition. The building is shadowed by stabling for four horses, built by the great-grandfather for £27; accounts survive, naturally. The stables survive too, constructed of Cotswold stone two feet thick, tiled by slate from the district before the veins were exhausted. 'Father used to go botanizing, as he called it, over all the big estates here – so it was in my blood, you see.'

Shortly after joining the Colonel, Oliver John Morris married Josephine, ' . . . a stranger from Ireland, Catholic and all, who'd come into service here'. They never did manage children of their own, so they adopted, Thomas and Mary Jo, both grown up. Today they live, Oliver John and Josephine, in their 400-years'-old cottage, wistaria at the door, blue lias stone flags from the Forest of Dean beneath their feet, a lovely mellow dresser stacked with pewter. A coal fire burns in the grate; move three feet away and the chill gnaws your bones. Cotswold stone houses are the devil to heat. Mr Morris eases his chair closer, a grey caterpillar of ash hanging from his cigarette.

'The Colonel and Mrs Jones hived themselves off to Monte Carlo after eight years . . . he's gone now, but she's still there, living in some hotel, I hear. Anyway, by that time every body wanted me – so I spread myself around, to Mrs Payton at Pear Tree House, Mrs Randall-Martin, Mrs Barrington, Miss Bilderbeck . . . the names change, but I sort of go with the house. Worse thing with new owners is them coming along ordering me to pull up and destroy a man's work willy-nilly. I tell them to wait and watch a while before they change it all.

'I don't care for regimental zinnias or African marigolds – too formal. A good mixed herbaceous border of lupins, peonies, pyrethrum, is what I like to see. A quarter acre garden is more than enough: lawn, herbaceous beds backed by shrubs. A garden must fit the house. People are patio-conscious these days – *barbecues*!' (He makes the word sound disgusting; it causes him bile.) 'Indoors is where you should eat, sitting up to it. I've seen them with their incinerated rubbish, black as the ace of spades, washed down with some mucked—about hooch. I don't know what's in eating like that and never will. Roast beef and Yorkshire pudding for me, eaten indoors at a table.

'June is the time in a garden, that's perfection. February is a deadly, horrible month. In November you're digging beds over, winter pruning – it's tempting to light a bonfire. It's no good working to a gardener's diary like Percy Thrower says on television – thing is to do it *now*. You can plant trees right through October, when the sap goes down, until March when the sap flows again. Use your own judgement.

'It's all to do with satisfaction. You start with a seed and you coddle it along –

237

it'll grow or it'll die, but you're the one. In a way you're working for posterity. Take a tree. It'll go on for centuries, you're leaving a mark, a bit of yourself. There's grandfather's pear tree out back and we're still eating the fruit. There's pear trees in this parish over 300 years old . . . plum only lasts 40 years. Plant pears for your heirs, that's what we used to do.

'I don't know what worries me. I'm a great muddler – I muddle on. I remember at the Colonel's we had a freak snow in June – filled the tulip cups with snow and they snapped off. It was terrible, but in a fortnight something else came along and that's what it's all about. You can't say it's happening to me . . . it's happening to everyone. I suppose I do have worries. In the war I worried about the wistaria, who'd look after it. I worry about leaving this house, coming back to find a swimming pool in the garden. But really I'm sinfully content with my lot. Except for change – you could say I live in the past.'

A walk along Broadway's High Street is evidence to Oliver John Morris's claim. Pera, his black labrador, tugs at the lead. 'Pera is Spanish for bitch, I'm told . . . he's a dog all the same. Pera the Third – we've had three, but never thought of another name.'

It must be hard for Broadway, known as one of the most beautiful villages in England. Call a woman beautiful, the chances are she will look in the glass more times than she should. Which may account for self-consciousness along this High Street. Which may account for Messrs Franklin & Cook calling themselves epicurians rather than grocers; why Small Talk, which sells bread and cakes,

carries a sign 'Tea Shoppe & Patisserie'. Perhaps it is why . . . 'I, Susanna Webb of Brigadoon, Orchard Terrace, Broadway in the county of Hereford and Worcester . . . hereby give notice that it is my intention to apply to the Licensing Sessions . . .': with any luck there will soon be Beaujolais to go with the sardines on toast at Susanna Webb's Cotswold Café.

In Oliver John Morris's youth a cobbler worked where today fine arts and antiques are displayed, spot-lighted and hung with Bond Street refinement. Richard Hagen sells 'Fine Paintings', so too John Noot, and Perigord; there are cashmere jerseys in H. B. Heyworth's window, Christmas tinsel at The Gift Shop, cocktail frocks at Corphée boutique, bed & breakfast at Inglenook Guest House. 'Gin palaces,' mutters Oliver John Morris, quickening his pace against the cold, his breath coming in Siberian gasps. 'Remember that cottage going for £75 – last sale it fetched £43,000.' Not once has he raised his trilby, because in his own village he has recognized no one and no one has recognized him.

'French ciggies!' is chalked on the blackboard outside Goblets Wine Bar. French ciggies to puff on, crêpes dentelles to chew, couture to dress in: this High Street is the veritable Champs Elysées of Evesham Vale. It is another era, an age away since a pig in the back yard was a symbol of survival and little girls in ribbons played hop-skip-and-jump on the green.

At the centre of it all is The Lygon Arms. Now here is a hostelry if ever there was: there can be few better in the land. Hospitality has kept travellers going since first reference to the inn appears in parish records of 1532. Charles I stayed here; Cromwell too, on the eve of the Battle of Worcester in 1651. In about 1830 General Lygon, who had served under Wellington at Waterloo, bought nearby Springfield estate and it is suggested that his retired butler took over the place, renaming it – from the White Hart, as it was previously known – after the family whose coat-of-arms, two lions passant with forked tails, now forms the sign.

Mind you, inflation has left its mark since 13 August 1767, when Lord Torrington entered in his diary: 'Most inns will do during the summer's heat, but there are not ten endurable in winter, when you come out of London; from register stores, and turkey carpets: tho' the inns now mend in their rooms and stabling, as we here begin to enter a fine fox and hare hunting country, to which many gentlemen resort in winter; nor are their charges unreasonable, as you may perceive by the following bill:

Tea	0	9
A chicken etc	2	0
Tart (apricot)	0	2
Liquors	2	3
Breakfast	0	9
	5	11

Served in your room, Champagne breakfast is now £6, a plate of roast Scotch rib of beef £4, and as for a bottle of Château Latour 1966 1er Cru Pauillac . . . and what else would you expect for the best? The dining room resounds with accents more from Arkansas than Chipping Norton but, as Oliver John Morris remarks, 'Broadway has always lived on the road'. And there's an end to it.

Yet The Lygon Arms breathes welcome; caring service is in its fabric. In room seven is an ogival-headed fireplace believed to be fourteenth century, twelve-inch-wide floorboards shine Beezwax bright, and massive old-fashioned baths empty with mad gurgling sounds of the Titanic going down.

Oliver John Morris views his village with a jaundiced eye. The sap, he implies, has been squeezed out of Broadway, replaced by thinner stuff, etiolated city blood. His birthplace has grown mercilessly picturesque, relentlessly quaint . . . a marshmallow village.

None the less there is a mood hereabouts from which one can never entirely escape. You might find it at nearby Bretforton, in what was, until recently, the coldest pub in the country, The Fleece. Set in a landscape of low cloud and daft sheep, the house was in Lola Taplin's family 600 years as a yeoman farmhouse; then, heaven knows how far back, they took on a licence. Miss Taplin ran it with the rod of a school marm: no sandwiches or crisps because of the crumbs, no putting down wet tankards on her sixteenth and seventeenth century treasures, not much heat either because that's no good to fine furniture.

Despite her ways and acid tongue, they came for miles around; and it can't have been purely for punishment. Miss Taplin chalked cabbalistic signs about her pub: beneath the grate to stop the witches coming down the chimney, on the flag-stones to keep them in their rightful place, down-under. Her marks are clear still. She lived with her sister and for the final twenty years they exchanged not a word. So it is told locally. Then the sister dies and Lola, with no good excuse, followed soon after. Maybe having no one not to talk to was her cause of death. Or perhaps they needed each other more than they knew.

Lola bequeathed The Fleece to the National Trust who decreed in their wisdom that it was unfit for human habitation. A board appeared – 'R. C. Hill: Builders and Contractors' – and drills pecked at the old place, plaster flying everywhere. Central heating, a snack bar . . . but one wonders whether trade will be as brisk as it was.

Lower Quinton is a few minutes away, and here the mood grows uneasy, for in 1945 the body of farm worker Charles Walton was found on Meon Hill. He was impaled on a pitch-fork, skewered to the ground, the sign of a crucifix scored across his chest. Fabian of the Yard headed the investigation, assisted by Detective Superintendent Alec Spooner. They discovered neither motive nor suspect, so the case was closed; but for nineteen years Mr Spooner returned to the village on the anniversary of the murder.

240

Farmer Basil Hall, two fields away from where Charlie's body lay, remembers the victim as an arthritic old man on two sticks. Now who'd want to do a thing like that? Naturally there was talk, suspicions, and they centred on a villager who died – when journalists, sightseers, a TV crew clustered round his grave. So unbearable it became that his widow removed the headstone. Cecil Alway, the vicar, begged her not to do it; but the widow had her will so that her husband should take his rest in peace. Charlie's grave was never marked, so even the vicar does not know its whereabouts. Neither does he want to know, nor even discuss the case. 'There are members of the family still here,' is as much as he will say. No one in Lower Quinton wants to talk about Charlie Walton's murder, which brought infamy and shame to this small province. It is still known as the Silent Village.

Oliver John Morris remembers it well. 'No,' he says, 'they'll talk to no one. Why should they? It's their business. Death's a private thing . . . and there's no life after. We're like plants – seed, germination, flower, produce seed, wither and die. Then the slugs come along and eat what's left. Much the same with us when you think about it. We're conceived – and at the end the worms have us. It doesn't worry me. It's the natural order. I live for today, muddling on.

'I believe there's something all right. If there wasn't a creator there'd be no garden. Fisons and ICI can't take all the credit. I'm a non-conforming Non-Conformist, if you like – the wife's Catholic and goes to mass . . .

'It's just I don't want to die. Father once told me he'd be satisfied to live the alloted span, three score and ten, and when he got to seventy I said, "Well, then – it's time you turned your toes up." But he said he'd changed his mind, and the old fellow went on till ninety-five. I'd like to do the same, only make it a hundred.'

Towards the end of the High Street, Oliver John Morris turns into the drive-way of Pear Tree House, opening a latch-gate into the garden. 'There's not much to see,' he says, 'not at this time of year, but in a garden you're always thinking ahead, planning the next season . . . with luck I'll be here to see it. Couple of years ago I had a heart attack. It was very hot and I was cutting the long orchard grass, heavy work. I knew I wouldn't die, it's not my time yet, but it cost me three months in bed and I got to thinking that this is where I was born and this is where I'll die, that's all I want. I told you I was a stick-in-the-mud.

'Travel? See a bit of the world? I haven't seen the Cotswolds yet . . . I haven't finished looking at Broadway.'

The Parson

The Reverend Geoffrey Cobley Smith

They buried Winnie on a bad day. There had been a storm, gales gusting to 100 miles an hour, so the wireless reported. A restless, treacherous sea scours East Anglian shores, shallower than most, more salty, truculent. Coastal people are unnerved by such winds because they know that lives are at stake. Some of these towns and villages survived entirely from fishing, when a man kept his family by what he took from the sea; if that man drowned, there would be no pension, no compensation, so women were in constant fear of widowhood and poverty. There is a nuclear power station at Sizewell, and American Air Force jets scream overhead, grey bats out of hell, loaded with atomic devices; but the sea, the wind are more respected.

And Winnie, late of Blythburgh in the County of Suffolk, had chosen the morning after such pandemonium to be lowered into her grave. This in the week before Christmas too, a count-down of ten days, that's all. Three deaths in the village in no time; three deaths and three interments . . . is there no consideration?

So the hedges around Holy Trinity Church were mangled, ruined branches littered the graveyard; the wind, ill-tempered still, drove rain into vicious sabre-lashing squalls. Not that Winnie, late of this parish, cared, cosy and snug in her wooden casket. It was a plain casket, nothing fancy; atop it a single spray of chrysanthemums, white as calico. She had a fine turnout, friends supporting her, come along to give a decent send-off. For Winnie was well liked: 'A natural helper,' said someone, 'friendly all round – and she had this lovely singing voice . . . wise old thing, she was.'

And a child that's born on the Sabbath day
Is fair and wise and good and gay.

Winnie certainly observed the Sabbath, so perhaps that is when she was born. She grew up, married, and their love lasted but a season; she was widowed, and she died. That is about the sum of it.

There was her poetry, of course; Winnie composed verses of her own and cut others from women's magazines . . . and after Hymn 134, 'Jesus lives!', and after Psalm 23, the Vicar read one of Winnie's verses. It wasn't very good, being concerned with young love and roses and dying, but it was moving and, glancing about, there were one or two dabbing handkerchiefs.

During the last hymn the sun appeared, drenching the church in clear prismatic light cascading from plain glass. Shadows and doubt went into banishment; it was like a benediction, Winnie's blessing. Four pallbearers, young men of Southwold with rugby players' biceps, shouldered the coffin, slow-marching behind the Vicar towards the grave, six-foot-six, trimly expectant.

'Man that is born of woman hath but a short time to live, and is full of misery. He cometh up, and is cut down, like a flower . . . ' intoned the Vicar as they lowered Winnie from view. The wind reared again, clawing the Vicar's words away from mourners, scattering them over the flooded marshes of Blythburgh below: 'Earth to earth, ashes to ashes, dust to dust . . . '

There was a turning away, mute acceptance, a resignation in bright artificial smiles; a hat blew off, roly-polying along a gravel path. Then tea and condolences, sandwiches of ham and rich fruit cake in some darkened parlour across the village street. Had anyone remained, he would have seen the gravedigger, Sam Miller, fastidious in his sense of decorum, come out of hiding, spade gleaming as it heaped soil upon the coffin, blotting out an East Anglian sky. But Winnie's eyes were sightless already, so no harm was done.

The Reverend Geoffrey Cobley Smith, Vicar of Blythburgh and Walberswick, attended to other duties to do with the souls in his care. A consultation with Churchwarden, Mr Muttitt, and with Parish Treasurer, Mr Collett, about the restoration fund; and yes, it had been nice to welcome so many to the funeral. Mrs Falck had come, and the Troughtons, Jordans, Onyetts, friends all.

Bill Muttitt knows a thing or two about this church, and not just through forty-two years as Churchwarden. By trade a carpenter, he has been involved with all restoration work since he was seventeen: 'I don't think there's been a nail driven I don't know about.' Mr Collett also has loose connections, one could say, with Blythburgh: such as the entry in parish records of the marriage between a forbear, Erasmus Collett, to Elizabeth Brooke in 1587 . . . who, on 8 February 1588, bore her husband a son, baptized also in the name Erasmus.

The Vicar shrugs into a cloak, anxious to stretch his legs in the lane outside, past a house known as The Green : 'Mr Malan lives there,' he informs. 'My other Churchwarden . . . he was a housemaster at Harrow. Mrs Pigeon was born in the house – she's still in the village.' The Priory comes next, where Mrs Hubbard, who used to be Peggy Grubb, lives with her husband. Opposite, exposed to the main road from the ports of Felixstowe and Ipswich unwinding to Lowestoft, is an overgrown orchard. Beneath apple trees lies an abandoned Suffolk wagon, glorious in its day, now disintegrating through neglect.

A fearsome thoroughfare, this main road, along which hurtle vast *camion* vehicles with *Fruehauf : Attention – Freins puissants* written over their swaying continental backsides. How cottages tremble at their passing, how careful you must be to dodge them on this blind bend. Surviving Blythburgh pedestrians deserve our keenest admiration.

Holy Trinity stands well above the road, while below, a fraction to the north, is the White Hart – the A12 separating them, an all man's land between hospitality and the hereafter. Not, according to the Vicar, that the White Hart is a real *village* pub these times, what with the number of Jaguars arranged beside the 'Please Park Prettily' notice. Yet it is a handsome building of the sixteenth century, where smoked trout is served, game pie, pâté and honest

Adnams beer. There are log fires, horse brasses, and pretty girls to serve; it is a roadhouse all the same.

A house on the road, or cottage rather, is The Stores, run by Mr Fox. The door is a bit stiff but once inside it is a wonderland of Vicks VapoRub and All Bran, Maltesers and Golden Syrup, Veno's Cough Syrup, fly killer and mousetraps; and villagers come in with string bags and alarming accounts of their infirmities. There used to be three shops, a post office and a blacksmith; now it is all up to Mr Fox, dispensing pensions with tinned peaches, postal-orders with more perishable goods.

On a high bank looking towards Angel Marsh and Bulchamp Marsh is a new development, six mini-mansions in exemplary taste, with integral garages and sun-bathing balconies; but stuff your ears to the mutterings of old cottagers whose view is now obscured. Apart from this dark muttering – and how East Anglians mutter: 'We talk with our mouths shut so's not to let this east wind in' – newcomers will find it quiet enough. Well, the school closed in the mid-sixties and the schoolhouse was transformed into a holiday house, five to nine year olds now attending class at Wenhaston. If anyone wants to convert another holiday heaven, the Primitive Methodist Chapel, opened in 1860 to be closed in 1976, might be available for offer. But do not expect the village bobby to direct you because the police, confident that the Mafia would be little interested in Blythburgh, pulled out in 1978.

A dead-and-alive place, you might think – and not be far wrong when winter's clutch is on the village. In June it is another tale. The world is at Blythburgh's doorstep in June. It is the month of the Aldeburgh Festival, when Holy Trinity – whose acoustics are held to be perfect – resounds to the chords of Rostropovich.

His tour of inspection over, the Vicar heads his Austin towards Walberswick, across gorse heaths that were once sheep walks. He could cross the Blyth by rowing boat from Southwold if he chose, but this takes time, a short commodity in the Vicarage larder. It is a 1931 vicarage, of no special virtue beyond the fact that it adjoins the ruins of St Andrew's, Mr Smith's second church.

'There really doesn't seem to be enough time,' he says. 'Reading is my chief indulgence but there's no time. I don't know where it goes. Perhaps it's to do with happening . . . I mean there are happening and non-happening plans. Walberswick is a more happening village than Blythburgh – which still hasn't actually bought the Silver Jubilee bench we collected for. It'll come one day, the Chairman of the committee assures me so. The day to day work of keeping the church going is very involved, perhaps it overwhelms us. Blythburgh church dominates the village, it almost swamps the village with a kind of daunting beauty. In some ways it hasn't helped – it's almost like the Golden Calf, almost a symbol of idolatry. Its size and importance are felt as a massive responsibility which has led to certain strains not encountered in less distinguished churches.

'Curiously, it hasn't intimidated me. Sometimes it even infuriates me because the maintenance of the fabric seems to be of more concern than the meaning of the place as a house of worship – we've raised over £50,000 in the past ten years. No, I can't honestly say it moves me as much as it seems to move some. I'm more fascinated by the people who come into it – it's a bit stark, austere to me after a High Church background. No, of course I couldn't try that sort of Anglo-Catholicism here just because I like it. They want simplicity, it's endemic to this part of the country. They hate change and they'd fight me, and I'd rather keep them in church than have them fighting me . . . it's only a case of the externals. We're also something of a tourist attraction, numbers swelled from all over the place when we floodlit the church sixteen years ago – I accept it as one of those things.'

The Reverend Geoffrey Smith is an accepting man. Born at March in Cambridgeshire, he accepted it when, at the age of nineteen, he was rejected at his interview for ordinands on grounds of immaturity. 'I wasn't hurt or surprised – I wasn't sure enough or ready enough.' Neither was he hurt nor surprised when the army rejected him for National Service because of a chest complaint. Instead, he became a junior railway clerk and met a girl called Elizabeth. 'I was drifting until I met her – she was a schoolteacher, we married and she settled me into a ten-and-a-half years' wait. I wasn't over happy as a clerk, but I had no skills so I was a clerk. It didn't shake my faith, the waiting – if one can say "God's cause . . ."'

'Then, all of a sudden at thirty-two, I knew it was right, so I offered myself for ordination to the Bishop's Chaplain for ordinands. I was accepted, went to Bishop's College at Cheshunt for two years and was ordained in 1965. But I never deviated, rejection hadn't affected me – I'd gained in experience, in the stability of marriage.'

After two curacies Geoffrey Smith was inducted into the livings of Blythburgh and Walberswick, where he settled with his wife, a Labrador bitch, Sandy, and a black cat, Nelson. They have five children. 'I don't know if we'd have had so many if we'd thought about it . . .' he trails off, as if the plurality of his brood astonishes him.

The vicarage is a functional house; not luxurious, but all the same, a roof, a home, somewhere to eat and sleep and say your prayers. There are religious prints, an upright piano, tea and biscuits on a tray. The vicar wears his cassock largely, it swells at the front, conforming to the beginnings of his convexity. He has a full head of dark hair which, at forty-nine, shows touches of iron; his face is filling too, the stirrings of dewlaps showing. One notices that the Vicar of Blythburgh and Walberswick has very red ears, perennially red ears. And soon one notices his transparent sincerity; it is impregnable, this sincerity. It is both his velvet glove and his sword. It is his secret weapon, so secret not even he knows. His sincerity and his innocence make him a formidable disciple of Christ.

He is neither intellectual nor theologian: 'If I had to appear on a TV show with an atheist and an agnostic, they'd wipe the floor with me in debate – but my faith would be the same . . . ' He is silent for a moment, reflective and somehow anxious.

248

Somewhere in the house a cuckoo clock makes bird-song of the hour, a staccato sound. He considers the proposition that his certainty is not unlike the story Dostoevsky tells in *The Brothers Karamazov*: Christ returns to earth, to Seville, at the time of the Inquisition. The Grand Inquisitor has him arrested. In a lengthy, irrefutably logical indictment, he explains to his prisoner why he cannot be allowed to continue his ministry. He concludes, 'We, the elect, are unhappy because we know how difficult it is to achieve salvation.But we have always kept this a secret from the people – who are not much better than cats and dogs, after all. Now you come back proposing to give the show away . . . I am afraid I shall have to have you quietly done away with and it is entirely your own fault. Prophets are all very well when they are dead, but while they are alive there is nothing for it but to burn or crucify them.'

As the Grand Inquisitor ends his case, Christ leans forward, kissing him on his pale lips. This is his reply: 'Your reasoning is powerful, but my love is stronger.'

'Yes,' says the Vicar, 'I'd say my own faith is like that . . . although I've never actually read the book. I have a tremendous love for people – I hate pi words, but yes it is love. Which is basically the parish priest's function – to bring God alive through Jesus Christ in terms of love, compassion and forgiveness. I'm told I'm quite good with people, particularly the elderly – I'm a good listener. But I'm no marvel . . . I'm tuned to the tenor of country life, so a Glasgow slum parish might not be for me. Horses for courses? Perhaps grace would be given . . .

'No, I'm not over strong on the intellectual side, but no one seems too fussed. I think what I say goes quite well. I don't find sermons easy . . . so I draw on other people's ideas, and there are books on sermon outlines . . . cribs. I think a lot of us crib a bit. I'm not a person with a lot of self-confidence, yet I seem to give the impression of being more capable than I am . . . and there's the strength I was given at ordination. I had a dreadful stutter as a boy, and it was difficult to read the lesson at theological college – but it's got so much better that people don't seem to notice any more.'

They do notice, of course, for the Vicar's stutter is pronounced. It is noticed and accepted with patience, for he is their Vicar and he has come among them, fifty-first of the perpetual curates of Holy Trinity, successor of Alexander of Dunwich in 1310, of Nathaniel Flowerdew in 1652, of Ralph Blois in 1735. Their acceptance is in the nature of things, immutable.

'And yet, you know, I'll never be quite one of them. There's an immense East Anglian reserve – they accept you but they hold something back. There's always something the villagers share among themselves that I'll never penetrate. If apparently I've made no impression on their church-going habits, they still take me as a familiar face. No door has ever been shut to me. Sometimes I get a bit down, a bit low, it's a personal thing. I'm in touch with so much decay and death, it seems that I'm only in touch with one end of life – there's not much youth around. It's lucky that my disciplined approach to the spiritual doesn't let my doubts hang about too long . . .

249

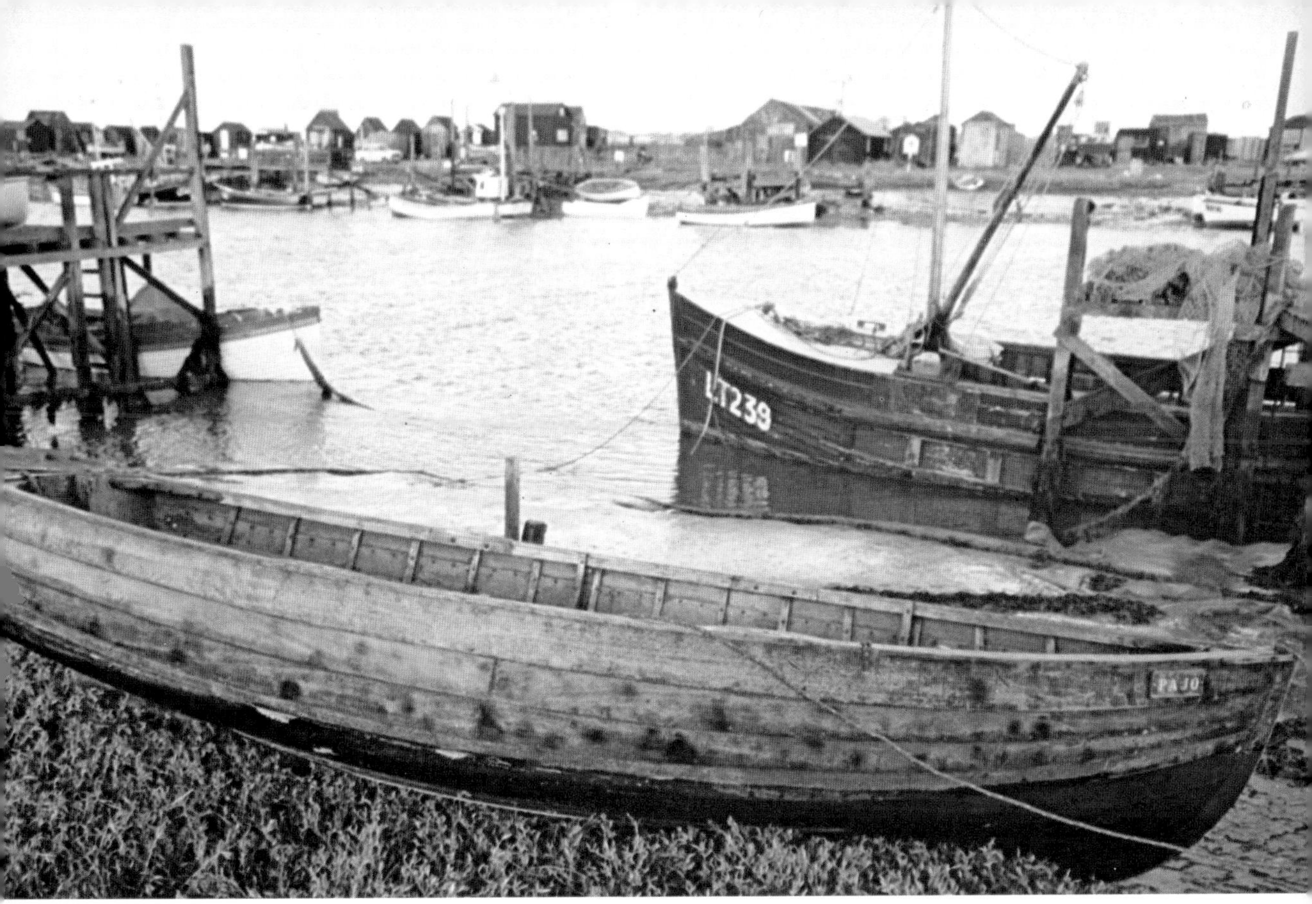
LT239
PAJO

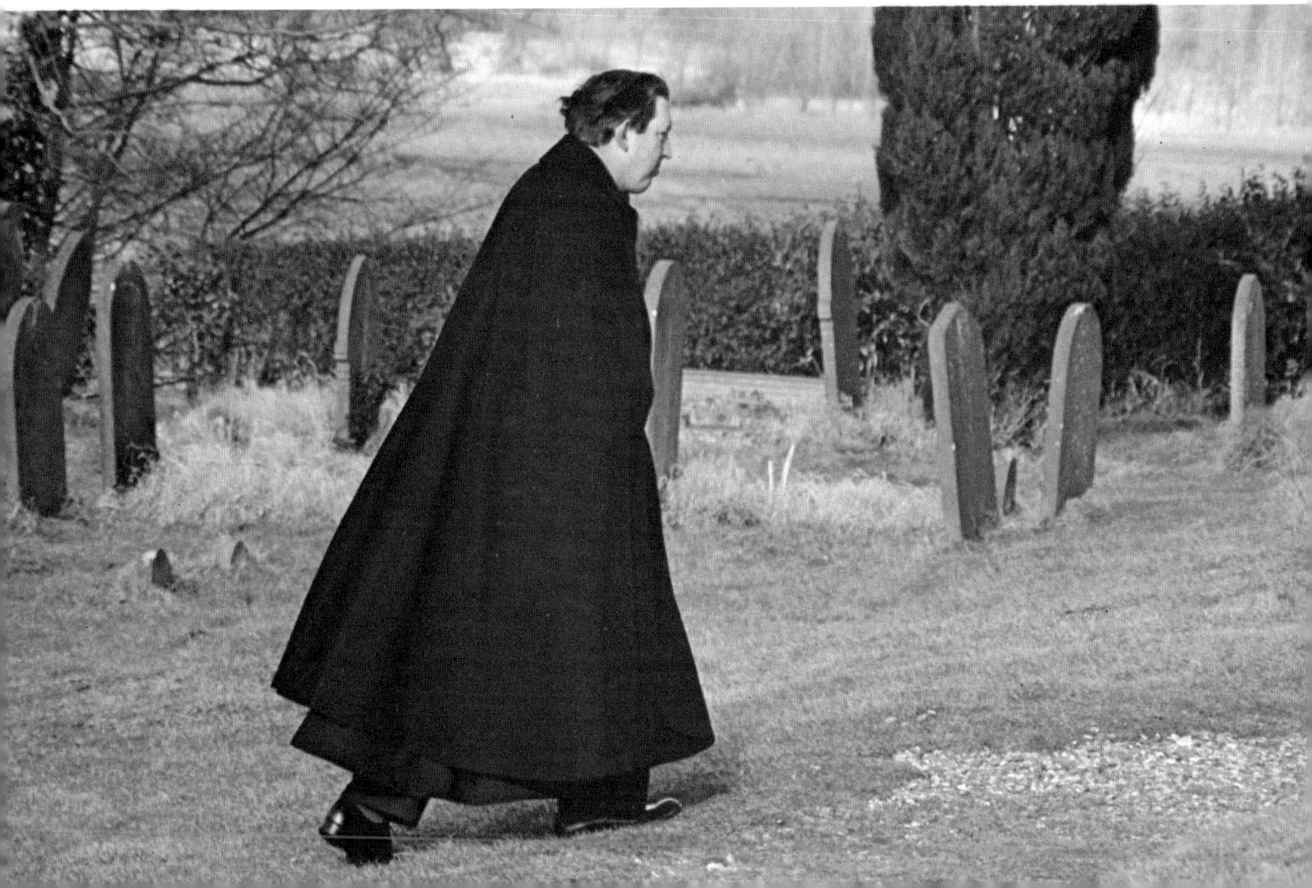

you see, I've made that leap of faith Thomas Aquinas talks about. I think he says that however much we argue intellectually there must be that leap of faith. I have no intellectual claims, I've made that clear – but the disciples were simple men, fishermen, farmers . . . the Lord can only work through the few able to spread the Christian message among those willing to listen.'

He sits back, his dewlaps giving him a petulant look. He seems anxious again, appealing perhaps to the heavenly graces for lucidity; or merely perhaps for divine intervention to put a stop to the interview so that he may return to the business of curing souls.

'What is the spirit of the age, the mood of the country? I don't really know. I'm very reliant on the media for that. We're rather off the beaten track out here, so it's all a bit second-hand. Strikes, divorce, crime – I've heard of them, but I can't pontificate about public morality from a backwater. By and large of the fifty million or so in this country, a huge percentage must lead relatively blameless lives.

'The family unit still holds together . . . that's the most joyous part of my life, family communion. I feel that the parish worships together as one family. The saddest? I don't think there is any real sadness in my job.'

In AD 636 East Anglia was ruled by King Anna, whose personal history is linked closely with Blythburgh and its church; so we may assume that a Christian church has stood here for over 1,300 years. The church, as it is today, dates from 1412 when a licence to build was granted by the King. We can, however, be sure that the tower, then steepled, survived from an earlier edifice (circa 1330) and that the fifteenth-century church was a 'graft' . . . until the steeple fell through the roof at the west end in the great storm of 1577.

Great storm indeed! Why, we all know it was nothing of the sort. The work of the devil, more like, for – as recorded by Stow in his *Annals* – this storm 'cleft the door, and returning to the steeple, rent the timber, brake the chimes, and fled towards Bongay, six miles off'. It also killed, in the congregation present at the time, 'a man of fortie and a boy of fifteene yeares', who were found 'starke dead'; others being discovered 'stricken down and grovelling more than half an hour afterward'. All bore marks of scorching, so that legend attributes the disaster to the devil in person, scorch marks visible on the north door being made by his fingers.

Some say the devil, some say Black Shuck, Odin's dreaded hell-hound, the monstrous spectral dog, breathing fire from his nostrils, who still wanders these marshes at night, looking for the spot where his master fell in battle. After a pint too many of Adnams ale at the White Hart, many a man has encountered Black Shuck.

The massive size of Holy Trinity – 127 feet long and 54 feet wide – was thought necessary by its designers to accommodate parishioners of what was then a town large enough to rate two annual Charter Fairs, to have its own Mint, a gaol, a busy town of houses and market stalls where quays bordered a river navigable to Blythburgh and to Halesworth beyond, crowded with craft from overseas, carrying on a thriving fishing and mercantile marine trade, and rearing, in the

252

surrounding pasturelands, flocks of sheep for the Suffolk wool trade. But fortune is capricious . . . as shipwrights built bigger ships traders began to look for ports which could accomodate heavier hulls and deeper draughts. The account roll for 1478 gives a pathetic instance: the receipt of '16d. and no more' is recorded 'because the Bretons did not come this yeare with salt'.

A heavier blow fell in 1528 when Cardinal Wolsey, son of an Ipswich butcher, received a Papal Bill authorizing him to suppress certain small religious houses, among them Blythburgh. The culmination of sad events came in the person of William Dowsing who, in April 1644 on the orders of his master, Protector Cromwell, set about the systemic spoilation of the church. Dowsing, who wrote in his diary of desecration, 'I brake down 3 orate pro animabus', while his men fired hundreds of bullets into the oak doors and the sculptured wooden angels riding remote and high above the hubbub. They smashed stained glass, mutilated pew-end carvings and had a generally lovely day. Well done, Sweet William, may you and your merry men rest in peace.

Yet Holy Trinity survived, most nobly so; and, as if to prove that good can come from bad, the quality of light falling through plain glass has a purity you never see in stained windows. The angels spread their wings, relatively unscathed, totally serene; and the Seven Deadly Sins depicted in the bench ends are recognizable as Avarice (sitting on his money chest), Hypocrisy (praying with open eyes), Greed (with distended stomach) . . . so really one could say that William and his vandals did not entirely have their hearts in the job.

Holy Trinity stands above salt marshes, tidal marshes which flood and ebb twice each day. They were water meadows once, grazing land before the sea claimed it. Broken gates and fences reach skeletal spines, like the limbs of drowning men, above the flood, black and foreboding. Look one way, it all belongs to the Earl of Stradbroke, who was Suffolk's Lord Lieutenant; in the other direction Sir Charles Blois holds the deeds. Blois: now that is a name hereabouts – the quick tending the land as they have for centuries, the dead taking a rest at Holy Trinity. There lie Eustace Blois, Gervase Ralph Edmund, Georgiana Isabella Francis, Dudley George, who never did make it back from the Somme.

A battle was fought here once, on this spot, by that King of the Angles, Anna, against Penda. Anna and his son, Firminius, were slain on the site of Bull Champ in AD 655. It is an untameable place where, on a peninsula, surrounded on three sides by water, sits a house called Bulchamp, untameable too. Approached by a rutted drive, Bulchamp has, over the generations, settled into the landscape with an air of unreality. Rub your eyes and it may disappear, swallowed by vapours rising from the marsh. Seeing the house for the first time is like experiencing a mirage – yet log fires burn, Mozart billows from the drawing room, and people live here.

There are Paul and Jude and baby Rory; there are Tim and Edward – and they make music and rocking horses, paint, and repair Morris cars, 'dying cars' as they

253

call them. Simon Loftus owns Bulchamp. Loftus and Adnams are the families behind the nearby brewery in Southwold. Simon is soft-spoken, wears a gold ring in his right ear and the look of a zealot who is a benevolent despot too. They are not a commune – he hates the word and the connotation; neither are they self-sufficient: 'Self-sufficiency has an isolating tendency, it cuts out shop, pub, milkman, reducing communication. We're simply a community of friends living under the same roof in order to keep the house alive. We're not trying to make any statement – the house is just too big for me, so we enjoy each other's company and privacy; it's an arrangement that works. It breeds phantasies locally, we're thought to "live in sin". I'm regarded as a freak.

'In my small space here I know what I want, and others can do as they want. If people don't agree with my ways here, they leave. I don't want to rule the world, only to live my way – which is why small personal friction is preferable to massive violence outside in the name of morality. Not that we encounter much violence – when we organized the Barsham Fair, 70,000 came in three days, without a single unruly incident.

'All politicians are self-interested, unscrupulous – and the idea of a Messiah to revive the country would be the worst possible solution. I'd like to see government abolished, to be replaced by the local community . . . yes, I know . . . it's a totally unworkable idealistic concept in a predatory world.'

Unworkable, idealistic, but not untypical of East Anglian character which has, since time began, 'done different'. It is the territory for dissidents, nonconformists breakaways; there is something inviolable in the way it juts its great jaw into the North Sea. There is something undefiled, inward looking about its people. Suspicious of clever modern men, they do not make a lot of fuss: 'Working a steady stroke', is their way of putting it. They have little time for the rest of the world, knowing in their hearts that it is a poor place by East Anglian standards.

Now it is Christmas Eve. The countryside is dark, dormant, awaiting rebirth. Holy

Trinity is floodlit. You can see it from a long way off, floating almost, ethereal. Mist creeps between tombstones, stealthy as a cat-burglar; the congregation enters through the north door, sliding into pews, shivering at the chill of midnight vigil. They have come in bulky coats with turned-up collars, in jeans and thigh-length boots from pub, in evening dress from dinner party. A blind man has come sweeping white cane before him like a mine detector. Sinners have come and, who knows, perhaps a saint or two. There are decorations of lilies, ivy, holly with berries bright as blood drops – bright as the blood of the New Testament which was shed for man, for his salvation.

The story, nearly two thousand years old, is acted out: the Reverend Geoffrey Smith, ears aflame, stutter no better and no worse than usual, addresses the crib. 'O come, all ye faithful', is sung, and throats are cleared and noses blown. Thoughts stray, for it is hard to concentrate with hands turning blue clutching *Hymns Ancient and Modern*. From the pulpit the vicar tells his flock of the power cut early in the evening as he put the finishing touches to his sermon – in this he saw symbolism: 'There are no power cuts with God – His light shines for eternity. Let Him not be extinguished.' The congregation kneels, and stands, and kneels again to drink that precious blood; and soon enough it is all over, with the Vicar's blessing for a Happy Christmas.

So Winnie is dead, and a child called Jesus lives. Death and rebirth: thus the Christian message. It seems as good as any; better than most. There is an order, a credence, in the ways of the Good Lord, or whoever is in charge of such things.